ERRATA

Greek Tragedy Into Film by Kenneth MacKinnon

Page 12 line 29
as to the viability of the theatrical film even within the context of

Page 23 line 8
ancients, thinking about contemporary theatre, from 'realist' views

Page 27 line 11
to life', although all acting is a matter of artifice and stylisation:

Page 29 line 12
ancient plays according to these prescriptions: 'An age which refuses

Page 36 line 17
tragedy as well as the Oedipus complex, for the former is conceived

Page 36 line 32
substitutes in the second — its dissemination means that tragedy —

Page 46 line 7
wearing a horned mask, and addresses Prometheus. Her exit is filmed

Page 48 line 18
the roof of the *skene* building).

Page 48 line 35
Ted Zarpas, is offered, shot so that occasionally the audience is in

Page 52 line 21
today, to be immediate forerunners of Darth Vader. Even the

Page 54 line 23
put it on celluloid', [11] or another, that, while Oedipus' and Jocasta's

Page 71 line 28
than the 'shots' which are 'heavily stylised', surely?) Another

Page 101 line 19
area it prefers to follow Racine rather than the Greek playwright.

Page 139 line 34
in his blindness. Angelo and he make the transition together to

Page 143 line 15
we have evidence that Pasolini wanted the soldier to be wearing

Page 158 line 6
pides heroine in the theatre at Delphi is recorded in a montage.

Page 170 line 5
fulfilment are not so overtly a matter of class, the situations of

Page 176 line 19
submission to the present powers but Electra is determined to

Page 195
Mast, Gerald and Cohen, Marshall (eds), *Film Theory and Criticism*, 2nd edn.
(Oxford University Press, 1979).

GREEK TRAGEDY INTO FILM

GREEK TRAGEDY INTO FILM

Kenneth MacKinnon

RUTHERFORD • MADISON • TEANECK
FAIRLEIGH DICKINSON UNIVERSITY PRESS

© 1986 by J.K. MacKinnon
Associated University Presses
440 Forsgate Drive
Cranbury, NJ 08512

Library of Congress Cataloging-in-Publication Data

MacKinnon, Kenneth, 1942-
  Greek tragedy into film.

  Bibliography: p.
  Includes index.
  1. Greek drama (Tragedy) — Film and video adaptations.
I. Title.
PN1997.85.M23 1986   791.43   86-13420
ISBN 0-8386-3301-3 (U.S. : alk. paper)

Printed in Great Britain

CONTENTS

Acknowledgements

  1 Introduction   1

  2 The General Problem: Theatre into Film   4

  3 Specific Problems   22

  4 Films in the Theatrical Mode   43

  5 Films in the Realistic Mode   66

  6 Films in the Filmic Mode   97

  7 Meta-Tragedy   126

  8 Conclusion   165

Appendices

A Ancient Greek Comedy into Film   169

B Brief Synopses of Ancient Plays on which
    Films have been Based   174

C Credits of Films of Greek Drama   180

Selected Bibliography   195

Index   197

PLATES

1. *Electra* (Cacoyannis)
   Electra (Irene Papas) with countrywomen chorus — formal groupings in natural landscapes

2. *Elektreia* (Jancsó)
   This highly choreographed version of *Electra* ends by bringing the tale into the twentieth century

3. *Iphigenia* (Cacoyannis)
   Army pressure on Agamemnon (Costa Kazakos) is realised in 'epic' visual terms

4. *Medea* (Pasolini)
   The centaur (Laurent Terzieff) is seen by Jason sometimes as ordinary man, sometimes (as here) in pre-rational terms

5. *Oedipus Rex* (Tyrone Guthrie)
   Guthrie's film of his play production renders chorus (and also actors) in broadly Hellenistic terms

6. *Oedipus Rex* (Pasolini)
   Sophocles' play exoticised: here, Jocasta (Silvana Mangano) is brought to Oedipus as reward for the sphinx slaying

7. *Phaedra* (Dassin)
   Phaedra (Melina Mercouri) and husband (Raf Vallone): business pressures replace divine control of events

8. *The Trojan Women* (Cacoyannis)
   Cacoyannis' Helen (Irene Papas) softens Menelaus (Patrick Magee) more by physical appeal than argument

ACKNOWLEDGEMENTS

The author and publishers would like to thank the National Film Archive, London for its assistance and Artificial Eye Film Companies Ltd, The Stratford Shakespearean Festival Foundation of Canada and Peter Darvill Associates for permission to publish stills from Jancsó's *Elektreia*, Guthrie, *Oedipus Rex* and Pasolini's *Oedipus Rex,* respectively.

Despite strenuous efforts to trace copyright holders and to seek permission for the publication of the other stills reproduced in this book, there has been no result. The author, publishers and editor would be glad to hear from any one not here acknowledged.

1 INTRODUCTION

Film-makers attempting to render ancient Greek tragedy are faced with a number of obvious problems, especially theoretical objections to the filming of works conceived for theatrical performance, and the intensification of these objections in the context of Greek theatre. Then, too, there is the problem of translating highly formalised works conceived within a particular set of conventions into a medium which has traditionally privileged 'realism'. Nevertheless, a number of world-famous directors — Pier Paolo Pasolini, Michael Cacoyannis, Miklós Jancsó, Liliana Cavani and Jules Dassin in particular — as well as less celebrated film-makers, have devoted themselves to the task of filming Greek tragedy, especially in the 1960s and 1970s.

Greek tragedy *has* been filmed. The question whether it ought to be, expressed in the wake of the fear that there may be something about Greek tragedy and/or cinema which makes them incompatible, may be less interesting than *how* it has been. Existence seems to precede essence here. The variety of approaches to the filming of Greek tragedy illustrates the range of tactics by which ancient culture is translated into modern culture, but especially the problems presented in filming what was once popular art, but what is now considered as 'high art'.

Few of the films have been screened outside the art-house circuit, or even the 'artier' channels and off-peak viewing hours of British television, in English-speaking countries: a notable exception is Jules Dassin's *Phaedra* (1961). That such international stars as Melina Mercouri, Anthony Perkins and Raf Vallone are in the film seems less an explanation of its commercial success than a consequence of the conception of the film. *Phaedra* demonstrates more clearly than any other film of Greek tragedy that, in order for such films to become 'popular', there must be a generic shift towards, for example, the highly popular cinematic genre of melodrama, as here.

Before analysing the individual films, before consideration of the problems allegedly inherent in the filming of Greek theatre, it is interesting to note that certain Greek tragedies are particularly popular with film-makers. Sophocles' *Oedipus Rex* is, predictably,

1

a frequent choice. Apart from Pier Paolo Pasolini's much studied version, made in 1967, there are those by Tyrone Guthrie (*Oedipus Rex*, 1956) and Philip Saville (*Oedipus the King*, 1967). The Electra story has also figured several times, perhaps because there are no fewer than four ancient Greek plays relevant to it — Aeschylus' *The Libation Bearers* (the second play in his *Oresteia* trilogy), Sophocles' *Electra*, and Euripides' *Electra* and *Orestes*.[1] No fewer than four films claim, by title alone, a relation with one or other of these plays.

The omissions are surprising. Among the most obvious is Euripides' *The Bacchae*, the obvious appeal of which to Western culture of the late 1960s suggests that it might even have been a popular success, under certain conditions. Another is Aeschylus' *Oresteia*, which Pasolini did propose filming. His preparatory research and statements about the planned execution of the film are preserved in *Notes for an African Oresteia* (1970).

Of the three celebrated Greek tragedians of whose work a small but significant portion survives, Aeschylus is least often filmed. This would suggest that drama which is 'anti-realist' in its ritualism and the importance of the Choral element, or drama which is too obviously embedded in fifth-century BC Athenian concerns is less likely to find favour with modern film-makers. The greater popularity of Euripides may well raise questions about his status as a tragedian in relation both to his own times and to modern society. Is it possible that he is the most attractive to film-makers because, according to one recent study,[2] he is deemed today to be the most 'anti-' or 'post-tragic'?

This book does not demand a specialist knowledge of the classics or of film studies, although it is hoped that both disciplines will benefit in some measure from it. Familiarity with the original plays is not assumed. For those who are uncertain of even the plots, Appendix B (pp. 174-9) provides short synopses of the tragedies relevant to the analyses of films in Chapters 3 to 7. The extended debates by classical scholars about interpretation of each play are seldom explored here, since the purpose of the book is to clarify the consequences of decisions of interpretation, rather than to validate or otherwise a particular interpretation. Inevitably, there must be some wrestling with the 'meaning' of the original, especially in relation to the discussion of Michael Cacoyannis (Chapter 5), where it will be argued that his film versions of Euripidean tragedies are paradoxically more 'tragic' than Euripides' originals.

The first films analysed individually (Chapter 4) are what sometimes seem like relatively transparent filmed records of theatrical productions. But they are not what they seem in that every choice of cut or camera angle mediates reception of the original production. It is the films which attempt to render Greek tragedy in less overtly theatrical fashion, however, that have proved more commercially viable and therefore — though only marginally in some cases — more popular with cinema audiences. It is from these that we can learn the strategies by which film-makers have attempted to release the originally-conceived theatrical works from the conditions of the theatre, and that we can arrive at some sort of estimation of the possibility, let alone of the virtues, of fidelity to the original plays. These films are discussed in Chapters 5–7.

Notes

1. Vassilis Fotopoulos' film, *Orestes* (1971), mentioned in Mel Schuster, *The Contemporary Greek Cinema* (Scarecrow, 1979), p. 304, seems to be impossible to trace.

2. Ekbert Faas, *Tragedy and After: Euripides, Shakespeare, Goethe* (McGill-Queen's University Press, 1984).

2 THE GENERAL PROBLEM: THEATRE INTO FILM

From the earliest days of cinema, there has been a close relationship between cinema and theatre. True, there was a tendency from the beginning to regard cinema as, *par excellence*, a realist medium. Lumière's short films of, say, a train entering the station at La Ciotat startled audiences into recognising the then unique power of cinema, which surpassed theatre in its ability not merely to represent but to record, and which surpassed photography by the addition of time, space and movement. Yet, at the same time as Lumière was photographing apparently unstaged events, another Frenchman, Méliès, saw cinema's potential as that of augmenting the marvels of theatre, or more particularly of the music hall. His aim was to outstrip the music-hall conjuror with the *trompe-l'oeil* trickery opened up by such cinematic techniques as editing. Rather than photographing everyday events, he would film his actors on such then fantastic exploits as a trip by rocket to the moon. Film studies, thanks to André Bazin, however, are inclined to question whether the seeming dichotomy between these kinds of cinema is valid. In Bazin's view, there is an essential realism in the medium of cinema which is as important in audience reception of the fantasy film as of the documentary. While Bazin's conception of cinema's essence has been repeatedly attacked by semioticians, for example, his questioning of the traditional Lumière/Méliès dichotomy remains valuable. If Méliès should be identified with what might loosely be termed a theatrical tendency in cinema, even Bazin's essentialism does not prevent the accommodation of both the theatrical and documentary tendencies under the heading of 'true' (for Bazin, realist) cinema. Moreover, it has been argued by Vardac[1], for example, that nineteenth-century drama and staging were marked by a striving towards a union of romanticism and realism, by which the glamorous or spectacular-ideas of playwrights were to be rendered credible in performance. If this is so, cinema in its beginnings can be discerned as the fulfilment and extension of romantic – realist stage practice. Not only need there be no unbridgeable gulf between theatre and cinema, but Méliès' sort of cinema is thus born from the dreams and needs of dramatists and stage directors.

4

While this conception of cinema's genesis could be thought partial and tendentious, there is no doubt that traffic between theatre and cinema has been common and at times heavy, ever since the last decade of the nineteenth century. Chaplin and many other comic giants of the silent cinema came from the music hall and imported to slapstick movies music-hall techniques. The advent of sound to cinema delighted some dramatists at the same time as it panicked others. We know, for example, that Pagnol in France and Shaw in Britain believed that the 'talkie' had the ability to record theatre plays and thus to introduce them to a much wider public than before.[2] Although as early as the 1930s it became normal practice to adapt stage originals considerably for filming, at least the initial practice of the 'talkie', when dealing with a stage original, can be described as producing 'filmed theatre'.[3] The relationship between screen comedy and theatre — particularly vaudeville in the United States — was continued in the sound era in the movies of the Marx Brothers, W.C. Fields and Mae West. Movies vitally influenced stage practice, too. Practitioners of drama — as well as artists and novelists — introduced elements of the cinema into their own medium. It could be argued that, if cinema represented the fulfilment of the popular theatre's romantic–realist tendency of the nineteenth century, dominant cinema practice in the twentieth century, by its romantic-realist near monopoly, forced theatre to turn in other directions, just as post-Cézanne painting eschewed representational art after the invention of photography.

Because theatre plays have been filmed so often, and because directors and actors and others move from theatre to cinema and sometimes back again (Olivier is one of the few who have worked in both capacities in both media), the question of the relationship between theatre and cinema is a vital and practical one, which has to be faced in some form every time a transition of this sort is made.

Hostility to cinematic adaptations of material conceived originally for the stage, if theorised, is based on notions of theatrical and/or cinematic specificity. Purists, so-called, must argue from the position that there is such a thing as cinema or theatre pure and unalloyed, an essence, and that therefore one medium cannot adapt itself to the other without betraying that essence. The dominant opinion,[4] up to 1940 at least, among those who gave thought to the relation of theatre and cinema was that they were 'separate but equal', provided that each maintained its purity by 'exploiting its "unique" artistic potentialities and developing within its "proper" stylistic and thematic domain'. [5] To judge by Pennethorne Hughes, writing in 1933, [6] this purist position seems so securely established that further debate is tiresome: 'that dead dog, the absolute independence of true cinema and theatre, has been flogged now into a nasty enough pulp to avoid any fear of further theoretical identifications of the mediums.'[7]

To examine the credibility of the purist position, we must rehearse the arguments for cinematic specificity. There are several key components in these, but probably the most fundamental and tenacious is the notion already alluded to (p. 4) in the context of Bazin's description of cinema — that of realism as cinema's essence. 'Realism', however, is a term which admits of multiple interpretations and applications, and some of the earliest theorists interested in the differentiation of the two media appear to argue in terms which, superficially, run counter to Bazin's position.

Thus, for example, Hugo Munsterberg[8] argued in 1916 that the theatre was undistinguished from nature in the sense that it was bound to obey the same temporal laws; whereas cinema's peculiar capability lay in freeing itself from nature, to demonstrate its power over nature's laws. For Munsterberg, the flashback demonstrates cinema's shaping by psychological considerations and its freedom from the necessities of temporal succession, while the close-up demonstrates an analogous freedom in spatial terms. In this sense, the representation of physical reality is theatre's, not cinema's concern.[9]

V.I. Pudovkin differentiates theatre and cinema on similar lines. He argues that the stage director deals with 'real processes . . . that take place in obedience to the laws of real space and real time';[10] while the film director, having as his material the 'pieces of celluloid on which these processes have been recorded'[11] may, through editing, create 'filmic time' and 'filmic space'.[12]

For Erwin Panofsky,[13] writing in 1934, the space of theatre is essentially static, while that of cinema is essentially dynamic. The two media are further differentiated for him by cinema's 'rigorous subjection' to the principle of co-expressibility and theatre's independence from it.[14] The decor of the staged play is, for Panofsky, a pre-stylised reality, whereas cinema's job is to photograph actuality. Thus, the verbal/visual primacy distinction traditionally applied to these media is underpinned in Panofsky by his analysis of the different functioning of space in theatre and cinema. His affirmation of cinema's concern with physical reality permits him to move closer to the classic-realist positions adopted by such theorists as Siegfried Kracauer, if not, quite, André Bazin.

Allardyce Nicoll, following Munsterberg in his recognition of cinema as representing the triumph of mind over matter, claims, in *Film and Theatre*,[15] that cinema's power over time and space is its fourth dimension. Ordinary time and space, which presumably are the province of the theatre, are superseded in cinema by new interrelations of past and present or by parallel actions.[16] Thus, cinema may give expression to subjective states, offering memories through flashbacks or wishes in visual imagery. One of the consequences he draws from his observation that cinema has greater credibility than theatre, in the sense that its material is treated by the audience as having a closer relation with actuality, is that film characters are much more individualised than those of theatre: 'practically all effectively drawn stage characters are types [while] in the cinema we demand individualisation . . . we recognise stage figures as types and impute greater power of independent life to the figures we see on the screen.' This happens, he says, because dramatic illusion is 'never . . . the illusion of reality: it is always imaginative illusion, the illusion of a period of make-believe.'[17] On the other hand, because cinema allows for an 'illusion of reality', 'we demand individualisation' of film characters[18] and 'greater complexity may be permitted without loss of sympathy.'[19]

Kracauer, like Panofsky (see p. 6), believes that cinema has a 'realistic tendency' in the sense that the dimension of physical existence is crucial to it.[20] He recognises that there is a tradition, accorded critical acclaim, within cinematic practice whereby a 'theatrical story' is told along the lines of such narration within the theatre. He dates this tradition from the formation in 1908 of a French film company, Film d'Art, dedicated to the attempt to make cinema evolve in accordance with theatrical practice, so that, for example, the position of the camera was fixed like that of the spectator in the theatre. Kracauer traces stageplay-based movies, such as *Death of a Salesman* (1952), or even such novel-based movies as *The Heiress* (1949) and *Great Expectations* (1946), back to the practice of Film d'Art.[21] Camera mobility may be assured in these, but the settings in which the characters move, despite their superficial realism, are 'painted canvases'.[22] Why, we might ask, since the decor looks solid enough? Kracauer believes that the *mise en scène* in these movies remains theatrical, and that theatrical *mise en scène* always *replicates* the world of actuality; that is, represents, but never is, that world; that decor in the theatre is limited to those parts of the world which 'sustain dialogue and acting';[23] that therefore the primary interest of theatre is in human beings, not settings; that when cinema treats decor in a similar manner it 'runs counter to the spirit of a medium privileged to capture "the ripple of leaves in the wind".'[24]

The profound difference for Kracauer between theatrical and cinematic *mise en scène* is related by him (interestingly for the subject of the present book) to Aristotle's *Poetics*. Aristotle approves of that form of drama which is an 'organic' whole — in which, in other words, the central section is unified with beginning and end by probability or necessity. Kracauer extends Aristotle's demand that dramatic episodes should be logically or necessarily linked with, though subordinate to, the central action when he concludes that theatrical decor must serve the ends of the plot's construction. Cinematic decor, on the other hand, is multivalent, not subordinated to a meaning demanded by the human action at the heart of a play. The 'theatrical' film, in treating its decor as illustrative of this action's meaning, cannot be truly cinematic. Kracauer quotes Proust with approval in this regard: the latter declares, 'our eye, charged with thought, neglects, as would a classical tragedy, every image that does not assist the action of the play and retains only those that may help us to make its purpose intelligible.'[25] The theatrical story, thus, cannot be truly cinematic (and most resistant of all to cinematic treatment, we might note, is classical tragedy!) because its *mise en scène* serves a presumably *a priori* significance, while in 'true' cinema decor, environment in general, cannot have its significance so narrowed without the danger of its becoming 'painted canvas'. The theatrical story can, in this sense, be classified as 'closed', the cinematic as 'open'. While Kracauer recognises the popularity of the theatrical story, he does not believe that such popularity proves its aesthetic validity.[26] It seems, paradoxically, that while it has always been an important part of cinema it is a denial of cinema.

Bazin shares a number of viewpoints with Kracauer, particularly the distinctness of theatrical and cinematic *mise en scène* and the primacy of the verbal element in theatre drama. Yet, his conclusions about what Kracauer terms 'the theatrical story' in cinema are far more optimistic. He sees only two possibilities for the filming of theatrical work: the photographing of the play, resulting in 'filmed theatre'; or adaptation of the original, resulting in a composite.[27] Masterpieces, he avers, demand that their texts be respected and this demand results in stress being placed on their theatrical character when they are filmed. ('Masterpieces' is less problematic than it might at first appear; Bazin implicitly identifies the category largely with the classical drama of France and England — Molière and Shakespeare, for example. Presumably, his analysis applies with as much force to films of Greek tragedy.) If the text, in his sense of the term, determines the mode and style of the cinematic production,[28] then, the text being 'theatrical', so should the production itself. Kracauer, it may be recalled (p. 7), objects to cinematic decor being reduced to 'painted canvases'. Surprisingly, perhaps, it is precisely when the decor is treated as painted canvas that Bazin can accept filmed Molière, for example.[29] Olivier's *Henry V* (1944) is cited by Bazin as an example of the right way to go about filming theatre, namely by emphasising, not disguising, the theatricality of the original. He notes that *Henry V* begins with a travelling shot plunging us into the courtyard of an Elizabethan inn, which establishes that the film's concern is the performance of the play, a performance ostensibly taking place in Shakespeare's own time. This opening, he believes, permits the film to use theatrical style and conventions, even when there is a switch from the world of the theatre to the battle of Agincourt.[30]

Bazin seems to accept Panofsky's (p. 6) view of theatrical decor as 'a pre-stylised reality'. Decor, in his opinion, constitutes the basic aesthetic problem of filmed theatre. The film-maker must 'give his [sic] decor a dramatic opaqueness while at the same time reflecting its natural realism.'[31] 'The subject of the adaptation', he goes on to say, 'is not that of the play' but rather 'the play precisely in its scenic essence'.[32]

To those who argue that specific to theatre is 'the impossibility of separating off action and actor',[33] Bazin replies that in cinema and television there is another stage between absence and the presence that the implied objection bases itself on. He accepts, nevertheless, that there are 'two psychic modalities of a performance',[34] that the theatre is based on the reciprocal awareness of presence in the audience and players, while the cinema involves watching a spectacle that is unaware of our existence. The self-consciousness of the theatre audience must be far greater than that of its cinema equivalent; and cinema stimulates audience identification, rather than spectator consciousness, through depersonalisation. Yet, Bazin asserts, cinema does have the capability of stimulating the spectator's consciousness.[35]

Panofsky, Nicoll, Kracauer, Bazin — all share the view that cinema has a closer relationship with 'reality' than theatre, that there is, thus, something inalienably 'realist' about the medium of cinema. Their attitude has been highly influential, being accepted by film critics of the 1970s for example. Thus, in their reviews of *The Trojan Women*, John Simon[36] writes about Cacoyannis's problem as being how to make 'this highly stylised play even moderately realistic for this much more realistic medium; or conversely, how to derealise the film medium; or, perhaps, how to work out a fusion of both modes'; while Tony Palmer[37] writes that the film version does not solve the problem of the Chorus in an 'essentially realistic medium'.

The questions about cinematic adaptation of theatrical originals, posed in particularly acute fashion when these originals are by Shakespeare or Sophocles, seem to come down to the 'purity' of these media and the 'essential realism' of cinema.

Susan Sontag places stress on the cinema as medium (as opposed to art), to remind us that, unlike the theatre but very much like television, cinema may render any of the performing arts with comparative transparency.[38] Still, controversy usually rages more energetically around adaptations rather than what she terms 'transcriptions', and it is to such controversy's grounding in notions of pure or essential cinema that she next turns. She draws attention to the covert political–moral position in the privileging of 'realism' and in cinema's alleged affinity for 'unstylized reality'.[39] She believes that behind the use of the term 'theatrical' lies a moral position which equates it with the false and therefore with lies, and a political position which associates the theatre with aristocratic taste and cinema with popular taste. While the traditional practice of cinema has been 'realist', she argues that this practice is not proof of the identity of cinema's essence. There has been a counter-tradition standing out against the identification of cinema's function as storytelling and arguing for artifice as cinema's future. (This tendency is associated with painters and sculptors, in particular, in Europe and the USA, and generally with the sort of intellectual avant-garde represented by, for example, German expressionism in the 1920s or surrealism in France in the 1930s.) The synthetic and theatrical need not be viewed as 'misplaced' in film, therefore, simply because it is so viewed traditionally.

Sontag, when arguing against the idea of cinema as primarily visual, by citing Ozu, Bresson and Godard,[40] when denying that the film spectator's perpetual motion justifies the radical dissociation of theatre from cinema,[41] or when expressing her doubts about the fairness of Nicoll's conclusion that the theatre deals in types, the cinema in individuals,[42] seems to be combating the underlying view that there is something unbridgeable between these media, something essentially 'cinematic' or 'theatrical'. Here she is on ground similar to Eric Bentley's when he disagrees with Allardyce Nicoll's distinctions between theatre and cinema: 'I think there is no radical distinction,' he writes, 'between stage and screen illusion. At best the difference is one of degree . . . On either stage or screen he [the director, author or producer] may choose . . . to be "naturalistic" or the reverse.' Or, 'What Mr Nicoll says is true of current movies and of many audiences, but not of all possible movies and all possible audiences.'[43] Bentley, in turn, by emphasising the quantitative rather than qualitative difference between cinema and theatre, is on remarkably similar ground to that of Eisenstein. By 1936, the latter is arguing that the use of 'frame and montage' in cinema 'is really an enlargement in scale of a process microscopically inherent in all arts'.[44] His conclusion is that 'film-specifics lie not in the process itself but in the degree to which these features are intensified.'[45] Sontag and Bentley agree that conclusions about the cinematic are drawn from popular practice rather then all possible cinematic practice. The cinematic and theatrical, they argue, have been identified merely with dominant practice. Thus they cast doubt on claims concerning the essence of cinema and theatre by objecting to arguments based on a single model of cinema or theatre.

Reminders that neither cinema nor theatre is a monolith are salutary, as is the emphasis on the need to separate the usual from the essential. Nevertheless, it is possible to overrate the potential or novelty of such arguments as Sontag's. After all, Bazin, who does argue for a cinematic essence, still allows for a plurality of emphases within his conception of realism, such that both fantasy and documentary cinema have legitimacy, and flourish by reason of what he discerns to be cinema's realist tendency. Then, too, Kracauer recognises that it is perfectly possible for there to be manifold actual examples of 'theatrical story' films, while he insists that there is such a thing as 'true' cinema, against which standard the many examples of the theatrical film may still be deemed as, presumably, 'false' cinema. Sontag correctly reminds us that the privileging of realism is no more than a prejudice, but all the same it is a prejudice with profound economic, political and aesthetic ramifications. To put it crudely, if a film-maker wants to be assured of a fair financial return — in other words, a substantial audience — for his/her film, the prejudice in realism's favour has to be considered seriously, whether the film is conceived in original cinematic terms or as an adaptation of a pre-existent theatrical property.

This observation may, in turn, be overstated, however. Perhaps because of television's inroads upon the popular audience and because of rapidly changing patterns in viewing habits, the notion of a mass audience for cinema is far less tenable today than it was when Bazin was writing. The Western cinema-going public is far more fragmented and stratified than it was before the 1950s. Since then, faith in the family audience has declined in favour of the young audience, and the once marginal art-house audience may be thought to play a significant role in cinema's survival in London, for example, in the 1980s. The more sophisticated, though less numerous, film-goers are demonstrably much more tolerant of what might be deemed anti-realist tendencies in cinema than the mass audience of the 1940s. Film-makers such as Godard, Fellini or, for that matter, Francis Coppola, none of whom could readily be termed realist in the senses that Kracauer or Bazin gave to the word, have a loyal following in Europe and North America, as well as further afield. What may have seemed minority practice in the 1920s and 1930s, conducted by a European avant-garde for an audience of avant-garde sympathisers, is much more widely disseminated today. Even on television, with its apparently in-built privileging of realism, the frequency of rock videos, not to mention advertising films often dependent on techniques pioneered by the French surrealists, affect present-day assumptions about the place of realism, even in the 'entertainment' context. In any case, Bazin has provided guidance as to the visibility of the theatrical film even within the context of his concept of realist cinema by demanding the foregrounding of theatrical 'reality' as an essential step to successful adaptation.

It seems mistaken both to despair of the possibility of bridging the two media and to underestimate the usefulness of a search for knowledge of usual — if not necessarily essential — differential emphases or elements helping to mark off the broadly cinematic from the broadly theatrical.

Distinctions in the following areas have all been considered as significant by one or several writers.

Time

Film editing means that time is far more obviously flexible in cinema than theatre. Flashbacks, even flash-forwards, multiple repetitions of the same moment, ellipses achieved often through montage, are all commonplace in films. Whether Munsterberg (p. 6), Pudovkin (p. 6) or, to some extent, James Hurt[46] is right in claiming that theatre is *bound* to follow 'natural' time seems dubious. Hurt himself concedes that there is time ellipsis in Aeschylus' *Agamemnon*. One could go much further, and suggest that Choral stasima in Greek drama, in the manner of blackouts or intervals in modern theatre, indicate the passage of whatever time the writer of the play requires to have elapsed between dialogue episodes. These thinkers may be referring, however, to sequential time. Even then, plays are not *bound* to deal in such time. Harold Pinter's *Betrayal*, a theatre play before it was a film, presented the stages of a love affair in reverse chronological order without discernible difficulty for the audience. Moreover, a play may provide the equivalent of a flashback by using, say, certain lighting techniques. It might be difficult not to make flashbacks signify as such by placing them within a scene, however, since the temporal reverse might have to be marked off from the normal time sequence by attention thus being drawn to it. Easier flashbacks could be achieved by use of costume and decor. A stage thriller might well benefit from such temporal switches. Practicable as these may be, the fact is that such time manipulation is seldom practised in modern drama. Yet, we have to set against this the conclusion reached by Vardac (p. 4) that nineteenth-century popular theatre manipulated time with much of the resourcefulness of cinema even before its invention:

From his [Vardac's] encyclopedic description of nineteenth-century stagecraft we can . . . infer that what are often considered to be 'essential' differences between film and theatre are actually quantitative rather than qualitative, differences of degree and not of kind. Contrary to Munsterberg and many of the Lessing-esque critics . . . the manipulation of time and space through parallel montage, flashbacks, flashforwards, and split-screen effects was a fundamental aspect of stage melodrama and spectacle as well as being a basic cinematic concern.[47]

Space

While questioning a number of conceptions of the essential differences between theatre and cinema, Susan Sontag suggests that, if
there is an irreducible distinction, it may be that theatre is confined
to the logical, or continuous, use of space.[48] Theatre may manipulate
space as easily as time, but in her view the only two spaces which
characters may be conceived to occupy are that represented onstage
and that which is 'off'. In that she accepts that cinema may create
alogical or discontinuous space through editing, she seems to be
arguing for a logical or continuous use of space onstage, or between
'on' and 'off' stage. That she has hit on an irreducible distinction here
is unlikely. Alan Ayckbourn's *Bedroom Farce* has three contiguous
bedrooms represented onstage, although the audience is not supposed to *perceive* these as spatially contiguous. Moreover, an alogical
relationship could be set up between on and off stage. Near the end
of *Un Chien andalou* (1928), the central couple step from a Paris
interior straight on to a beach. This is easily achieved by editing in
that film. It would be relatively easy to create an alogical space out
of on and off stage relations, however. Recorded sound of waves
breaking, seagulls crying and lighting to indicate sunshine, for
example, could suggest the existence of a beach immediately outside
a Paris apartment interior represented onstage.

A more promising differentiation of space could be suggested,
however. A film camera may record action taking place in an
actual Paris apartment or, for that matter, the Eiffel Tower, while
apartment or Tower would always be represented in the theatre.
Thus, film space may be 'real' in a way denied to theatre space, which
is always representational. Even this distinction is not absolute. In
Tom Stoppard's *The Real Inspector Hound*, the stage space which
has been the setting for a highly conventional 'whodunit' suddenly
becomes the 'actual' stage at the point when one of the critics
(during the interval, as it were) nervously ventures on to it to answer
a real telephone which, during 'the play', had been a conventional
prop. Stoppard is mischievously upsetting convention here though,
and the laughter which greets the critic's answering of the telephone
is partly attributable to the audience's shock in realising that the
stage space is no longer representational.

Bazin[49] differentiates stage and film space in terms of frame and
mask. The proscenium arch at least acts in the same manner as a
picture frame, he argues, while the rectangular frame of film is

actually less frame than mask. If the camera moves to right or left, the continuity of cinema space is normally 'proven'. Again, the camera movement could do quite the opposite, as in Monty Python TV shows, and show the huddled director and technicians rather than more of the same exterior. Once again, it could do so, but seldom does. On the other hand, Bazin's interest in what he discerns as the frame of stage action emphasises a seemingly crucial point, that viewing positions are relatively fixed in theatre and relatively fluid in cinema. While both audiences normally stay seated in the same positions throughout the performance, the perspective is constantly changing for the cinema viewer thanks to multiple changes of angle, varieties of shot (long shot, close-up, etc.), the use of crane or zoom lens, etc. A theatre audience may be permitted to walk about among actors, but it is a matter sufficiently surprising to receive much publicity when it is. A cinema audience may find its viewing position relatively static in certain films of Dreyer, notably *Gertrud* (1964), or Straub-Huillet, for example, but the sense of fatigue or irritation which this induces testifies to the abnormality of the practice.

Mediation

This last point is relevant to consideration of whether cinema or theatre is more unmediated. It might be argued that, since almost everything that is placed or made to happen on stage is the result of somebody's decision, theatre is mediated in a way that cinema, which admits the random through the use of the mechanical device of the camera, is not. Crucial to the argument about mediation, however, is the fact that point of view, literally, and perhaps metaphorically, is determined for the audience by the film-maker. Theatre audiences facing the relatively static stage space may still have their attention drawn to areas of that space by lighting or by sound, whereas cinema operates not only by showing but dictating how what is shown is to be seen. This property of cinema is considered so fundamental that Laura Mulvey, for example, argues that a patriarchal point of view is inscribed within the cinematic apparatus of Hollywood cinema.[50] (Further work needs to be undertaken, all the same, on the relation of visual and what might be termed psychological perception.)

Transience/Permanence

Roger Manvell argues that, while both film and theatre involve re-enactment of stories before an audience, each theatrical performance is a unique event, while the film offers exactly the same experience to audiences all over the world.[51] At first glance, these statements seem acceptable enough. Though one might quibble with the implication that there are perceptible differences in each performance of, say, a West End play put on by seasoned professionals, it is literally true that each performance is unique. The conclusions which may legitimately be drawn from the observation are worth examining, all the same. Raymond Williams is unimpressed with the related argument that film cannot be 'real drama' because there is no fruitful participation by the audience in a filmed performance. While Williams does not dispute the absence of an audience from the filming of a drama or its presence in the theatre, he argues that the 'effect of an audience on the *creation* of a work . . . has almost certainly been overstressed',[52] and that ideally the 'inspiration to great performances' should 'arise from the actor's response to the whole emotion of the work' instead of to the audience.[53] As far as absence of audience from filming goes, there appears to be an assumption that once a performance is recorded on film (or, presumably, video), it becomes (barring technical problems) permanent. So far, so good. The question is whether its 'meaning' is thus fixed and homogeneous. If signification is a matter of interaction between text and audience, it is constantly shifting rather than stable. The same film may be perceived quite differently in New York and London; still more differently in London and Bombay. A film made in 1945 is 'different' in 1985, not simply because the print may be inferior due to the passage of time, but because questions of class, race, individual psychology and other factors which could be subsumed under the label 'history', affect the reading of that film.

Identification

It is customary to consider theatre as a cooler medium than cinema, to use McLuhan's term.[54] This is partly because theatre involves the presence of actors and audience and the awareness by each of the other's presence. A theatre audience has more 'work' to do, in that it has to deal with such conventions as theatre space being representative (p. 14), whereas the cinema audience is thought to be more likely to surrender its individual consciousness to the spectacle which is recognised as having no awareness of that audience. Thus, the cinema audience is placed in a more voyeuristic relation to the spectacle; its experience has also been compared with that of dreaming. While identification is much facilitated by these conditions, it would be a mistake to believe that wish-fulfilment and identification are essential parts of the cinema-viewing experience which are denied outside the cinema (is the rock concert not a form of theatre?). Brecht has affected cinema as profoundly as theatre, it seems. Audiences are often 'distanced' in modern films and television productions by devices which, for instance, draw attention to the cinematic nature of cinema's narration.

Acting

Roger Manvell's differentiation of scale in acting in the two media[55] is valid enough in general terms. The reason why performances need to be scaled down when they move from theatre to film can largely be identified with the importance of both 'realism' and audience identification in dominant cinematic practice. With the sort of modernist inroads into that practice achieved since the 1960s and referred to above (pp. 11-12), however, the theatrical, in performance at all levels, may be foregrounded as legitimately as it has habitually been modified.

'Seriousness'

In the 1950s and earlier, the recognition of the economic importance of the mass audience suggested that 'serious' dramatists were trivialised when their works were adapated for cinema, and that intellectual matters were best left to the theatre. The assumptions behind this thinking deserve sceptical questioning. Broadway and the West End also wanted to make a profit (or at least break even) so that commercial pressures were hardly unknown there. Moreover, since *Cahiers du Cinema,* and the increasing sophistication of Andrew Sarris's so-called *auteur* theory, it is no longer safe to argue that 'entertainment' movies need not, *ipso facto,* be taken seriously.

In any case, this model of cinema and of its audience seems outdated today, when films are addressed to more specialised audiences and when the *Verfremdungseffekt* has manifested itself frequently in cinematic terms, breaking the assumed encouragement in 'entertainment' movies to audience passivity and loss of consciousness.

Verbal/Visual Primacy

Just as the privileging of realism is easily discernible in the practice of cinema and television of the western world, so the privileging of the verbal is not hard to detect in Anglo-Saxon culture. Part of the underlying reason for the reservation of the serious to theatre could well be the assumption that theatre is primarily a verbal and cinema primarily a visual, medium.

'Proof' of the importance of the verbal in the theatre is sometimes suggested to be embodied in the fact that play scripts are not only published and bought far more regularly than film scripts, but are also studied in academic institutions as a branch of literature.[56] Further evidence is found in the fact that dramatists are far more celebrated than screen writers; that the cinema advertises its stars and directors rather than its scenarists.[57] These points should not go unchallenged, however. Roger Manvell, who appears to argue for verbal primacy in the theatre, concedes, for instance, that one of the reasons for the celebrity of the playwright was that he used to be charged with the production of his own play[58] — this was certainly the normal expectation in ancient Greek theatre production. Moreover, the academic practice of analysing drama in relation to its verbal element exclusively could be viewed as detrimental to the comprehension of it as a performed art. (This emphasis has been almost exclusively the rule in classical study of drama until at least the 1960s.)

Jack J. Jorgens attempts to redress the balance at the outset of his study of films of Shakespeare plays,[59] and questions the wisdom of undue attention to the play script:

> Students of Shakespeare's plays as literature . . . might consider that the plays were conceived and written for performance, that the script is not the work, but the *score* for the work . . . we cannot rest easy with a view of the plays which gives complete

emphasis to the word and denies the essentially collaborative nature of the drama.

He then proceeds to link film performance with live theatre performance in the ability of both to alter the emphasis of (i.e. to mediate) the unperformed script: 'Like live performances, a film can help us focus not only on what is said, but on how, why, and to whom it is said. It can help to expand the term *imagery* to include much more than verbal imagery.'[60]

This reminder of the importance of the non-verbal in theatre performances and the questioning of confinement of imagery exclusively to the verbal is timely for the present subject. In addition, the identification of the cinema as the art of visual communication received a considerable set-back with the coming of sound, since when the importance of dialogue has had to be recognised. Dialogue *may* be crucial to a film's import, the non-verbal to a theatre performance's. While it would be absurd to neglect the visual dimension in any film, the verbal in any play, it is not far short of absurd to limit attention to those areas.

Plays have throughout the history of cinema been adapted for that medium. There is, therefore, no practical bar to such adaptation. Whether or not there is a theoretical bar should emerge from the analysis offered in this chapter. It would appear that there is not. Jack J. Jorgens suggests that there are several degrees of adaptation, which he categorises into 'modes':

1. Theatrical mode: that which uses film as a transparent medium with the ability to record. The space of the action seems static, the frame analogous to the proscenium arch, the meaning generated largely through dialogue and the actors' gestures.
2. Realistic mode: the most popular of these possibilities, partly because it is the most popular mode in cinematic practice. Emphasis is shifted from actors to actors in a setting, that setting being 'objective'.
3. Filmic mode: that in which the film-maker becomes a poet in his or her own right, using non-theatrical techniques, but emphasising film's potential for artifice rather than as a 'realist' medium.[61]

Jorgens identifies the primary task of the film-maker to be first 'presentation'; second, 'interpretation'; and third, 'adaptation'. Whether a distinction can usefully be maintained through these terms may be doubted, but this categorisation, while not watertight, promises to be useful in the organisation of this book. In any case, the various films are difficult to distinguish in 'watertight' fashion. The modes may best be treated as predominant tendencies, whose limits of applicability may constantly be questioned even while they are used.

Before we can proceed to the analysis of Greek theatre into film, however, a number of more specific obstacles to that enterprise seem to need examination.

Notes

1. A. Nicholas Vardac, *Stage to Screen: Theatrical Method from Garrick to Griffith* (Harvard University Press, 1949).

2. See Roger Manvell, *Theater and Film: A Comparative Study of the Two Forms of Dramatic Art, and of the Problems of Adaptation of Stage Plays into Films* (Fairleigh Dickinson University Press, 1979), p. 31.

3. See ibid., pp. 31–2.

4. According to Gregory A. Waller, *The Stage/Screen Debate: A Study in Popular Aesthetics* (Garland Publishing, 1983).

5. Ibid., p. 27.

6. Pennethorne Hughes, 'The historical inception of stage and film', *Close Up*, 10 December 1933, pp. 341–4.

7. Ibid., p. 341; quoted in Waller, *The Stage/Screen Debate* p. 94.

8. Hugo Munsterberg, *The Film: A Psychological Study* (Dover, 1969).

9. See Gerald Mast and Marshall Cohen (eds), *Film Theory and Criticism*, 2nd edn, (Oxford University Press, 1979), pp. 345–6.

10. V.I. Pudovkin, *Film Technique*, tr. Ivor Montagu (1929) (Bonanza Books, 1949), p. 55; quoted in Waller, *The Stage/Screen Debate*, p. 206.

11. Ibid., p. 56; in Waller, p. 206.

12. Ibid., p. 59; in Waller, p. 206.

13. Erwin Panofsky, 'Style and medium in the motion pictures' (revised), *Critique* 1, no. 3, January/February 1947.

14. See Mast and Cohen, *Film Theory and Criticism* , p. 345.

15. Allardyce Nicoll, *Film and Theatre* (Harrap, 1936).

16. See Manvell, *Theater and Film* p. 265.

17. Allardyce Nicoll, 'Film reality: the cinema and the theatre', in James Hurt (ed.), *Focus on Film and Theatre* (Prentice-Hall, 1974), p. 30.

18. Nicoll, *Film and Theatre*, p. 165, quoted in Waller, p. 238.

19. Ibid., p. 170, in Waller, p. 238.

20. Siegfried Kracauer, *Theory of Film: the Redemption of Physical Reality* (Oxford University Pres, 1960, 1979) esp. pp. 221–2.

21. Ibid., pp. 217–8.

22. Ibid., p. 217.

23. Ibid., p. 218.

24. Ibid., pp. 221–2.

25. Ibid., p. 216.

26. Ibid., p. 230.

27. André Bazin, 'Theater and Cinema', in *What Is Cinema?*, vol. 1, tr. Hugh Gray (University of California Press, 1967), p. 83.

28. Ibid., p. 84.

29. Ibid., p. 86.

30. Ibid., pp. 87–9.

31. Ibid., p. 111.

32. Ibid., p. 115.

33. Ibid., p. 95.

34. Ibid., pp. 101–2.

35. Ibid., p. 100.

36. John Simon, *New Leader*, 27 December 1971.

37. Tony Palmer, *Spectator*, 29 January 1972.

38. Susan Sontag, 'Film and Theatre' in Mast and Cohen, *Film Theory and Criticism*, p. 360.

39. Ibid., p. 361.

40. Ibid., pp. 363–4.

41. Ibid., p. 362.

42. Ibid., p. 365.

43. Eric Bentley, 'Realism and the Cinema', in Hurt, p. 54.

44. Sergei Eisenstein, *Film Form: Essays in Film Theory*, ed. and tr. Jan Leyda (Harcourt Brace, 1949), p. 5, quoted in Waller, p. 284.

45. Ibid., p. 4, quoted in Waller, p. 284.

46. Hurt, *Focus on Film and Theatre* pp. 10–11.

47. Waller, *The Stage/Screen Debate* p. 337.

48. Sontag, in Mast and Cohen, *Film Theory and Criticism*, p. 366.

49. Bazin, 'Theater and Cinema', p. 105.

50. Laura Mulvey, 'Visual pleasure and narrative cinema', *Screen*, vol. 16, no. 3, Autumn 1975; and 'Afterthoughts on "Visual Pleasure and Narrative Cinema" inspired by *Duel in the Sun*', *Framework* nos 15, 16, 17.

51. Manvell, *Theater and Film*, pp. 23–4.

52. Raymond Williams, 'Film and the dramatic tradition' in Raymond Williams and Michael Orrom, *Preface to Film* (Film Drama, 1954), p. 13, quoted in Waller, *The Stage/Screen Debate*, p. 352.

53. Williams, p. 14, quoted in Waller, *The Stage/Screen Debate*, p. 352.

54. See Hurt, *Focus on Film and Theatre*, p. 9.

55. Manvell, *Theater and Film*, pp. 53–4.

56. See, for example, ibid., p. 25.

57. See, for example, ibid., pp. 29–30.

58. Ibid., p. 29.

59. Jack J. Jorgens, *Shakespeare on Film* (Indiana University Press, 1977).

60. Ibid., p. 3.

61. Ibid., pp. 7–11.

3 SPECIFIC PROBLEMS

Ancient Greek Theatre into Film

The problems which have been claimed to dog the transference to film of any play conceived for live theatre performance are considered to be intensified if the play in question is a Greek tragedy. David Wilson,[1] for example, believes that Greek tragedy 'compounds the problem of theatre into film'. This problem, in the various forms under which it has been identified, has been the subject of Chapter 2, but it could be asked if 'problem' is a fair term. It is, only if a purist view of either medium is maintained, or if dominant practice is taken effectively to exclude all other possibilities.

It might be instructive to consider Wilson's explanation of the compounded problem:

> How [to] represent, in an age of realism, a drama which was formal, quasi-religious, rooted in ideas rather than character?

Several of the assumptions here could be questioned. Are we in 'an age of realism'? We are in an age, certainly, when realism is the privileged but not the only mode in cinema and television (see p. 12). Moreover, Bazin, who believed that cinema was indeed essentially realist, saw no obstacle to the filming of classical tragedy, provided that its theatrical reality was respected (pp. 8-9). Greek tragedy is fairly described as 'formal' and its religious origins are highly likely;[2] yet, despite all its formality, ancient commentators on tragedy seemed sufficiently unperturbed by its conventions not to think of it in terms other than mimetic — in other words as having a direct relationship with life. Plato, in *The Republic,* went so far as to convict Greek tragedy of telling lies about the gods and heroes, which implies that tragedy was generally taken to have a close relationship with actuality. (Why else would the philosopher have worried about misinformation invading the lives of the Guardians of his ideal state?) Aristotle, in the *Poetics,* demands probability or necessity of superior tragedy's structure and attributes the achieve-

22

ment of catharsis to the arousing of intense pity and fear through what we would term identification, which in turn demands the credibility of the narrative. Although mimesis is a problematic term which deserves far fuller analysis than can be offered here, these Greek philosophers at least talk about tragedy in a manner that is curiously close to that in which realist cinema is discussed. Yet, what is understood to be 'realist' may be very different to the ancients' thinking about contemporary theatre, from 'realist' views of, say, Hollywood or Italian cinema. (It is useful to remind ourselves that realism is a convention which alters in time and in different media, and that it is an aesthetic choice with often profound political implications rather than an unavoidable necessity.)

Is tragic drama 'rooted in ideas rather than character'? Aristotle lists action as logically prior to character, but puts these components at the head of his list of six. His argument is that by their action we arrive at an estimation of the character of those who act. Morals are drawn (usually by the Chorus) in the course of tragedies, but whether these views are authoritative readings of the tragedy is another matter. Aristotle's emphasis may well be legitimate, although our expectations of action are belied in 'tragic action'.

> How [to] deal, in the flat plane of the cinema, with the essentially circular presence of the Chorus, so integral a part of Greek drama that the theatres were built in the round?

Taking this question in its most literal sense, we could ask whether it might not be rephrased to consider the rectangular frame rather than 'the flat plane'. All projected film images are literally flat (though it is not simply 3D movies which are *perceived* as having depth); all theatre performances three-dimensional. The question is clearly more searching than that, though. Wilson seems to be asking how such a defiantly formalist area of Greek tragedy as the Chorus, without which no tragedy was presented, may be accommodated within a medium which privileges realism and whose formal properties have no obvious equivalent for this. The Chorus does deserve to be viewed as a candidate for 'problem' status, the problem being at its most acute when a 'realistic' rather than 'theatrical' or 'filmic' mode is chosen (see p. 19). While Wilson is justified in drawing attention to the centrality of the *orchestra* (the Chorus's performance area within the ancient theatre) he may thereby be exaggerating the centrality of the Chorus to every tragedy performed in the theatre.

It is noteworthy that by far the greatest concentration — in Aristophanes' ridiculing or criticism of tragic writing, in Plato's *Republic,* or in Aristotle's *Poetics* — is upon the dialogue spoken by the actors and not the lyrical expressions of Choral thought. Aristotle expects the Chorus to be 'integrated', but Euripides, the tragedian whose works survive in greatest quantity despite Aristotle's evidently stronger interest in Sophocles, disappoints this expectation, most notably perhaps in his *Hippolytus,* where the Chorus appears to be an irritating necessity.

What to do with those awkward last-minute interventions of the gods?

A fair question, though it should be stressed that by no means all extant tragedies end with a *deus ex machina* and that, even in Euripides' time, the sudden intervention by a god must have been discerned to disrupt the organic wholeness that Aristotle seems to demand of good tragedy.

Jack J. Jorgens' experience of critical attitudes to films of Shakespeare allows him to conclude tentatively that these are automatically praised or blamed because they have been made in a particular mode. It seems wise, he suggests, 'to avoid elevating our own particular sensitivities to the status of universal laws'.[3] While not explicitly stated as such, there seems to be a ban in Oliver Taplin's review of the National Film Theatre season, in June 1981, of filmed Greek tragedies[4] upon any film made in the filmic mode (see p. 19), and particular interest in the theatrical mode, perhaps because of Taplin's well-evidenced enthusiasm for modern theatre productions of Greek tragedy.[5] David Wilson ends his summary of the problems in a mood of greater tolerance (as well as greater imprecision) than his article originally promised:

It is not a question of whether one version of a play is more 'authentic' than another. What matters is the film-maker's creative response to a theatre which, in confronting ancient myth, confronted also the eternal contradictions of the human mind.[6]

Conditions peculiar to Greek Tragedy

'Authenticity' — whatever that means precisely in the present context — is said not to be obligatory, particularly for film-makers choosing to operate within the filmic mode. Yet, it seems important for at least those attempting the realistic mode to know what elements of Greek theatre were essential or more frequent and may be most resistant to adaptation. (The theatrical mode shifts the desirability of such knowledge from the film-maker to the producer of the stage version, on the other hand.)

The most significant of these would appear to be the following, listed in no particular order:[7]

Chorus (see pp. 23-4)

The Chorus, already an integral part of many occasions celebrated by the community as well as of the religious festivals at which the plays were put on, 'lent ceremony and depth' to these occasions, and thus to drama.[8] The oft-remarked integral part of the Chorus should not be taken to imply that it is integral to the dramatic action. Its use has been well described as 'to relieve, amplify, intensify, or complicate [the] drama — and to mislead simple readers who habitually look for the "moral" of the tragedy.'[9] Taplin's synopsis of the function of Choral song in relation to the action of the play is that it provides a sequence 'of associative, often emotional, links'.[10]

Masks

Although the reasons behind their use in Greek tragedy take us back to pre-dramatic times, the use of masks seems likely to have made for less incongruity when female characters were played, as always, by male actors. However, it is suggested[11] that their use encouraged a tendency to typing rather than individualising of characters. While this is possible, we should beware of making assumptions about typology in ancient drama simply because it does not deal in the idiosyncrasies of characterisation which, say, the novel has made us expect. The characters of tragedy pre-exist these dramas since they come[12] from heroic myth. A novelist has to create character and, in the traditional novel, that character's credibility each time he or she introduces one. Clytemnestra, however, was the faithless wife who killed her husband Agamemnon centuries before Aeschylus wrote *The Oresteia*. A character's psy-

chology may still be interpreted differently in each play. The Clytemnestra of Euripides' *Electra* seems, for example, a far less strong-
willed and single-minded character than in the Aeschylean trilogy.

While we should be on our guard against modern assumptions
about character as we try to analyse the function and effect of the
use of the mask, these assumptions are highly relevant to modern
readings of masks, as well as of the characters whose faces were
represented by them in fifth-century BC drama.

Costume

The costume of Greek tragedy was formal and conventionalised,
and did, as Muller suggests, occasionally include head-dresses (to
mark the foreign-ness of Medea, for example), but Muller is mistaken in believing that high-soled buskins were used on the classical
stage. All the archaeological evidence suggests that footwear was of
no significant height, and that it is not until Hellenistic times that
high-soled footwear appeared in tragedy.[13]

Conventions

As well as those listed under Masks and Costume, above, other
conventions of ancient production include:
1. The stock Messenger, whose function is generally to report in an
objective manner an actual or threatened catastrophe which has
occurred offstage.
2. The three-actor limit — the conservatism about number of actors
in tragedy may be explicable in terms of drama's origins in ritual;
whatever the reasons, parts had to be divided among no more
than three actors, a practice that must have occasioned particular
awkwardness in Sophocles' *Oedipus at Colonus*.[14]
3. Stichomythia — a formal passage of dialogue in which exchanges
between characters are expressed in a line of poetry apiece.

Theatre

The most significant aspect of the ancient theatre may for today
simply be its size — capable, for example, of holding the entire
population of Athens at the Great Dionysia. Performances were in
the open air, the audience being seated in the tiered, horseshoe-
shaped *theatron* looking down on the *orchestra* and, behind it, the
actors' area in front of the *skene* building. A play was normally
performed only once, presented with others in competition to a
vast audience celebrating a religious festival but also aware of its

ostensible civic cohesion and ready to consider political and ethical, as well as more obviously religious, questions.

Acting

All of the factors discussed above seem relevant to any theory of ancient dramatic acting which may be constructed — these, together with the evidence of the plays themselves and the conception of mimesis which underlies the discussions of tragic poetry in Plato's *Republic* and Aristotle's *Poetics,* for example (see pp. 22-3). Oliver Taplin, in his discussion of acting, makes the valuable point that every age thinks of its actors as unprecedentedly 'natural' or 'true to life', although all acting is a matter of artifice and stylisation, thus, 'natural' performances are indicated by certain conventions within the repertory of a particular theatrical style.[15] Classical Greek acting is supposed by many to be particularly stylised, on the evidence of the use of masks and certain other conventions, but especially because of the size of the auditorium. The question cannot be considered simply in unexamined terms of stylisation, however, since it is the audience's perception of acting conventions that may be crucial rather than what our culture in the 1980s discerns as specially stylised. In other words, what is artificial to us may have been 'read' as sincere and life-like by an Athenian audience of the fifth century BC. Taplin reminds us that such stage machinery as the *mechane* (or crane) was invented so that characters said to fly in the script could be seen to be 'flying', and that, therefore, the case for an interest in realism would thus seem to be strengthened.

Subject matter

Tragedies based their plots almost exclusively (see note 12 below) on heroic myth, a vast body of legends which seem to have been commonly known in advance by theatre audiences. Oliver Taplin makes some sense of Aristotle's claim that they were known to only a few[16], however, by pointing out the tremendous variability of oral and literary traditions and the great difference between myth and 'plot'.[17] The effect of such prior knowledge as has already been noted in the context of characterisation (p. 25) must also have produced opportunities for tragic irony in such plays as *Oedipus Rex.* Muller points out that these stories were history, not poetry, for the Greeks.[18] This might be questioned. Heroic myth might have been taken to represent some level of historical truth, but this is differentiated sharply by Aristotle from the poetic, or universal, truth of tragedy. The elasticity with which individual playwrights treated the same myth suggests also that it may be simplistic to imagine that the Greeks viewed dramatic plots as based on historical actuality. Muller's point in talking about historical veracity is to suggest that Greek tragedy is more realist than it has traditionally been taken to be. This valid point could be argued, however, without recourse to this interpretation of myth.

Ancient into Modern Theatre

The central question, at least in commentaries on modern productions of Greek tragedy, seems always to be that of fidelity to the original, whether it is feasible and, if so, whether it is desirable. If it is the central question, it might be worth examining it in more detail. A more extended discussion than usual is provided in Oliver Taplin's *Greek Tragedy in Action*[19] in the section entitled 'Round plays in square theatres' (pp. 172 ff.). An examination of these arguments ought to prove useful.

Taplin poses the question, 'Authenticity or freedom?', suggesting that it is a question relevant to all play productions, unless the author is also the director. In relation to ancient drama, he sees the opposite poles as, on the one hand, the closest possible reproduction of the original performance and, on the other, 'uninhibited rein to modern reframing'. Modern theatre being a director's theatre, he claims, the choice is often the latter alternative, resulting in a play which is 'openly and unashamedly rewritten' until it is a new work 'inspired' by the old one. In productions which do claim fidelity, Taplin concludes that there is a split between verbal and other dimensions, so that there is fidelity to the original verbal text but aural and, especially, visual elements are decided by the director and, to a lesser extent, the cast: the visual dimension 'has no necessary connection with textual fidelity'. More, it can obscure or militate against the author's meaning. The result of inattention to the author's 'visual and scenic meaning' is that the modern production uses, adapts, 'improves' on the author's work, without making the audience aware of this interference. Still, the other extreme also has serious pitfalls, the most obvious being that a carbon copy of the original production is impracticable and that the performance could not be authentic since the modern audience is 'inauthentic'.

Since the extremes in production are so unsatisfactory, Taplin next examines a middle position, allowing an 'interplay of past with present'. This is achieved by respect for the author's meaning, inextricable from his 'communicative purpose'. However, since we are necessarily not the original public or even similar to it, the 'real search is for what the author's meaning has to say for us now'. In practical terms, he prescribes the following:

1. The director and the actors should respect the author's words, by translating but not altering; and

2. the visual meaning is to be elicited, the author's explicit and implicit stage instructions to be given due emphasis, invention and interpolation of stage business to be shunned.

He ends this section with a rebuke for those who have not produced ancient plays according to these prescriptions: ('An age which refuses to learn from the past, or which uses it merely as an inanimate raw material without regard for its integrity and life, is an age of tyranny, narrow-mindedness and arrogance.'

The equation of the invention of stage business, or of visual and aural dimensions, with tyranny, narrow-mindedness and arrogance seems like overkill even within the terms of the argument. The simple fact is that, before the appearance of the book from which this discussion is culled, there was almost no guidance other than the plays themselves as to the visual dimension of staged Greek tragedy. Moreover, Taplin's own work, valuable for an understanding of productions within the theatres for which the plays were written, gives little sustained help for producers working in quite different conditions.

Taplin is at his best on the points where he itemises the reasons for the impossibility of total fidelity (our ignorance of certain conditions of production,[20] the fact that the Theatre of Dionysus is now damaged, etc.), and especially when he draws attention to the mighty difference in audiences, so that 'what was new is now old', and what was immediate 'is now distanced'. These arguments are, paradoxically, the best defence against charges of arrogance or tyranny. Taplin whips up feeling against those directors who invent the visual dimension by comparing this sort of activity with the revamping of a Rembrandt painting or of a Shakespeare sonnet, and by convicting them of 'dictatorial patronising'. This seems overstated criticism of the tendency. A Rembrandt painting may be viewed by today's art lovers, a Shakespeare sonnet read by poetry lovers. No ancient production exists. The painting may also be filmed, videoed or televised, raising problems of mediation, the latter recited on stage, film and television. Would this recitation, which retains Shakespeare's words but presents a new visual dimension, be condemned as 'revamping'? Would the film-maker, having no clues from Rembrandt or from Shakespeare about how best to record the painting or sonnet, be tyrannical, patronising or narrow-minded if he or she invented, out of necessity, a visual dimension?

While decrying inauthenticity in visual matters, Taplin suggests that there is little problem about verbal authenticity. Any reader who, therefore, imagines that there is a definitive verbal text for even one ancient drama is in for a big disappointment. Much of classical scholarship can be epitomised as the unending search for credible readings of much (or even slightly) disputed passages in ancient authors. Arguments about preferable readings of passages where the manuscript tradition offers various possibilities assume the author's meaning or attempt to elucidate it, but also, it should be remembered, help to create it. A Sophocles play emerges from centuries of debate about the credibility of the hundreds of variant readings in the transmitted text. As long as textual criticism of this sort is practised, the play is, to an extent, fluid, the author's meaning a process, if it is not indeed a construct of many scholars' informed surmises. There is also an industry in books arguing often widely divergent interpretations of ancient playwrights' work. This suggests that, even if there were a definitive text for each play to be produced, the meaning of those words would be quite unstable and open to debate. A still more obvious point is that modern productions, at least if they are to make any financial return, are always in translation. Translation itself may aspire to verbal fidelity but that must remain only an aspiration. It is not merely words that are translated but concepts and concepts which were meaningful to a fifth-century BC Athenian audience may well have no equivalent today.

Lest this summary of the difficulties inherent in the notion of verbal authenticity lead to an exaggerated reaction against the aspiration to authenticity, it should be said that there remains a difference between productions which use *a* translated version of an original and build upon interpretations arising from a close study of that version, on the one hand, and, on the other, productions which abandon such study to offer a quite different experience of a dramatic version of the myth. Taplin's separation of the two is not without validity or usefulness, but the promotion of the first sort of production rests on a far less secure basis than he allows for.

At the end of this discussion, it seems that the question remains as open as ever. A modern producer cannot produce a 'carbon copy' ancient production, agreed, but he or she has many choices thereafter between or within the extremes of whether to seek fidelity, as far as that is achievable, or to base a new work on the original ancient play. It does not seem possible to attach values to different approaches beforehand but rather, if one insists on evaluating, to examine what is afforded as a result of those different choices. Even then, we have to be aware of our assumptions in such evaluation. At the simplest level, we should know whether we are looking for an educational experience, whereby modern audiences are illuminated as to fifth-century BC drama and the conditions (in the broadest sense) under which it was produced, or for some sort of 'dramatic' experience analogous to the cathartic experience attributed by Aristotle to classical tragedy. One need not exclude the other, but evaluations seem in practice to favour exclusivity.

The 'death of tragedy'

If audiences of either modern stage productions or films relating to Greek tragedy are to enjoy a 'dramatic' experience, let alone achieve catharsis, the question of tragedy's viability in our times seems crucial. Before considering that question, however, we ought to consider the much-contested definition of tragedy, since those who have tackled the debate about the feasibility of modern tragedy inevitably rest their arguments on a definition, explicit or implicit.

A definition of tragedy as a dramatic genre is expectedly elusive. What may be more surprising is that a definition even of ancient Greek tragedy is extremely hard to maintain. The three major surviving tragedians, Aeschylus, Sophocles and Euripides, although having many formal components in common, and sharing the habit of dramatising incidents from heroic myth, seem to construct their plots differently, to take up vastly differing attitudes to the ethical, religious or socio-political questions raised by the mythical material as interpreted by them. Aristotle's *Poetics* attempts a description of tragedy (as well as other sorts of poetry) when it is not offering prescriptions for 'good tragedy', and yet, viewed in the context of the surviving plays, the *Poetics* seems to offer a brilliant analysis of *Oedipus Rex*, a largely fair description of Sophocles' methods and a singularly unhelpful description of tragedy if we attempt to use it for the comprehension of Aeschylus' or Euripides' dramas. He gives this definition of tragedy in Chapter 6:

Tragedy . . . is a representation of an action that is worth serious attention, complete in itself, and of some amplitude; in language enriched by a variety of artistic devices appropriate to the several parts of the play; presented in the form of action, not narration; by means of pity and fear bringing about the purgation [catharsis] of such emotions.[21]

This raises as many questions as it solves. What, for example, is 'an action that is worth serious attention'? The actions of tragedy are given serious attention, largely (some of Euripides' plays treat themes or incidents more light-heartedly than might be expected within tragic practice), and these actions must, presumably, be worth serious attention. But if Aristotle is to rescue himself from tautology, he must be suggesting that there are actions which are *intrinsically* serious. Whether actions can be serious or trivial until they are perceived as such is doubtful, but if we take the commonsense line, that death (or more especially kin murder, incest, pollution) are all 'worth serious attention', we find that the Oedipus story which, in Sophocles' treatment of it, involves all of these elements, is treated as a subject for comedy in Aristophanes' *Frogs*:

Euripides [reciting]:   A happy man was Oedipus at first —
Aeschylus: Was he at any time? When even before he was born Apollo had decreed that he should kill his own father? You call that being a happy man?
Euripides [reciting] — But he became the most unfortunate
                    Of mortal men.
Aeschylus: He didn't become so, he *was* so all along. Look at his story. First of all, as a new-born baby, he is dumped out in the cold, cold snow in an earthenware utensil, to prevent him from growing up and murdering his father; then he comes limping to Corinth with both his feet swollen: then he marries a woman old enough to be his mother; and then, as though that wasn't bad enough, he finds out that she *is* his mother. And finally he blinds himself.[22]

In other words, the elements of the story are serious when treated as such, comic when treated as such. (Death or nuclear annihilation would seem, on a commonsense view, to be intrinsically serious subjects today, but if so we have to reckon with the comic treatment afforded to them by Joe Orton's *Loot* and Stanley Kubrick's *Dr Strangelove* (1963), respectively.)

If the conception of Greek tragedy is nebulous, then and now, we can hardly expect a cogent description covering everything claimed as tragic from Aeschylus to Arthur Miller. Ekbert Faas agrees with Barthes that tragedy is Western man's 'most daring effort to justify the human dilemma under the guise of some metaphysical scheme'.[23] Faas conceives of the tragic as purposive rather than pessimistic, in that suffering and death are shown to serve a meaningful purpose. He is supported in this by Taplin and John Gassner. Taplin concludes that a sense of understanding is the 'message' of tragedy,[24] pointing out that the intellect is engaged as well as the emotions, that suffering is placed within situations of moral conflict.[25] Gassner's view is similar: 'The therapy of tragic catharsis could no more be complete and conclusive without intellect than any form of psychotherapy which brings the patient's inner tensions to light without enabling him [sic] to understand and master them.'[26] 'To adopt Nietzsche's terminology from *The Birth of Tragedy*,' he continues, 'Greek tragedy imposed . . . the Apollonian world of light and reason upon the Dionysian world of passion.'[27]

Herbert J. Muller directs the discussion, in attempting to define the tragic spirit, incidentally away from questions of form — which might be a promising direction, at least for ancient tragedy — and towards seriousness and universality: 'tragedy might be defined as a fiction inspired by a serious concern with the problems of man's fate',[28] he offers, proceeding to exclude the sensational from the serious, and the adolescent, the abnormal individual, the representative of a type or social class, from the man who is the subject. (He says nothing of woman.) 'Above all, tragedy is centred on the problem of his "fate" . . . his relations to his total environment, his position in the universe, the ultimate meaning of his life.'[29]

The point of Muller's stress on the universal is partly to set up criteria by which modern tragedy may be judged, and found wanting. He argues that it is the common practice of modern tragedy to focus on questions of social and political injustice. The problem with this practice, for Muller, is that these questions are soluble, that such a theme is too 'timely', whereas a tragic writer ought to be bringing out the 'timeless implications'. The writer imbued with the tragic spirit would identify the problem not with a particular society's workings but with the age-old problem of 'man's inhumanity to man', because 'there will always remain suffering beyond remedy'.[30]

In his stress on the eternal or 'timeless', Muller agrees with Hegel and Schopenhauer, although these philosophers reached opposite conclusions concerning rationality within the tragic universe.

The more detailed definition of tragedy worked out by John von Szeliski[31] covers the following points:

1. The central character, not always virtuous, must be dramatically central and in a position to enact something concerned with the meaning of the questions about existence raised by his [sic] crisis.
2. The crisis must therefore centre on the chief character's suffering.
3. The outcome of this suffering must be emotional or spiritual destruction, or complete physical destruction.
4. The theme must be serious — the meaning of life, a question of universal relevance.
5. The action should be at least slightly fictionalised.
6. The spoken text must attempt to express the tragic in terms of man's [sic] fate.

Once again, a definition has been attempted, largely on the basis of Greek and Elizabethan tragedy. This tendency is especially odd in Muller's case, since he disputes the notion that Tragedy has an existence transcending the works claimed to be tragedies: 'There is no eternal Idea of Tragedy existing independently of the works of men, but only a host of works that men have called tragedies. Neither is there any such thing as a "typical" tragedy'.[32] Yet, Muller attempts to use his definition of the tragic against modern works 'claimed to be tragedies'. The inconsistency of his logic becomes all the clearer when he writes,

> As for modern tragedy, critics still argue that it is not 'really' tragic by some canon derived from the practice — or more often the theory — of the ancients. The fair question is whether, in the new terms imposed by modern knowledge and conditions of life, it still affirms equivalent values and affords an equivalent pleasure.[33]

Von Szeliski justifies the confinement of his definition to 'traditional' tragedies by arguing that there is necessarily a relation between modern and traditional tragedy: 'Unless some playwright wishes to claim he has invented a new genre . . . any attempt to write "a tragedy" is at least partly based on producing the essential satisfactions which were present in past, successful tragedies.'[34] It seems a weak defence. It would be curious to arrive at an understanding of Shakespearean tragedy by emphasising only the 'essential satisfactions' present in Greek tragedy. Yet, he sees what he claims as the inbuilt pessimism of modern tragedy as 'a problem for tragedy' because 'such men's natures drastically cut down identification due to their highly specialised relation to life. We are not drawn to their power or spirit or potential because . . . they are not expected to be powerful or successful.' Are pessimism and reduced possibilities of identification inimical to tragedy, then? But how can they be if they are key elements in self-proclaimed modern tragedy? Von Szeliski comes dangerously close here to creating an 'Idea of Tragedy' that exists independently of its (modern) practitioners.

What seems to emerge from the examination of definitions of tragedy is that modern tragedy is different from previous tragedy. Some would argue that it is not so much different as dead, killed off by one or more of the following:

Marxism

If the tragic spirit has some connection with human recognition of the inexorable — whether this be termed Fate or Necessity — then Marxist hostility to it is readily appreciated: 'Necessity is blind only in so far as it is not understood.'[35] Thus, the tragic theatre takes on the appearance of the pre-rational,[36] and the tragic becomes 'an obsolete mode of perception'.[37] Georg Lukács's explanation of the existence of tragic conceptions at certain points in history is that these mark 'the moment in which an existing social order is dialectically dissolved'.[38] Marcuse argues that Marxism effects 'the end of Christian idealistic tragedy'.[39] Tragedy can be deemed 'Christian' only in the loose sense that it is describable as 'purposive' despite its concentration on human suffering, or that an ultimately benign divine providence may be anticipated by struggling humanity. (This last notion is truer of Aeschylus than could credibly be claimed for Sophocles or Euripides.)

Brecht is 'anti-Aristotelian' without necessarily being, therefore, anti-tragic. His challenge to the principle of unity or to the emotional function of tragedy as propounded by the *Poetics* finds its expression in his 'epic theatre'. (These Aristotelian principles could be thought already to be challenged within the context of Greek tragedy's practice, none the less.) Where he could be claimed to be anti-tragic — and this depends on one's understanding of 'the tragic spirit' — is in his confidence in the perfectibility of humankind, in the power of rational inquiry or concerted action.

Freudianism

Freud shares with Marx the view that tragedy is a product of a disadvantaged age. Where Marxists may look upon tragedy as a relic of a pre-rational phase in human history, Freud would analyse it from a psychoanalytic, scientific standpoint. Tragedy, according to Freud, alongside morality, society and religion, results from the primeval crime of parricide:

> After the band of brothers kills and devours the father for keeping all the women to himself, their contradictory feelings of hatred and admiration for the deceased first engender remorse. In order to allay this . . . they institute the totemic system, whereby the totem or father-substitute comes under special protection against repetitions of the original crime.[40]

The killing of the father, for Freud an historical event, engenders tragedy as well as the Oedipus complex, for the latter is conceived by him to be a ritual where the crime, through the use of a totem or father-substitute, may be regularly and safely celebrated. The murdered father who haunts the memory of the killer sons and their descendants is transposed into god, king, hero, in mythology. The hero of Greek tragedy is viewed by Freud as this father reincarnated as scapegoat for the original crime: 'He had to suffer because he was the primal father, the hero of that primordial tragedy . . . and the tragic guilt is the guilt which he had to take upon himself in order to free the chorus of theirs.'[41]

However credible or otherwise this account of tragedy may appear — and the variety of tragic actions, as well as the frequency of tragic heroines, would at least require further explanation, as would the identification of 'guilt' with the Chorus in the first place, and with the father-substitute rather than some putative brother-substitutes in the second — its dissemination means that tragedy, at least that based on heroic myth — may no longer be approached 'innocently'. As Steiner puts it, one of the 'notable discoveries of the modern temper is that the ancient fables can be read in the light of psychoanalysis and anthropology. By manipulating the values of myths one can bring out from within their archaic lineaments shadows of psychic repression and blood ritual.'[42]

Modern Attitudes

When we turn from intellectual history to popular beliefs, the tendencies encouraged by Marx and Freud seem to be marked, though less rigorously argued, if at all.

It has been claimed, as noted above (p. 33), that modern writers tend to look for answers to their protagonists' crises, in social or political reform, for example. This is only one aspect of intolerance of the irremediable or of the Romantic desire for a happy ending. Steiner traces a link between Rousseau, with his presumption of the origins of evil as discoverable in social rather than metaphysical causes, and the closure of the Hollywood movie, with its lovers moving hand in hand towards marriage.[43]

If the possibility of finding an answer, with the consequent promise of ultimate happiness, is inimical to tragedy, precisely the opposite tendency in modern writing is thought to be as likely to frustrate the composition of tragedy today. An entire book[44] has been devoted to the preponderance of pessimism as an attitude in modern 'tragic' writing, while traditional tragedy tempered its fascination with suffering by means of intellectual exploration/enrichment so that it could be thought of today as 'purposive'. Joseph Wood Krutch argued in 1929 that, the universe being soul-less and mankind being a creature of reflexes and complexes, there was no possibility of interest being taken in questions of human fate.[45] The despair that infects modern writers and which runs counter, it is claimed, to the spirit of tragedy is traced by von Szeliski to 'Darwinism, Freudianism, cut-throat domestic and international economics (and politics), agnosticism and atheism'.[46]

In any case, the protagonist of traditional tragedy was heroic, while at the centre of today's tragedies is most commonly found a petty bourgeois.

> Reality says there are no heroes. Our politics says all men are created equal. Politics and expedient theology say that nobody ought to be far more important, far richer, or far more gifted than anyone else. We reject the superman as we reject Naziism's super-race. Democracy, unionism, socialism, and even Christianity have often made the 'common' man the central character of contemporary education, religion, government, and culture. The contemporary hero would be a freak.[47]

Lack of Community Audience

One (Romantic) explanation for the alleged failure of Europe to produce tragic drama after the seventeenth century has been taken to be the lack of a suitable audience for it. This audience would, according to this view, be one made up of members of a community sharing a culture agreed on the significance of human existence, the kind of audience thought to have witnessed Greek or Jacobean tragedy. In fact, we know too little of the beliefs of these audiences to declare that they were a community in the Romantic conception of it, but George Steiner does accept that a profound change in European society was occasioned by the French Revolution and the Napoleonic wars, whereby ordinary humanity was plunged into the stream of history and thus laid open 'to pressures of experience and feeling which in earlier times had been the prerogatives of princes, statesmen, and professional soldiers'.[48] While the release of the middle classes into the mainstream of history created strikingly different theatre audiences from those that had attended performances of Racine, for example, other changes are just as significant for the question of tragedy's imagined decline. The loss of a 'unified' audience is not merely a matter of social and political change, but also a matter of technological advance. During the nineteenth century, low-cost, mass printing might be discerned as a principal reason for the abandonment of the 'serious' theatre to minority audiences, since the 'serious' writer might well channel his or her energies into the writing of novels rather than plays. 'The spectator had become the reader' is Steiner's succinct comment.[49]

So many reasons to explain the death of tragedy. But it is timely now at last to ask if tragedy did die. Or rather we ought to ask, with Ekbert Faas, what exactly died, if anything. Was it a literary genre (some would prefer to think of it as a dramatic genre), he asks, or an entire vision of life?[50] He points out that tragedy, if it has died in modern times, also died several times before. The first of these deaths was once thought to be as early as the fifth century BC, in the works of Euripides! This useful reminder of tragedy's multiple deaths and obituaries is supported by Muller's observation that periods of tragic production have been very rare: 'By general consent, there have been only four important periods, all of them brief: the ancient Greek . . . the Elizabethan . . . the French classical . . . and the modern, inaugurated by Ibsen'.[51] Muller also points out the narrow localisation of the phenomenon, its confinement to the Western world.

Rather than think in terms of a single death, Faas suggests that we should think not even of multiple deaths but multiple repudiations. He believes that such repudiations occur *within* tragic writing. The anti-tragic bias which is discernible in twentieth-century playwrights such as Ionesco, whose *Victims of Duty* is described by Faas as 'more radical in its anti-tragic stance than Marxism and Freudian psychoanalysis',[52] is not, he stresses, confined to the twentieth century. It can be discerned in Shakespeare, whose *King Lear* is, for Hegel, 'a vision of absolute evil and depravity'.[53] It can be discerned in Euripides, whose plays taught Montaigne the 'volubilitie and incomprehensibleness of all matters'.[54]

Where does this examination take us? It could be objected that the multiple repudiations of tragedy hardly alter the position claimed for modern theatre, that tragedy is incapable of being written for it. This would be to underestimate Faas' contribution, though. He shows not simply that reactions against tragedy have happened before. Much more crucially he shows that anti-tragic drama has a symbiotic relation with tragedy, that it gains validity from the prior or contemporaneous existence of tragedy, and that to understand anti-tragedy an audience or commentator needs to understand tragedy. This opens the door to the performance of even classical Greek tragedy in a modern context, and especially to fairer consideration of the films of tragedies which are too lightly dismissed as 'betrayals', or which, because deemed 'anti-tragic', are therefore no longer seriously discussed.

Faas creates two categories, 'anti-' and 'post-tragic'. For him, tragedy is 'purposive'. Anti-tragedy, he says, 'tends to misguide the spectators . . . it confuses and shocks, where its counterpart provides us with cathartic or otherwise meaningful effects.' It also tends 'to portray life in its situational and psychological singularity rather than to subsume it under all-encompassing schemes packaged in consistent plots.' Those who create anti-tragedy have in common 'a basic denial — or at least questioning — of the tragic vision of death and suffering, as somehow meaningful in the general order of things'. While Faas defines anti-tragedy in relation to tragedy, post-tragedy, he claims, 'affirms an independent vision' where suffering is 'neither meaningful nor absurd in an ultimate metaphysical sense. It simply and unavoidably exists.'[55]

Euripides produces genuine tragedy in his *Hippolytus* or *Iphigenia in Aulis* by these definitions, but makes forays into the anti-tragic with his *Ion* and *Electra*, or into the post-tragic with *The Bacchae*, according to Faas, who attempts to demonstrate that there is no chronological progression from the tragic to the anti-tragic, or vice versa. One could go farther than Faas and suggest that different parts of his plays demonstrate differing tendencies towards the tragic and anti-tragic. If Faas' basic points about anti-tragic tendencies coinciding with the tragic are acceptable, the mystery of Nietzsche's identification of Euripides as the destroyer of tragedy while Aristotle shows no awareness of this destruction even though he is not always complimentary to Euripides, seems less puzzling.

One of Euripides' most abiding monuments is, paradoxically, New Comedy. While all of Euripides' dramas were presented in the tragic competitions and not in comic contexts, it seems clear today that there are links between certain tendencies in Euripides and the genesis of Greek New Comedy. The playwright's 'bourgeois realism', his interest in the individual, his theatricality and 'artificiality', his sentiment, have all been cited[56] as elements which reappear in New Comedy. The most celebrated exponent of New Comedy, Menander, is never afforded the status of Aeschylus and Sophocles or, for that matter, Aristophanes. But New Comedy is Euripides' most enduring achievement in that this sentimental drama survives today, where it may be discerned in television sit-coms, for example. It might equally be possible to see the anti-tragic tendencies in Euripides, but particularly his bourgeoisification of tragedy, as laying the foundations of melodrama, the most popular 'serious' form of drama in today's cinema and television.

While further detailed consideration of Euripides should be held up until appropriate points are reached in the discussion of those films based on his work, this summary suggests directions in which modern productions of ancient tragedies might go; directions in which some films based on these tragedies can demonstrably be seen to have gone.

Film-makers, wishing to popularise tragedies, might well be expected to recast the original plays in terms of melodrama, shifting the centre of interest from heroic characters' relation to questions of divine or cosmic justice on to bourgeois characters' interaction without appeal to divinity or a sense of Providence. An obvious example of such an attempt is Jules Dassin's *Phaedra* (see pp. 98–105). A more stimulating direction, however, might be to question or comment on tragedy from a more modern, anti-tragic standpoint.

This seems to be the line chosen by Pasolini, for example, who evolves a kind of meta-tragedy, depending on knowledge of classical tragedy but viewing it from a modern standpoint which takes account of Marx, Freud and Frazer.

Our review of the reasoning behind the claims of tragedy's death could lead us to believe that the reports are somewhat exaggerated. In any case, rather than anticipating a succession of anachronistic films desperately attempting to breathe life in to a livid corpse, we may now look forward to an exploration of the strategies by which tragedy's rich potential, as embodying a view of life against which that of modern works may measure itself, is exploited.

Notes

1. David Wilson, 'Greek tragedy on film', National Film Theatre programme, June 1981, p. 18.
2. See A. W. Pickard-Cambridge, *Dithyramb, Tragedy and Comedy* (Clarendon Press, 1962), for discussion of origins of tragedy.
3. Jack J. Jorgens, *Shakespeare on Film* (Indiana University Press, 1977), p. 15.
4. Oliver Taplin, 'The Delphic Idea and After', *The Times Literary Supplement*, 17 July 1981, pp. 811–12.
5. He is the author of *The Stagecraft of Aeschylus* (Clarendon Press, 1977) and *Greek Tragedy in Action* (Methuen, 1978).
6. Wilson, 'Greek tragedy on film', p. 18.
7. Most helpful for the present endeavour have been Herbert J. Muller, *The Spirit of Tragedy*. (Alfred A. Knopf, 1956), esp. pp. 49–53; and Oliver Taplin, *Greek Tragedy in Action* (Methuen, 1978), esp. pp. 13–16.
8. Taplin, *Greek Tragedy*, p. 13.
9. Muller, Herbert J., *The Spirit of Tragedy* (Alfred A. Knopf, 1956), p. 49.
10. Taplin, *Greek Tragedy*, p. 13.
11. By, for example, Muller, *The Spirit of Tragedy*, p. 50.
12. There are exceptions, such as the characters of Aeschylus' *Persians*.
13. See, for example, Kendall Smith, 'The use of the high-soled shoe or buskin in Greek tragedy of the 5th and 4th centuries BC', *Harvard Studies in Classical Philology*, 1905.
14. See Muller, *The Spirit of Tragedy*, p. 50.
15. Taplin, *Greek Tragedy*, p. 15.
16. Aristotle, in Aristotle, Horace, Longinus, *Classical Literary Criticism*, tr. T. S. Dorsch (Penguin Classics, 1965), p. 44.
17. Taplin, *Greek Tragedy*, p. 163.
18. Muller, *The Spirit of Tragedy*, p. 52.
19. See note 5, above.
20. Our ignorance of the music and details of choreography seems especially salient when it comes to staging the stasima.
21. Aristotle, in Aristotle, Horace, Longinus, *Classical Literary Criticism* pp. 38–9.
22. Aristophanes, *The Frogs and other plays*, tr. David Barrett (Penguin, 1964, 1975), p. 199.

23. Ekbert Faas, *Tragedy and After: Euripides, Shakespeare, Goethe* (McGill-Queen's University Press, 1984), p. 4.

24. Taplin, *Greek Tragedy*, p. 170.

25. Ibid., p. 169.

26. John Gassner, *The Theatre in our Times: A Survey of the Men, Materials and Movements in the Modern Theatre* (Crown Publishers, 1954), p. 53.

27. Ibid., p. 55.

28. Muller, *The Spirit of Tragedy*, p. 12.

29. Ibid., p. 12.

30. Ibid., p. 17.

31. John von Szeliski, *Tragedy and Fear: Why Modern Tragic Drama Fails* (University of North Carolina Press, 1971), pp. 11–12.

32. Muller, *The Spirit of Tragedy*, p. 10.

33. Ibid., p. 250.

34. von Szeliski, *Tragedy and Fear*, p. 11.

35. George Steiner, *The Death of Tragedy* (Faber & Faber, 1961), p. 4.

36. Ibid., p. 342.

37. Faas, *Tragedy and After*, p. 13.

38. See ibid., p. 14.

39. Ludwig Marcuse, quoted ibid., p. 13.

40. Sigmund Freud, *Totem and Taboo*, quoted ibid., p. 15.

41. Freud, quoted in Muller, *The Spirit of Tragedy*, p. 30.

42. Steiner, *The Death of Tragedy*, p. 324.

43. Ibid., pp. 135–6.

44. von Szeliski, *Tragedy and Fear*.

45. See Muller, *The Spirit of Tragedy*, p. 244.

46. von Szeliski, *Tragedy and Fear*, pp. 33–34.

47. Ibid., p. 106.

48. Steiner, *The Death of Tragedy*, p. 116.

49. Ibid., p. 118.

50. Faas, *Tragedy and After*, p. 4.

51. Muller, *The Spirit of Tragedy*, p. ix.

52. Faas, *Tragedy and After*, p. 17.

53. Hegel, quoted ibid., p. 21.

54. Montaigne, quoted ibid., p. 22.

55. Ibid., pp. 6–7.

56. By, for example, Muller, *The Spirit of Tragedy*, p. 130.

FILMS IN THE THEATRICAL MODE

Prometheus in Chains (Directors: Costas and Dimitrios Gaziadis, 1927/1971)

By far the earliest filmed record of a modern theatrical production of Greek drama, this short's particular value is in partially preserving a key moment in the history of drama. The filming technique as well as the quality of the film stock would justify Oliver Taplin's description of the original film (1927) as 'exceedingly primitive',[1] but the event filmed, 11 minutes in all from the production of *Prometheus Bound* (by 'Aeschylus') at Delphi on 9 May 1927, has unusual significance. Mrs Aglae Mitropoulos, the guardian of the Greek Film Archive, considers that this production constitutes the rebirth of tragedy.[2] The claim of rebirth should not be taken to mean that the Delphi production was the first occasion that an ancient drama was enacted in an open-air theatre in modern Greece: Sophocles' *Antigone* was performed in the newly-excavated Herodes Atticus theatre in 1867.[3] Until this production, however, there was no 'living dramatic movement'[4], previous productions having been antiquarian exercises for an élite. This one, however, has been credited with inspiring all subsequent productions of Greek tragedy, particularly those at Epidauros.

Prometheus in Chains was part of a wider enterprise espoused by the poet, Angelos Sikelianos. After his marriage to the rich American, Eva Palmer (who was sympathetic to his 'Delphic Idea' in which the world 'might be saved from rationalism and industrialism by "the female principle", blended with Orphism, Buddhism, Dionysus, Pindar and Aeschylus'[5]) the couple conceived the dream of making Delphi the centre of the world. (The sacred precincts had been taken to be 'the navel of the Earth' in ancient times.) A university was to be established at Delphi, offering teaching that would propagate the 'Delphic Idea'; but the first notion realised in practice was the Delphic festival in 1927 and another in 1930, at which Aeschylean productions were offered. This short film (32 minutes in its 1971 version) preserves certain key moments of the 1927 production, which took place in the ancient theatre of the sacred site. Although the Greek authorities showed little interest in the work of Eva and Angelos Sikelianos, and Eva eventually left Greece in disgust, the attempt to restage Aeschylus in an ancient theatre had important repercussions.

The film begins with an exposition of the Sikelianos dream, while the audience is shown photographs of Eva and Angelos. The exposition continues with the information that the *Prometheus* production was intended to inaugurate their dream's realisation and that games (some snatches of which are shown) and exhibitions of Greek craftsmanship were also part of the project. The originality of having the Chorus as part of the production, in line with the interest taken in it by Plato and Aristotle, is stressed. The audience is then informed about the rationale for decisions about what was and was not to be filmed in 1927. The Oceanid Chorus was to be recorded, while long speeches were not to be included in the film. (The fact that the 1927 film was silent helps to explain this decision, as well as the fact that the characters wear masks so that the audience cannot even guess at what is being said when lips are obscured.) The 'Aeschylean' text is missing in the 1927 version, but the movements of Hephaestus' arms and head give the masked character life, and the dance of the Oceanids (who are 'inaccurately' without masks) is shown in this introduction to the film.

Also explained in this introduction is the contribution in 1971 to the original film, when sound was added. A particular *coup* was that George Bourlos, the actor who played the original Prometheus, was able, despite illness, to supply the voice of Prometheus for the new soundtrack. Also he and some of the women who had been Oceanids in 1927 were able to supply details of the production. The 1971 film operates, the introduction finally informs the audience, partly by freezing some scenes (to add dialogue, for example). The film then proceeds to contextualise, by means of a commentary, the scenes chosen for filming in 1927.

The opening scene, where Kratos and Bia (Strength and Violence personified) drag Prometheus out to torment is described and his crime, the theft of fire, mentioned in a written summary. The scene that we are shown has Kratos, Bia and Prometheus emerging from a rock cave, with Hephaestus limping behind. An impressive rock formation has been artificially created onstage as the actors' area, as opposed to the Chorus's. In the film, it is particularly instructive to see this man-made rock against the background of the actual landscape of Delphi, Mount Kirphys and the valley of the Pleistos, since this could forcefully remind us that the demarcation line between theatre spectacle and the world of actuality surrounding the theatre may have been very thin. Because the ancient theatre was open-air, the audience may well have had an unusually strong sense of the events staged within it as vitally connected with the world often visible outside. In the fragment of film, Hephaestus is seen to speak, and Prometheus' hands seen to be beaten by Hephaestus' hammer, indicating that he is riveted to the rock, crucified between Kratos and Bia.

The *parodos* (the opening Choral song sung as the Chorus enters the *orchestra*) of Oceanids and their father Oceanus was the next element in the 1927 production selected for filming. During the *parodos,* four lines of women enter the *orchestra*, two from each side, singing and moving in rhythm. The physical relation of the height on which Prometheus is pinioned to the *orchestra* is demonstrated by this fragment, and members of the audience can clearly be seen on the other side of the *orchestra*.

Intertitles next summarise the substance of Prometheus' speech to the Chorus leader, explaining why he is suffering, and indicate that Oceanus is advised of the uselessness of any intervention by him, after which there are some feet of 1927 film showing the Chorus leader, who is then held in freeze-frame. Prometheus is filmed in close-up in dialogue with the Chorus leader. The white-beareded Oceanus, replete with stick, appears among the rocks looking up at Prometheus, while the Chorus sits attentive to the dialogue, after which it sings and dances the first stasimon (already summarised by the intertitles). One of the noteworthy features of this section is that three physical levels of action have now been established — the *orchestra,* the height of the rocks on which Prometheus is riveted, and the lower portion, where his interlocutors enter and exit. The ancient theatre would be most unlikely to have provided a 'naturalistic' rock formation for Prometheus and the other characters, but the three levels could easily have been part of an ancient production. The *orchestra* would have been a focal point of the theatre then, as in 1927 (or as now at Epidauros, for example) but also available would have been the *skene* building as permanent 'scenery'. The façade of this building as it faced the *orchestra* would presumably stand for the rock against which such characters as Oceanus make their appearance; its roof would serve as a height on which gods could appear or, here, where offenders against Zeus' decrees could be crucified as an example to others.

The film proceeds by summarising the subject-matter and then showing brief 1927 film footage of the second episode and then second stasimon, in which the Chorus dances in couples, with its leader spatially separated, on part of the rock formation.

In the third episode, the tormented, horned, mortal maiden Io appears. In the 1927 production, she enters on a path in the rocks, wearing a horned mask and addresses Prometheus. Her exit is filmed as a fall behind a rock, while the 1971 soundtrack allows her utterances to continue (voiced by H. Hatziargyri). The chorus is then recorded visually, singing in rectangular formation, then adopting a more circular pattern.

The dénouement of the Aeschylean play is summarised in intertitles, according to which Prometheus, having prophesied Zeus' doom, is summoned to Zeus by Hermes, at which point, amid thunder, the surrounding rocks collapse and bury him.

The 1927 film shows Hermes, dressed in white, mounting the rocks to speak to Prometheus, who is then filmed in close-up. This image is held in freeze-frame while Bourlos's voice continues his speech. Next, we are shown an extraordinary sequence in which the Chorus, in a line, mount the rock (obviously by concealed steps) right up to Prometheus, passing Hermes on its way. Finally, it stands in a zigzag formation that runs from the bottom to the top of the rocks. The chained Prometheus is seen to speak. The top of the rock formation is then shown collapsing and falling in, along with Prometheus.

The short ends with the written information that eagles came and hovered over the theatre at the cataclysmic end.

Prometheus in Chains demonstrates economically the value that the 'theatrical' film possesses as evidence — permitting a present-day audience access to information it could not gain so succinctly from any other medium. As a record of the 1927 performance, it suffers from all kinds of disabilities which the 1971 additions actually emphasise. Only those parts especially suitable for filming were believed worth preserving. Even if voices have been added by a largely new cast in 1971, the verbal medium of the original performances is totally absent, and, in order to accommodate the relevant portions of the verbal text, the 1927 sequences have to be 'frozen' on certain frames. Yet, what is suggested about the aesthetic decisions involved in this seminal production of Greek tragedy proves highly informative, possibly helping to explain the direction in which theatre practice and critical opinion regarding the staging of traged-ies have tended in the decades following it.

Although Greek tragedy's formal properties are manifold (see pp. 25-7) and although the possibly pseudo-Aeschylean *Prometheus Bound* is one of the most formal of the extant tragedies in any case, certain decisions were taken in this production which helped to shape the future course of modern staging of classical tragedy. The *skene* building of the ancient theatre of Delphi has long since vanished. Therefore, a production in that theatre was faced with the question of whether to abandon even the rudimentary 'scenery' which the *skene* building façade provided for the ancients, to reconstruct that façade, or to substitute for it a more naturalistic construction. The decision was to adopt the latter, and thus an impressive rock formation was built. Characters find their way up or down the rock, while Prometheus is fixed at its peak, dominating the rock as he dominates the play. At the end, an attempt is shown to have been made to simulate the collapse of the rock, even if the effects are limited to its peak. When earthquakes, as in Euripides' *Bacchae*, or thunderstorms, as here, are indicated in Greek tragedy, it is almost certain that no visual correlative would have been practicable. An earthquake is assumed when there is verbal indi-cation of its occurrence, but it seems highly unlikely that a stone theatre with a stone *skene* building façade could have provided any visual impression of natural catastrophe. The decision to build an impressive rock and to 'destroy' it at the end of the production indicates that naturalism is thought to be appropriate to modern production, even in an open-air theatre.

A curious result of this decision and one made evident by the 'randomness' that affects the camera as recording device, is that to an audience which can see (as the film audience certainly can) the actual landscape around Delphi at the same time as the artificial landscape against which the drama is acted out, that rock, for all its naturalism, must look artificial, constructed. For this particular production no problem is raised by that (possibly unforeseen) percep-tion, since the landscape of the play is not that of Delphi or Greece in general, but 'the remotest region of the earth,/The haunt of Scythians, a wilderness without a footprint' [6] in primitive times. So distanced is the world of the play from that of even the original spectators that the character Io is unusual in not being an immortal. None the less, the choice of naturalism in setting, even if the effect of that choice is rendered more complex in practice by the wider setting, must have been highly influential not merely on later theatre productions but on the cinema's forays into the 'realistic mode' of filming Greek tragedy. Cacoyannis's *Electra,* for example, seems a direct inheritor of the 'naturalist' bias of this production, in that the action there is set against the dusty, dry landscape of the Greek countryside.

While there is an emphasis on 'authenticity' even in the choice of the ancient theatre of Delphi as the venue for this production, there are also signs of independence from a strictly faithful conception of the staging (were fidelity practicable, in any case). Thus, the Chorus sings and dances without the encumbrance of masks, and that singing and dancing must inevitably be a modern creation of likely equivalence to fifth-century BC choral performance elements. It must have been known that the zigzag formation which the Chorus finally adopts before the cataclysmic end of the play was impossible in the original theatre conditions, since no Chorus could possibly dance up the façade to join Prometheus (placed, presumably, on the roof of the *skene* building!).

Two *Electra*s (Directors: A. Meletoupolos, 1938; Ted Zarpas, 1962)

The only other 'theatrical' films which attempt to record a modern production within an ancient theatre deal with Sophocles' *Electra.* Oliver Taplin writes,

> It was in 1938 that the National Theatre first put on a perform-ance, Sophocles' *Electra* at Epidaurus, a site at that time well off the beaten track. Mrs Mitropoulos again produced a few minutes of film from her archive. Even without sound, the sight of Katina Paxinou clinging to the urn which she thinks houses her dead brother is powerfully stirring. . . . It is curious to see the great auditorium less than a quarter full for that historic occasion.[7]

The more substantial of the two films, however, is a record of a later production (in 1961) of the same play at the same site, again by the National Theatre of Greece. The film opens with a brief documentary on the theatre at Epidauros. Then the play production, directed by Takis Mouzenidis, and filmed by the Greek-American Ted Zarpas, is offered, shot so that occassionally the audience is in view.[8]

It is noteworthy that the publicity on the film provided by J. N. Film Productions Inc. says nothing about this *Electra* as a film. Almost the entire promotion concerns the National Theatre's history and celebrity. Oliver Taplin writes:

> A tragedy was filmed in its entirety during public performance at Epidaurus in 1961: Sophocles' *Electra* again. It is not a technically distinguished feat of photography, but it gives some idea of the accomplishments of the National Theatre and of the atmosphere of its performance, down to the eerie piping of the Epidaurus frogs. The play is built on the varied passions of one woman, and Anna Synodinou's performance pulls its audience into a vortex of anguish and exaltation (though Orestes is played by the same actor as in 1938, and the camera ruthlessly turns to bathos Electra's complaints about Orestes' long-delayed vengeance). Her slow, full movements are all weighted with feeling; but above all it is her voice — her control of pitch, timbre, pace and volume — that grips even those with no knowledge of modern Greek. [9]

The film is treated therefore as quite 'transparent' by its own publicity notes, purely a record of an internationally famous company's achievement at Epidauros. Taplin moves rapidly from the undistinguished photography to an appraisal of the dramatic merits of the production in terms that would be appropriate to a theatre review. Interestingly, though, he draws attention to the fact that the film's soundtrack records for posterity not only Synodinou's voice but the noises of the frogs. More interestingly still, he shows how the film medium, with its ability to direct visual attention where it could not be thus directed in a stage performance, can alter the perception of a drama. The presumably aged, and therefore ludicrously long-waited, Orestes is revealed as such only by the closer scrutiny of the camera. This observation is a reminder that even the 'theatrical' film with ambitions only to record a distinguished production by the means open to it acts upon the original material. Choices are constantly being made about the angles and distances to be adopted in the filming, since the option of a static camera is not entertained even by the first filmic record. It is at moments like these when an actor is revealed as less youthful than the part demands, that the 'natural realism' of the cinematic medium seems proven. What is really being highlighted, though, is the difference in theatrical and cinematic space, but particularly in spectator positions, and the effects of that difference upon reception of the material. Taplin's remark about the frogs, or the observation by another commentator that the audience is sometimes part of the film, could be seen as serving to remind us of the difference in control that appears to obtain normally between film and theatre. The sophistication of sound-recording equipment or cost of multiple takes on several evenings would help to explain the frog pipings on the soundtrack — an economic decision, in other words — but their presence could as easily be taken as an aesthetic decision, helping to provide the 'atmosphere' of the Epidauros experience, as Taplin says, like the inclusion of shots of the audience.

Our looking at the theatre audience with the knowledge that we are not part of it shapes our response to the theatre production, reminding us that we are an audience, but not the audience at whom the production is aimed, reinforcing the awareness of the film as film, not merely 'transparent' record. This problem, of the placing of the film audience in relation to the theatre audience within the film, is met constantly in Hollywood musicals, as Jane Feuer[10] demonstrates. She shows at various points how the film audience is eased into its peculiar relationship with the show within the film through 'physical' (camera-created) positioning. It is first permitted to feel part of that audience and to look from its viewpoint, but it is progressively given a freedom from the fixity of that viewpoint and can eventually accommodate overhead shots or shots from the wings. No such easing into a 'liberated' position is built into the 'theatrical' films of Greek tragedy, so that when an angle or relatively close position offers up information that would not be available to the theatre audience we cannot accommodate it within our conceptions of the film's design. We feel almost as if we were eavesdropping, able to see things that we are not meant to. Hence, the (justifiable) attribution of 'bathos' to the film when we see Orestes too close for illusionism to prevail. Ultimately, the voyeuristic analogy would seem to apply here more convincingly than any notion of cinema's 'essential realism'.

One final point that should make *Electra* valuable for the history of theatre productions is that Epidauros (which is widely taken to be a standard against which other productions measure themselves) takes native Greek productions further along the naturalist path observable already in the Sikelianos production of 1927 by allowing not only the Chorus, but the actors, to perform without masks.

Oedipus Rex (Director: Tyrone Guthrie, 1956)

A remarkable change in direction, both in terms of stage production and filming, occurs in Canada, in 1956, when Tyrone Guthrie commits to celluloid his production of *Oedipus Rex* at the Stratford, Ontario Festival seasons of 1954 and 1955. This production could hardly be less naturalistic. Not only does it reinforce the conventions of ancient Greek theatre, but it adds a great number of its own. For Aristotle, all art is mimetic; Sophocles' *Oedipus Rex,* presumably, a supreme example, since it is, for the philosopher, the supreme example of tragedy. Yet, such distancing as the ancient theatre might achieve by its formalism has been augmented considerably in this production.

While only the actors wore masks in the 1927 production of *Prometheus,* nobody in the Epidauros productions was masked. In Guthrie's *Oedipus,* everybody is elaborately masked, from the Chorus to the humblest character. These masks are constructed to cover the entire head of the performer, although the generosity of the space at the mask's mouth puts much emphasis on the actors' lips and teeth. Even here, the true mouth of the player is not permitted any 'naturalistic' force. Jocasta, for example, at one point indicates misery by turning the corners of her mouth down until her face becomes that of the Roman mask of tragedy. It is noteworthy that the abundant archaeological evidence for fifth-century BC masks indicates that they are remarkably 'naturalistic'. So alike are masks and real faces of the actors, as depicted in vase painting, for example, that uninformed observers of such paintings might think they were witnessing the effects of decapitations on a large scale, since masks, looking for all the world like human heads, often lie at the feet of actors portrayed 'before performance'. No doubt, the faces of the actors in these paintings are stereotyped, but the important point for our purposes is that, whatever the conventions, masks are painted in a way that permits them to be easily confused with real human heads. Yet, Guthrie emphasises the artificiality of the masks by making them disproportionate to the bodies of the actors — too large — as are their arms for their torsos. Not only that, but he differentiates the masks, like the characters generally, by colour. Thus, Oedipus' mask, surmounted by a gold crown, has as its dominant colour, gold. The face and beard are those of a young man, but the mask looks eyeless long before the moment in the play when Oedipus discovers his 'crime' and puts out his own eyes. His hands are gold, as are his lengthy finger nails (like those of all central characters and the Chorus). Creon, linked with Oedipus in royalty though not yet king, wears a gold mask which has a greenish tinge. Jocasta's mask is blue, while her hair is a greyish-blue. Tiresias has a slightly more naturalistic mask, in that he is given a bald pate, with tufts of white hair at the base. Surprisingly, perhaps, the Chorus's masks are not uniform. Although the play calls for a Chorus of Theban elders, this Chorus has sufficiently differentiated, though stylised, masks to suggest a range of ages.

Differentiation by colour goes well beyond masks, however. Gold is the dominant colour of Oedipus' robes until he puts his eyes out. At this point, he reappears in red, no longer wearing his gold crown, but with a black veil over his red mask. His daughters appear at the end of the play also in red robes. Creon's dominant colour is a darker gold, Jocasta's blue. The Chorus wears drab colours; there is no uniformity in the individual colouring, but all are distinguished from the principals by the dullness of hue of their costumes. The Corinthian wears a greyish white, while the retainers who manhandle the herdsman and later the messenger who announces Oedipus' blinding are dressed in black mail, menacing figures who seem, today, to be immediate forerunners of Darth Vadar. Even the herdsman's features are given stylisation through colour — brown skin against white hair. However, while the Chorus and all the principal characters are given outsize arms and talon-like, coloured finger nails, the herdsman's real fingers are visible, peeping through homely mittens.

To increase the stylisation of his players' appearance as well as to render their movements less and less 'life-like', Guthrie has equipped the main actors (but not the Chorus) with high-soled footwear. In doing so, he is going right against classical practice, but maintaining consistency by opting (as with his masks) for maximum stylisation within and beyond the possibilities afforded by the Hellenistic theatre.

As in ancient Greek theatre, but probably to the point of greater austerity, scenery is minimal, confined to a mauve-coloured curtain at the back of the stage, and doors of the palace. The stage is divided, again following ancient custom but with much more sparing effect, into upper and lower levels, connected by steps. The Chorus normally occupies the lower level, but actors too, such as Tiresias, may occupy that level on occasions.

Acting is consistent with the extreme stylisation observable in every aspect of the production. Movements in particular are highly mannered. The Chorus bobs and wheels, with often puppet-like movements (emphasised by its disproportionately large heads and hands), writhing and crawling at moments of extreme tension. Hand movements seem particularly expressive among the principals, and to be more balletic than the movements of feet and legs. The actors declaim, using a variety of rhetorical devices which eschew naturalism. They habitually look away from one another, even when, as it were, communicating. At one point, the script talks about the tears shed by Oedipus' daughters, but no tears or sign of emotion appear on their masked faces. Instead, they perform a sort of ballet of grief.

All of this is filmed without any concession to the traditional methods of 'theatrical' filming. Thus, there is no audience within the film for this utterly stage-bound event. The angles at which the action is viewed often defy realist convention. When Jocasta first appears, for example, there is an overhead shot of the actors and Chorus grouped round Oedipus. After her exit, there is another overhead shot of the Chorus singing, sometimes individually, sometimes in unison.

Some detailed samples of the production ought to indicate the rigorously anti-naturalist methods employed. In the scene in which Tiresias (Donald Davis) confronts Oedipus (Douglas Campbell) to warn him of his future, the Chorus moans in the background as he delivers his speech. There is a close-up of Oedipus pronouncing the question, 'Who was my father?', and immediately thereafter a shot of the Chorus leaning forward to hear. Later, as Tiresias crawls forward to cry out, of the unknown polluter, 'That man is *here*', the Chorus quickly retires from its positions. Tiresias then falls right back to end up with his head resting on the step lower than his body. He rolls down the step a little, while the Chorus wheels and whirls, hands raised in horror.

After Creon's (Robert Goodier) departure, Oedipus and Jocasta (Eleanor Stuart) are alone together on the upper stage. When they speak, however, they are spatially isolated from each other. Then, as Oedipus runs to her to tell her what Tiresias has been saying, he moves his head in the manner of a little boy (he is running to his mother to be comforted, after all!).

At the point where Oedipus recalls his deeds on the way to the throne of Thebes, there is a sudden long shot at the moment where he describes his going to Delphi. Then, when he talks about the prophecy of marriage to his mother, the camera holds Jocasta in close-up, while next the Chorus is filmed with its hands over its ears. Oedipus stamps about the stage in a transport of rage, and yells three times in animalistic passion, 'I killed them all,' as he describes the killing at the crossroads. Then he sinks to his knees and recoils from Jocasta's hands. Her reaction is to move away from him with her hands raised in the air. She then stands motionless while the Chorus addresses Oedipus. Throughout its utterances and often during its periods of silence, the Chorus moves gently, undulating slightly. (The effect is similar to that of a mobile frieze.)

At the moment when Oedipus hears the last piece of evidence required for him to know the truth, he is entirely isolated spatially. When the tale ends, the actor utters a chromatic scale, 'AIEEE'. His utterances are practically sung as this point. The word 'accursed' is hissed out, though. The old herdsman falls on his side as Oedipus disappears into the blackness beyond the palace doors. The Chorus then moves round the herdsman lying in a foetal position. A semi-choir addresses the camera direct, and then the other semi-choir takes up the chant. When they sing in unison, the effect is like that of chromatic chanting, moving up and down the scale.

It is extraordinary to read, in a hostile review of the film, the charge, 'Guthrie has not made a movie of "Oedipus"; he has simply put it on celluloid',' or another, that, while Oedipus' and Jocasta's masks are acceptable, 'the rest . . . are absurd — more the debased imaginings of twentieth-century degenerates than the stylised countenances of the citizens of Thebes.'[12] The author of the second statement criticises Guthrie also for choosing W. B. Yeats' 'so-called translation'. The fault in this choice is that it 'intrudes upon Sophocles' sobriety a garish and anachronistic Celtic symbolism'. The alleged sobriety of Sophocles is not what Guthrie seeks to emulate at any point in his production. It is all of a piece, garish and anachronistic possibly, or, more fairly described, highly stylised and anti-classical.

Dilys Powell is very nearly right when she says of the film, 'The camera edges forward, circles, leans; it can read nothing in these fixed features. No scenery; no action except for the hieratic gestures of the theatre — yet such is the intensity of the familiar drama that all the rules of the cinema can be broken with impunity.'[13] What these 'rules' may be she does not indicate, but there is, indeed, something audacious and defiant in both theatrical and cinematic terms about Guthrie's production. To attribute the power of the film to 'the intensity of the familiar drama' seems wrong-headed, though. The film distances, prevents catharsis, or even pity and fear. Its success is its achievement in defamiliarising the familiar.

The Persians (Director: Jean Prat, 1961)

Another highly stylised production of Greek tragedy is that of Aeschylus' *The Persians,* a play produced in 472 BC, filmed in 1961, and strikingly unusual in its subject-matter since it is the only extant Greek tragedy which concerns historical incidents and characters. As in the Guthrie production, masks are used. Thus, this production's stylisation seems to be in keeping with the decision to have the performers masked.

There may be quite different reasons, however, for the two productions to be so stylised. Taplin locates the reason for Jean Prat's decision in his over-impressiblity: 'He had read that early tragedy was like an oratorio: so his Chorus scarcely moves. . . . The costumes, obedient to the book, are "statuesque" '.[14] Guthrie is dismissed in the same paragraph. His use of masks results in 'specious authenticity', in that 'their design, like the rest of his production, came from his strange imagination rather than from any textbook.' Presumably, there is specious authenticity evidenced in both cases — in Guthrie because he follows his 'strange imagination'; in Prat because the textbook was wrong. (If the authenticity of Prat is not specious, on the other hand, he must presumably be disapproved of for making an aesthetic error in keeping his version of *The Persians* 'authentic'.) While Taplin's description of Guthrie's method is fair comment, his dismissal of it is less so. A reader of Aeschylus' *Persians* and Sophocles' *Oedipus Rex* could hardly fail to notice the very different structures of the two plays. Although they have formal elements in common — most noticeably, as in all Greek tragedies, the use of a Chorus — and although we know that masks would have been used in both ancient productions, the Aeschylean drama seems almost without plot, the Sophoclean one to be plotted with unusual deftness and brilliance. One offers some details of the sense of desolation in Persia after its defeat at Salamis, while the other offers an archetype of the detective thriller, in which the 'detective' painstakingly solves the answer to Thebes' pollution, as he had earlier the Sphinx's riddle, only to reveal himself as the guilty man. It is likely that the performance of these plays in the ancient theatre was very different, with more stress on credibility (if we judge from Aristotle's later analysis of drama on the model of this play) and verisimilitude in one than the other. While Prat's textbook would be oversimplifying if it suggested that all drama was oratorio-like and all acting or Choral performance 'statuesque', it is not necessarily wrong in its surmises about the production of *The Persians*. Therefore, Guthrie in taking the most celebrated of all Greek tragedies and making it defiantly anti-Aristotelian is stamping the production as his own and rendering the familiar in unsettlingly unfamiliar guise, while Prat may be aiming for an authenticity less spurious than Taplin suggests.

The ancient Life of Aeschylus makes it evident that the tragedian was believed to be seeking grand effects and to have little interest in the creation of empathy in his audience. If this is so, he presents a problem for those who would use Aristotle's *Poetics* as a means to understanding the effects of tragedy. Tragedy, according to Aristotle, aims at catharsis by stimulating pity and fear, and these emotions are encouraged in the audience if there is the possibility for the play's spectators of what we call identification with the characters in the play. Unity of action is explained with reference to probability or necessity, the emphasis on probability reinforcing the notion that credibility is a prime requirement of the successful dramatist. In practice, though, Aeschylus seems to have offered a rather different experience to his audiences. His *The Suppliants* relies heavily on the Choral element of the play to carry the burden of its message. Group is ranged against group. Personal identification is rendered difficult. In *Prometheus Bound*[15], he dramatises the struggle of Prometheus against the tyrannical rule of Zeus, confining the action almost exclusively to the world of the gods. By keeping Zeus offstage, and having Prometheus static perforce (by being pinned to a rock at the opening of the play) he minimises the chances of the audience's feeling excitement of the sort that a busier plot might inspire. Lest we imagine that modern conceptions of tragic action or empathy have intruded upon the ancient theatre and that he was viewed quite differently in his own times, we have the considerable evidence of Aristophanes' comedy, *The Frogs*, for perceptions of him in at least the late fifth century BC. Even allowing for comic distortion, we find a consistent attitude towards him as 'bombastic' and too lofty in his drama to trouble with the creation of 'ordinary' people as characters or, presumably, with questions of empathy and identification. In other words, tragedy changes between *The Persians* and

Oedipus Rex and it is not impossible that production style also underwent changes. What is appropriately 'statuesque' in 472 BC may well have looked, fifty years later, old-fashioned and inconsistent with the kinds of plays written at that time.

Prat therefore had a number of possibilities open to him, one being the credible choice of the 'statuesque' as the dominant mode of production at the time of the play's performance, particularly in the light of its near plotlessness. This choice should not be prejudged. Such authenticity as it may produce need not be spurious. Whether it is wise to choose 'authenticity' so that a kind of drama results which is not conducive to arousing a modern audience's interest, let alone empathy, does need to be considered. A fairer question might, however, concern the wisdom of the choice of such a play for modern production. The 1927 production of *Prometheus Bound* at Delphi attempted to naturalise it. The 1961 *Persians* rejects naturalism, partly because, the choice of play having been made, it is almost impossible to see how it could have been naturalised. The Persians of the play, although they speak Greek, are emphatically 'different' from the Athenian audience. They are suffering the consequences of hubris; they are royal in the special sense of being anti-democratic; they do not belong in the world of Greece as the Athenians picture it. Hence, the strangeness and feeling of alienation is appropriate. It should be remembered, however, that these Persians are interesting to the Athenians because they are a recently defeated enemy. Their otherness of political and religious customs may be fascinating since it is because of those attitudes that their defeat is taken by the Athenian audience to have significance, other than that of pure patriotism. A French audience is deprived of that point of contact with the material chosen; attention is held, or not, purely by reason of the alien nature of the production and of the original material, which is not mythic in the usual sense, but mythologised history given a political and religious interpretation.

The black and white, French-language film, appropriately for a 'statuesque' production, opens focusing on Persian sculptures, with a soundtrack of dramatic music (composed by Jean Prodromides), music performed with special emphasis on brass instruments. Immediately after the title, the camera pans to the set in which the whole play is performed. There is a back-cloth representing the sky. The set has some relation with the physical conditions under which the drama may originally have been performed. For the major part of the production, use is made of two stage levels. Two flights of steps, one to the right, the other to the left of the upper stage, connect it with the lower level. Behind the upper-level stage is a building from which the Chorus and characters supposed to reside within the Persian palace emerge. Stage left, on the upper level, is another entrance, used by the Persian messenger or the returning Xerxes. This entrance is flanked by statues of creatures with horses' bodies but human, Persian (as conceived in this production) faces.

Use of this set is formalised, as it must have been in the original production. The Chorus moves down to the lower level after its entrance to the first, higher stage; while Atossa, for example, takes up her position more frequently on the upper level, addressing the Chorus below.

At the point in the play where the shade of Darius is invoked, Atossa enters the palace, while the Chorus follows her in single file. The film takes us inside the palace where an almost identical arrangement of levels is found. There may well be a single set (with variations, as with the presence or absence of the 'horse statue' entrance) in operation, although the film creates the illusion of the interior set's near mirror image of the exterior.

The Chorus is made up of seven men and one coryphaeus (François Chaumette). The seven men may speak individually or chant in unison. When they are closest to Choral song, the music is reminiscent of Carl Orff, the voices of operatic quality. Their movements are choreographed so as to be minimal, but also uniform and stylised. When they chant the *parodos,* their opening song, they stand in profile with hands raised. When they moan at news of Persian suffering, the sound that they make is foreign to any naturalistic or Western expression of grief, a sort of extended 'O-O-O-A-A-A.' The wailing of the Persians in this play seems to have struck the Athenian audience as funny, in both senses of the word, to judge from Aristophanes' *Frogs:*

> *Dionysus:* I loved that bit where they sang about the days of the great Darius, and the Chorus went like this with their hands and cried 'Wah! Wah!' [16]

The masks which the male Persians wear furnish their faces with hair, beards and earrings, but leave the actors' faces exposed from nose to chin. The Chorus, like the messenger (Maurice Carrel), wears high-soled boots, anachronistic for this period of tragedy, but defensible to mark off these characters as strange and foreign.

Atossa (Maria Meriko) expresses grief in a highly formalised manner. Her characteristic posture is one which involves holding her arms at an angle of 45 degrees to her body and a fixed gaze, her eyes almost unblinking. The fixity of body and gaze remains unchanged even when the messenger brings dire news to the Persian court. Her most signal reaction to ill tidings is the bowing of her head. The messenger, on the other hand, is permitted greater 'naturalism' in his delivery, particularly in the speech relating the battle of Salamis, during which there are energetic movements of his body, and especially his arms.

Darius, a ghost in the play, is no more stylised than his living counterparts. He is given the mask of an old man, although his mysteriousness is suggested by his cry being heard offstage before he is seen, and then by the crucified position of his arms as he begins to address the Chorus. Xerxes' (Claude Martin) passion is expressed in the volume of his delivery or by his outstretched arms. His performance is consistent with the other royal characters, though. It is appropriate, therefore, that when he talks of his 'rags' there is no sign of damage to his formal clothing.

The filming of this production is as 'artificial' as the production itself. For example, there is an unusually long close-up of the already motionless Atossa during one of her speeches. There are overhead shots of the Chorus, and when the action of the play moves from palace exterior to interior, there is a tracking shot high enough to have been achieved by the use of a crane, to the tomb of Darius.

The ending of the film is worth recording. Xerxes demands that the Chorus mourns with him. He stands on the upper level looking down at it as he bids it to cry aloud. This it does, with fists raised. As the men of the Chorus are ordered, they strike their breasts in unison. (They are also ordered to tear their hair, but no attempt is made to simulate this.) The breast-beating and Xerxes' orders continue. Each time they strike their breasts a lashing sound can be heard on the soundtrack against the music. The Chorus move in a circle, reciting 'Malheur!', and its self-beating becomes the more formal act of driving one fist into the other hand's palm. Xerxes whips up its grief, as the camera moves into a full-facial close-up of him.

The next shot is of rocks and sea, as the credits roll. At the end of the credits, the camera pans upwards from the rocks to look out to the open sea from an inlet. The natural world is thus sharply contrasted with the world of the play, since it has been rigorously excluded until the last words are spoken, but the movement from particularised to generalised locality after the credits serves as an analogy for the relation of the drama of the Persians to that of the world outside the royal court.

Electra (Director: Jean-Louis Ughetto, 1972)

In 1972, Jean-Louis Ughetto filmed a stage production by Antoine Vitez of the latter's translation of Sophocles' *Electra*. The play is largely in French, although there are 'parenthèses' (by Yannis Ritsos) and brief passages in modern Greek. It was originally produced in 1971 at Le Théâtre des Amandiers, Nanterre, and subsequently the production was taken round Europe. The film of the play was made at the Cité Universitaire Internationale.

While this, like other films in this chapter, is a film of a stage production, it is unlike the others in several respects. For one thing, the film makes little effort to establish detail of the stage set. So low is the lighting that it is not until well into the film that some notion of the stage space (there is, in fact, no set of the usual sort) emerges. There seem to be a couple of walkways placed at right angles to each other, so that a cross shape is created for the action. Actors may speak on one of the walkways, while actors on the other may be 'out of sight', listening to the first group. For example, it appears that Orestes and Pylades observe Electra unseen from their walkway, at one point in the play. The film concentrates on individuals, often in close-up, refusing to allow a sense of spatial relations throughout, or even at times to permit a confident identification of the characters.

Then, too, the other films have been of productions which seemed capable of being placed in one dramatic tradition or another, where aesthetic decisions were made that accorded with the principal strategy of the production. This production is highly eclectic, establishing itself out of time and space by its throwing together of French and Greek, by its mix (in terms of period and country) of costumes and by its inclusion of modern idiom within a largely classical register. Just as the acting space and its filming are out of the ordinary, so too are the treatment and behaviour of the audience. So close are the spectators to the acting area that at times the players and audience are indistinguishable. We see a man and woman at the front of the audience exchanging smiles, or hear much coughing in a scene where the tension slackens. While such carefully controlled stagings as that filmed in *The Persians* make awareness of the camera something of a shock, as when we notice that the operatic voices of the Persian Chorus are out of synchronisation with its lip movements, here there are so many curious juxtapositions of the mode of utterance or of costume and such casualness concerning the audience's relation to the action, that the capricious filming of the play seems once more to be appropriate to the style of the production, and the obvious intrusion of, for example, modern microphones at the climactic moment of Aegisthus' murder is easily assimilated. As the stage space is little separated from the audience space, so the camera makes no effort to establish the acting area for the film audience. As characters move in and out of spotlights in the production, so the camera may hold a character in close-up, allowing the film audience no notion of the activity or characters surrounding him or her. If the Epidauros *Electra* seemed like an 'official' production, and the Tyrone Guthrie *Oedipus Rex* like an anti-classical production, even to the extent of eliminating the audience altogether from the film, the Ughetto *Electre* has a post-1968 feel to it. It seems to be populist without any sign of popularity in its commonest sense; to be attempting to bridge the void between a modern intellectual (student?) audience and the Athenian populace at the Theatre of Dionysus by disallowing any sustained classicism. 'Non, je ne regrette rien,' cries Clytemnestra (Arlette Bonnard) defiantly at Electra (Evelyne Istria), when her daughter questions her conduct. Before telling a false tale of his own death, Orestes (Jean-Baptiste Malartre) waits for his moment of activity, comforted to know that the water for his early morning coffee is on the boil. The Tutor, at the point where Electra asserts her intention to die in despair at Orestes' death, reads from a loose-leaf notebook, behaving more like the play producer that he is than the character that he, Antoine Vitez, plays at that point. Orestes, on his first appearance, wears jeans beneath his 'eastern'-style jacket. While, then, the eclecticism of the visual and verbal idiom eases a modern audience into the play, it is jarred out of identification by such (Brechtian) tactics. Of all the filmed play productions, this is the most modernist — as unsettling for a film audience hoping to see a staging 'transparently' recorded as the staging must have been to a theatre audience expecting to see Sophocles' play simply translated from classical Greek to modern French.

Pylades (Colin Harris) is filmed reading a quite modern-looking publication, in which there is a reference to Mycenae and to a coach trip there. Electra will suddenly leave off her writhing on the floor or whirling in passion to whisper intimations about her intentions directly to the audience. 'I'd forgotten the number of the house, even the telephone number,' she admits to Chrysothemis (Jany Gastaldi) during a violent exchange with her sister. In Electra's encounter with Clytemnestra, several of the original Sophoclean arguments are retained but Clytemnestra's address to the audience, filmed from behind her head, is un-Sophoclean. The intimacy between characters and audience is a logical outcome of their spatial closeness but is also aided by the removal of the Chorus, its function being taken over — partly at least — by such characters as the Tutor.

When Clytemnestra beholds the box that takes the place of the original urn supposedly holding Orestes' ashes, Orestes informs the audience that 'the retribution scene is about to begin'. The false story is related to Clytemnestra with much gesticulation and stage business by the Tutor, warming to his task in actorly fashion, becoming particularly loud and excited as he describes the race in which Orestes is supposed to have been killed. By means of this vivid description of the living Orestes' death, instead of the original Tutor's 'objective' report, the cruelty of the scene, by which the future victim is teased with the energy of his invention, is greatly increased. His excited utterance is accompanied by equally excitable camera movement. 'Can a mother not grieve?', Clytemnestra asks at the story's end, although Electra and her sister doubt her sincerity. But the joy with which she embraces Chrysothemis and expresses her relief to be free of Electra's threat undermines her show of grief. Electra's eyes are picked out by the light as she witnesses her mother's reactions. She and Chrysothemis embrace each other and talk of the action they will take, now that Electra has been encouraged by Chrysothemis' certainty that Orestes is alive and has made offerings at the tomb: 'I knew it was Orestes. Take heart, dearest one.' Electra's response is to crawl animal-like around the sleeping bodies of Clytemnestra and Aegisthus, encouraging her sister to kill them. When Chrysothemis rejects her, Electra is held in close-up as she resolves to do the deed alone. The camera swings from Electra to Chrysothemis and back to Electra again, and we glimpse Aegisthus running offstage after Clytemnestra.

It is the Tutor, not the original Chorus, who subsequently lectures Electra on the duty of the young to their parents. The camera pans to Orestes and Pylades listening to the reproof. Sometimes, then, the Sophoclean Chorus is played by a character within the original drama, or the Chorus becomes a voice from offstage, as immediately after, when Electra's mourning over the urn is interrupted by advice from an unidentified voice bidding her not to weep too much. Just before the recognition scene, in which Orestes reveals his true identity, there is a tussle between brother and sister over the possession of the urn which is unserious enough to have the Cité Universitaire audience laughing loudly on the soundtrack. The recognition itself is accompanied by the voice offstage speaking of the joy of reunion.

The play reaches its appointed close, with Clytemnestra's despatch an easy execution behind a curtain. 'Ruling had become too big for her in time', the audience is told. With Electra's encouragement, Orestes stabs Clytemnestra who screams, but any doubt about the matricide seem to be silenced by Chrysothemis' reaction (taking the Chorus's place), that she cannot condemn her siblings. Unlike the Sophoclean play, this production culminates in Aegisthus' (Christian Dente) death, to a general shout of acclaim, and a voice offstage proclaiming freedom.

Vitez's production, in eliminating the Chorus but retaining its function, or rather redistributing various aspects of its function among characters of the original play, in making the characters at one moment modern, another ancient, at one time on intimate terms with the audience, at another remote, oscillates constantly between familiarisation and distance. It is ultimately far more demanding and unsettling than the consistently defamiliarised Guthrie production. The film, denying information about the staging, moving a character out of frame but not necessarily offstage with the same casualness as it isolates a speaking character from her hearer within the play, is appropriately disorientating. More work is demanded of the viewer than in the other productions where it is possible to settle back and ignore the camera's mediation of staged reality. In *Electre* neither the original production nor the 1972 film permits any comfortable relationship between spectator and event.

These films in the theatrical mode offer a surprising variety of possibilities both from theatrical and cinematic viewpoints. On the one hand, we have the 'official' dramatic production of *Electra* performed at Epidaurus, with its roots in the tradition established (or reinvigorated) at Delphi in 1927. The ancient acting spaces are adhered to, with certain qualifications, and the production is conceived in terms which seem appropriate to the ancient theatre, in that 'naturalism' seems to be the dominant mode, whether it be an 'Aeschylean' or Sophoclean drama that is produced. On the other hand, we have a defiantly avant-garde *Electra* to contrast with the Epidauros version, or a resolutely untraditional *Oedipus,* moved out of the classical towards the Hellenistic or even Senecan theatre and then beyond, or a possibly more traditional than traditional *Persians.* It would seem as if the debate about the 'acceptable' methods of filming tragedy is prefigured in the theatrical context, where there appears to be much variety of practice in staging of Greek originals. Some of this variety is explicable in terms of the circumstances of production. Where an ancient theatre is used and a vast, largely Greek, audience is anticipated, though not always realised, 'authenticity' seems to be the ideal. This authenticity may be more apparent than real (it is arguable that Prat's *The Persians* could be seen as more Aeschylean than the Sikelianos *Prometheus*) but it seems safe to conclude that audiences would perceive the productions as attempting fidelity of staging. Where a less impressive, or even tiny, acting area is available and a self-selecting audience, which may represent a cultural élite, is anticipated, experimentation seems more likely. Sophocles' *Electra* may be the link between the Epidauros and Cité Universitaire Internationale presentations, but a chasm exists between them in practice.

The filming of these theatrical events raises a number of interesting questions, which would cast doubt on the assumed transparency of film as a recording medium. A principal question might concern the psychological placement of the film audience in relation to an original audience. In the Guthrie *Oedipus,* the only audience is that in the cinema, but the drama takes no cognisance of that or any other audience. In the Ughetto film, the intimacy between theatre audience and actors is observed but not necessarily shared by the cinema audience. Even when the theatre and cinema audiences are placed apparently in similar relation to the great theatrical event filmed, as at Epidauros, there are several points where the difference in experience is underlined, the most obvious perhaps being that alluded to by Taplin (p.49). While both audiences may hear the Epidauros frogs, only one is in the physically closer position to see the bathos of Electra's lamentations for her long-awaited brother. How does our awareness of ourselves and of the medium of film at these moments affect the indentification aimed at by the more prestigious productions? How do the differences between our experience and that of the original audience, and our consciousness of those differences, affect our relations to the drama filmed?

Notes

1. Oliver Taplin,'The Delphic idea and after', *The Times Literary Supplement*, p.811.

2. Mrs. A. Mitropoulos, National Film Theatre programme notes to *Prometheus in Chains*, June 1981.

3. Taplin, 'Delphic Idea', p.811.

4. Ibid.

5. Ibid.

6. Aeschylus, *Prometheus Bound and Other Plays*, trs. Philip Vellacott (Penguin Classics, 1961, 1975) p.20.

7. Taplin, 'Delphic Idea', p.811

8. 'Electra', *Variety*, 5 September 1962.

9. Taplin, 'Delphic Idea', p.811.

10. Jane Feuer, *The Hollywood Musical* (British Film Institute/Macmillan, 1982).

11. Arthur Knight, *Saturday Review*, 26 January 1957.

12 Courtland Phipps, 'Oedipus Rex', *Films in Review*, vol. VII, no.8, October 1956, p.416.

13. Dilys Powell, *Sunday Times*, 26 August, 1956.

14. Taplin, 'Delphic Idea', p.811.

15. I am aware of the debate about the authorship of *Prometheus Bound*. Whether or not it was written by the historical Aeschylus, the point that it was believed to have been bears out my arguments about conceptions of Aeschylean drama.

16. Aristophanes, *The Frogs and Other Plays*, tr. David Barrett (Penguin Classics, 1964), p.194.

5 FILMS IN THE REALISTIC MODE

Oedipus the King (Director: Philip Saville, 1967)

This chapter begins with a problem of classification. Philip Saville's version of the most famous of all Greek tragedies, *Oedipus the King* (1967), could at times appear to be a film in the theatrical mode. Much of the drama, after all, is shot in the amphitheatre at Dodona where the players dispose themselves in acting areas that sometimes recall those of ancient dramatic performances. The fact that there is no audience within the theatre is of no great relevance to this question, since, for example, Tyrone Guthrie's version of the same play (see pp. 51-5) is acted out in what looks like a (modern, indoor) theatrical space without an audience witnessing it. On the other hand, as the film proceeds, there is less and less attention to acting within the acting areas. The tiers of the ruined theatre are used by the performers as readily as the *orchestra* or the space between *orchestra* and *skene* façade, even though these tiers constituted the *theatron* or audience area of the ancient theatre.

More crucially, we find ourselves in the 'actual' Greek countryside frequently in the film, particularly during Choral stasima. From the beginning, Saville's strategy seems to be that theatrical reality and 'actuality' are to be intermingled, so that what happens within the theatre space of Dodona is an extension of activity beyond the theatre, in the 'real world'. Again and again, events or speeches within the amphitheatre are heard or reacted to by peasants or plague victims in an unstylised, natural landscape, so that, while a differentiation is established but not always maintained between two kinds of reality, theatrical and 'actual', the dividing line between these realities is faint. Olivier's *Henry V* was praised by Bazin (see p. 9) for beginning in a reconstructed Globe Theatre and, once the occasion of a particular play performance in the Shakespearean age is established, moving on to such scenes as Agincourt. By this method, Bazin claims, the scenes outside the theatre are given a theatrical reality, so that exteriors of the film are not so much 'natural' as natural within the conventions of the Globe as imagined by Olivier. *Oedipus the King* seems to reverse this procedure. By

Plate 1. *Electra* (Cacoyannis)

Electra (Irene Papas) with countrywomen chorus — formal groupings in natural landscapes

Plate 2. *Elektreia* (Jancsó)

This highly choreographed version of *Electra* ends by bringing the tale into the twentieth century. By permission of Artificial Eye Film Companies Ltd

Plate 3. *Iphigenia* (Cacoyannis)

Army pressure on Agamemnon (Costa Kazakos) is realised in 'epic' visual terms

Plate 4. *Medea* (Pasolini)

The centaur (Laurent Terzieff) is seen by Jason sometimes as ordinary man, sometimes (as here) in pre-rational terms

Plate 5. *Oedipus Rex* (Tyrone Guthrie)

Guthrie's film of his play production renders chorus (and also actors) in broadly Hellenistic terms. By permission of The Stratford Shakespearean Festival Foundation of Canada.

Plate 6. *Oedipus Rex* (Pasolini)

Sophocles' play exoticised: here, Jocasta (Silvana Mangano) is brought to Oedipus as reward for the sphinx slaying. By permission of Peter Darvill Associates

Plate 7. *Phaedra* (Dassin)

Phaedra (Melina Mercouri) and husband (Raf Vallone): business pressures replace divine control of events

Plate 8. *The Trojan Women* (Cacoyannis)

Cacoyannis' Helen (Irene Papas) softens Menelaus (Patrick Magee) more by physical appeal than argument bringing plague victims at the film's beginning from the authentic Greek landscape into the theatre to supplicate the King, Saville seems to suggest that the theatrical performance is simply a crystallisation of issues which belong in the real world, and, if ever the conventions of Greek tragedy threaten to divorce audience from a context of actuality, the conventions are underplayed so that the 'authentic' dimension may come to the fore.

The most resistant convention of all is probably the Chorus. Saville does not eliminate it, or even 'rationalise' it, as Cacoyannis does increasingly in his films of Greek tragedy. The Chorus is multiple, garbed in conventional costume, may chant rather than speak, tends to move in unison, but often when the soundtrack is devoted to the Chorus, and we listen to the words written by Sophocles, the visuals are those of the Greek countryside, used often to 'illustrate' the phenomena of which the Chorus speaks. Thus, the lyric element, which most resolutely refuses to be incorporated into the generally mimetic framework of tragedy, is at least half-naturalised in its new context. While the stasima remain and interrupt the dramatic action as in ancient times, the film attempts to ground the lyrics in actuality, to 'explain' and motivate them. The result of such a strategy is the reverse of respecting a theatrical reality even in scenes shot on 'convincing' locations. Instead, it is the imparting of a sense of actuality to events that are clearly staged within a theatre. The theatre, by its emphatic links with the world of Greece just beyond it, and often inseparable from it even in spatial terms, is rendered less theatrical. The realism of the film guarantees, to some extent, the 'credibility' of the performance. For this reason, the film may more confidently be placed in a realistic tradition of filming of Greek tragedy than in a theatrical, despite superficial evidence to the contrary.

Although several critics have remarked on the fidelity of the film to the original play, at least in modern English translation, the filming involves several striking alterations. The absence of masks means, for example, that Jocasta must look old enough to be Oedipus' mother. The close-ups of Lilli Palmer raise obstacles which would have been less likely to occur in the original production. A common sense reaction to Oedipus' marriage to Jocasta, often experienced in the seminar room from students who have merely read the play, is that he has behaved foolishly, if not wrongly, in marrying a woman old enough to be his mother. There is an Aristophanic quality to such an attitude, but it is much more likely to be raised for discussion in response to this film version by virtue of its 'realism', which extends to the psychological treatment of the characters at certain key moments. 'For once, we have a mother sufficiently seductive to go to bed with,' John Coleman[1] writes in praise of Lilli Palmer. The sexism of the remark, all too familiar in film criticisms even today, when Barry Norman on BBC television seems incapable of reviewing a new movie without informing his audience of the degree of lust the female star has inspired in him, is possibly what the film deserves. Oedipus' (Christopher Plummer) problem in this film is almost exclusively guilt for murder, while Jocasta is saddled with the guilt for incest. This, at least, seems to be the point of additional sequences within the palace, in which she feels haunted by Laius' ghost. Her union with Oedipus inspires such guilt in her that she commits suicide. Oedipus' destruction of his sight, on the other hand, is largely because he, like the film audience, could only see in part the meaning of the murder at the crossroads and the identity of those involved. It is perpetrated in sorrow for the loss of Jocasta rather than a sense of guilt. The woman, it seems, must expiate the guilt of incest, while the man's world is that of action. When the truth can no longer be hidden, Oedipus curls up in a foetal position within the bowl of the amphitheatre. He is as helpless as a baby, but also as innocent. Jocasta, in this production, as possibly in the original play, guesses the truth of her relationship before Oedipus knows of it, and immediately takes the guilt upon herself. No protection in the womb for her. She leaves the amphitheatre and faces guilt and death alone in the palace. Her destruction removes Oedipus' sanctuary — a point that Seneca underlines at the end of his *Oedipus* by having Jocasta strike at her womb, instead of hanging herself, as a means of suicide.

The functioning of the amphitheatre in the double capacity of ancient theatre (with its regular acting areas and entrances marked out and used as such) and ruined setting can be puzzling. It is possible to argue that the use of the *theatron* as an acting space has some significance within the terms of the ancient theatre's conventions. Thus, when the Chorus is at its most spectator-like, it occupies the seating area and watches the action in the *orchestra* or on the 'stage'. When Oedipus is at his most formal and statesman-like, he transacts business in the acting areas; when he seeks companionship and intimacy, he removes himself to the audience area. This argument would not hold up at all times, however. The confrontation with Tiresias (Orson Welles) is at the top of the seating area, and the all-important final revelation by the Theban shepherd (Roger Livesey) happens at roughly the same part of the theatre. Most confusing of all, if any link is made with the way that the theatre was originally used, is the entrance of the Chorus or of Tiresias and his guide from the top of the *theatron*. This would have been unimaginable in the ancient theatre, since the Chorus or players would have had to be in that position before the play began for them to make an entrance from there. Such concealment of a masked figure, let alone a masked Chorus, in an open-air, day-lit amphitheatre is so unlikely as to be ruled out as a feasibility. If the theatre were simply a ruin where actors have assembled in the film to act out a production of *Oedipus Rex,* well and good but there are sequences where the theatre functions in its ancient capacity and seems vital, where it is a real acting space, not just ruined architecture.

By far the most serious problem, however, is the one with which this section began — Saville's choice of 'the realistic mode'. The appeal of this method is comprehensible, and, even in terms of the conventions obtaining within the ancient Greek theatre, there appears to be some sense in it. If Aristotle, like Plato, discerns mimesis to be the fundamental aim of Greek tragic theatre, then there was likely to have been an expectation in its audience that life in the theatre would have some relation with that outside it. The trouble with Saville's film is that there is a literal-mindedness about the realisation of this relation which casts doubt on the wisdom of using it. One of the classic problems of realism arises when it lays claim to some special proximity to truth. In certain examples of documentary cinema, for instance, truth then has to be narrowed down to what can be photographed. In other words, the Dodona performance is 'authenticated' by the filming of life in the country-side in its external manifestations, by the presentation of the sights and, to a lesser extent, the sounds of the countryside around the amphitheatre. Aristotle argues that tragic art deals in a different kind of truth from history. Artistic credibility would seem to depend, in his opinion, on obedience to laws of probability or necessity while historical truth is a matter of the possible. What has happened is obviously possible. The possible may not, however, according to Aristotle, be probable and is not therefore always suitable for drama. The film attempts to collapse the distinction between theatre and 'actuality', as if by showing the effects of plague on peasants beyond the theatre walls and then inaugurating within the theatre an inquiry into the cause of the plague the credibility of this inquiry would be guaranteed. What we are shown as happening outside the theatre — the plague, Tiresias descending from an actual Greek mountain, Oedipus, blinded, moving off into exile, for instance — is certainly possible, historical in the peculiar senses in which the cinema allows these terms to be used. If the camera shows us these things in a clearly 'real' location, then they are happening for our purposes. But what they become once within the acting spaces of the theatre in this film is still a matter of possibility. The insistence on the guarantees of reality provided by landscape tends to sap the 'credibility' of the theatrical reality. What Aristotle deems to be the probability or necessity of Sophocles' play seems at times merely possible. The relationship of the dramatic to the actual is subtler in Aristotle (and, probably, in Greek practice) than that of sight and sound within the theatre to sight and sound beyond it.

Rather than imbuing his landscape with theatricality which would allow no barrier in the passage from the amphitheatre to the country, Saville constantly (though possibly unconsciously) calls into question the authenticity of the dramatic action. Why are those sore-ridden peasants marching into the theatre to assemble in the *orchestra?* Why is that mountainous priest striding down from his home to argue with an actor on the grassy upper tiers of a ruined amphitheatre? Why are the afflicted peasants' interests represented by such stiff-postured, stave-carrying, theatrically old men (their leader is, after all, the then fairly youthful Donald Sutherland) taking up these unlikely positions in the auditorium? Parallel questions would be unthinkable in *Henry V*. We meet the 'actors' first in their own peculiar surroundings with peculiar conditions attaching to these. King Henry is obviously playing at being a king. Agincourt may look 'convincing', but if it turns out to be a thing of cardboard and back projection no great jolt will be experienced. In *Oedipus the King,* people become actors; suffering, which we accept in human terms, is expressed in language that the same human beings would scarcely understand, let alone speak; hillsides and valleys narrow into the man-made bowl of the amphitheatre.

Some of the critics were kinder about this adaptation of *Oedipus Rex* than they were about Tyrone Guthrie's film of his stage production. John Russell Taylor, for example, calls this 'a film of the Sophocles tragedy, not a mere filmed record', whatever that means precisely and, more particularly, whatever 'mere' suggests. He praises the acting performances; the Paul Roche translation, for its compromise between archaism and modern colloquialism; the closeness of the screenplay to Sophocles' original; the way that the Chorus is made acceptable in filmic terms; and says in conclusion: 'If you have come to doubt whether any performance of *Oedipus Rex* these days can be more than a reverent visitation of a tomb, this is the film to make you think again.'[2] This laudation of the film manages to steer clear entirely of the crucial business of its location, or more especially dual locations.

A number of others were not only less happy with the achievements of the film than this critic but attempted to pinpoint its failures. Michael Armstrong senses a conflict between what he discerns as the stylisation of the original and the film's modification of that stylisation in an attempt to humanise the story, which 'inevitably' in so doing conflicts with the play's strengths of stylisation.[3] He may be wrong in believing that the play's strengths reside in its stylisation. Guthrie, for example, seems to be *introducing* elaborate stylisation into a play that at the time seemed to be remarkably free of it, and to be highly mimetic (although what we would regard as stylised today could have been read in the fifth century BC as mimetic). However, he is on surer ground when he discerns the essential problem as that of compromise. The actors sometimes use a naturalistic gesture, at other times a stylised one, he says. The camera may suggest 'realism' through foregrounding the hand-held aspect of the camera, or by psychologically searching close-ups, but this is compromised by the heavily stylised shots of the Chorus spaced on the amphitheatre steps in symmetrical patterns, Armstrong argues. (Though it is more the disposition of the Chorus than of the 'shots' which are 'heavily stylised', surely?) Another critic declares, 'Philip Saville courts disaster by attempting to steer a middle course between formalism and naturalism', and comments particularly on the decision to emphasise the open-air, part-of-the-landscape aspect of the amphitheatre: 'this is not a play which can grow out of the landscape as *Electra* could [a not unchallengeable judgement, incidentally]: it needs an enclosed setting.'[4] The setting may, of course, be 'enclosed' while being open-air. The film records of the theatrical performances at Delphi (p. 43) and Epidauros (p. 48) may have offered incidental views of the surrounding terrain, but the dramatic action was entirely limited to the world of the theatre.

What is being felt in these accounts, though expression is not as clear as it could be, is that the mingling of actual with theatrical landscape is unworkable as done in this film. The problem is of the conflation of the theatre's architecture and natural scenery without apparently the will to derealise one or the other.

Antigone (Director: George Tzavellas, 1961)

George Tzavellas's film of *Antigone,* shot in black and white, was made in and around Athens. It is set in 'natural' surroundings, those of the Greek landscape or a 'realistic', albeit to some[5] an unimpressive, set of Thebes. In line with this decision to 'naturalise' the action of Sophocles' play, Tzavellas has dealt with the more resistant elements, such as the Chorus of Theban elders and the messenger, by rendering what he believes to be the essential information provided by these in cinematic/realist terms. The Chorus is dealt with in various ways to make it unobtrusive, so that, paradoxically, it is much less like a Chorus than a number of individuals offering motley opinions about the central action. The first stasimon in the play is 'split up among a number of speakers and presented conversationally' while 'one or two others work well as reflective monologues; and three [Choral speeches, presumably] are treated . . . as commentaries on the soundtrack accompanying bridge passages in the action, visually presented.'[6] What the Chorus does not do in this film is to move in choreographed fashion or sing. However, 'the effect of the Chorus as commentary remains, in the person and voice of an elder of King Creon's court, and in an off-screen voice intoning in moments of transition.'[7] While the Chorus is somehow largely integrated within a realist convention, the narratives of the sentry and of the messenger in the original are cut while their information concerning the progress of events is presented in purely visual terms.

The realism of the film appears to be that of costume drama, in that ancient costumes are employed. In a film of this nature, it is all the easier to understand the reason for the question from one reviewer, 'why festoon the Chorus of elders in crêpe hair which makes them look like Spirits of Christmas Present in summer moult?'[8]

Tzavellas's *Antigone* is admired by Penelope Gilliatt, who seems to believe that the director, by adopting the tactics that he does, has solved the predicaments of those faced with the task of filming Greek tragedy. 'It's no good simply shooting a stage performance at Epidaurus; this is what people call "Art-cinema" when they are meaning to be rude. Nor is it much good half-modernising the legend as Jules Dassin did in his absurd "Phaedra". George Tzavellas chose better.'[9] Dilys Powell felt less comfortable with his choice. Complaining of the way that the action swings from what she calls 'stage-palace' to natural setting of hillside and plain, Powell writes, 'these half-measures are a mistake. The choice lies between . . . complete liberation from the conventions of the theatre — Cacoyannis's approach — and . . . performance in the manner of the classical stage.'[10] At least this critic shows a greater tolerance of theatre conventions than Gilliatt, who is sufficiently deterred by putative popular reaction that she does not consider 'filmed theatre' any further. Whether Powell is right in believing that Cacoyannis's films are 'completely' liberated from theatrical conventions remains to be discussed.

The assumptions behind the attitudes to this film need to be considered further. The principal point claimed in favour of Tzavellas's methods is that he has got rid of the more intractable (because 'anti-realist') elements of the original without any damage. In brief, he has rendered visually what the original described verbally. Since the tone of the messengers' speeches is usually more objective than that of any others in the ancient plays, it may seem safe enough at first consideration to render visually what is originally depicted verbally. Whether the Choral lyrics are a matter of narrative information or of scene-setting, whether they are 'objective' in the way that the messenger speeches could be argued to be, would seem to need more careful consideration than the critics normally accord the questions when they congratulate the director. It is one thing to praise a film of *Antigone* without reference to the detail of the original, another to state, as Gilliatt does[11], that Tzavellas 'put a gag on the Chorus without sacrificing anything interesting that it had to say'. 'Interesting' may be the operative word here. Gilliatt does not claim that nothing is sacrificed, only that nothing interesting is sacrificed. By 'interesting', she appears to signify elements that relate to narrative thrust. If this interpretation is correct, then the Chorus could be cut altogether since its opinions about the action or the general meaning of it have precious little to do with forwarding the narrative. What she seems to be arguing is a case for films which tell the stories of the ancient tragedies. She adds that the 'images of the text' are retained in Tzavellas's much edited script, meaning, presumably, that he has translated verbal images into visual terms.

The fundamental question, then, is whether showing something by visual means is equivalent to verbal description. The assumption that it is, without further argument, is naïve, surely. In drama, all descriptions are offered by a person or persons, a character or chorus. Even if that character is a messenger, he speaks from a point of view, not from the quasi-objective angle of, say, a nineteenth-century novelist, but from the point of view of, not surprisingly, a messenger in Greek tragedy. In 'realist' cinematic practice of the traditional kind, what is shown is 'true', or rather taken to be so. Point of view is ubiquitous in cinema, but it is seldom recognised as such, and a subjective, possibly distorted, point of view has to be specially signalled by cinematic devices in dominant practice. Thus, a hand-held tracking shot may indicate a break in the traditional, 'objective' manner of shooting, suggesting that a particular character, possibly in flight or pursuit, is seeing events in a highly personal way. Realist cinema works by *seeming* to be free of ideological implications, or else by making them seem 'natural', to reinforce with particular potency the political *status quo*. Ideology, when masked, is permitted to masquerade as 'objective truth'. The political effect of the realistic mode is profoundly important because of its very invisibility.

Cacoyannis's Euripidean Trilogy

Michael Cacoyannis has filmed three Euripidean tragedies. His *Electra* (1961) and *The Trojan Women* (1971) are based on Euripidean originals of the same name, while his *Iphigenia* (1976) is based on Euripides' *Iphigenia in Aulis*. As far back as 1963, there is on record[12] his intention of making a trilogy of Greek tragedies, although *The Trojan Women* at that point was not considered; instead Euripides' *Orestes* was. The three films realised by 1976 were shown in the National Film Theatre season on 6 and 7 June 1981, in reverse order to that in which they were made, for the obvious reason of narrative coherence. *Iphigenia* concerns an incident involving Agamemnon, Clytemnestra and their daughter, Iphigenia, on the Greek expedition's voyage to Troy to commence the war. *The Trojan Women* relates the suffering of the female victims of that war immediately after the Trojan defeat. *Electra* depicts the revenge killing of Clytemnestra and her new consort, Aegisthus, by her

children, Orestes and Electra, for her murder of their father, Agamemnon, after his triumphant return from Troy.

Whether Cacoyannis has made a trilogy (rather than three separate films based on Greek tragedy) is doubtful. The Euripides plays
were certainly not written as a trilogy, even if *The Trojan Women*
is the final play in a (quite other) trilogy. Although each dealt with
incidents concerning or arising from the Trojan war, the same
incidents or characters might be treated in quite different ways in
different Euripidean plays. Moreover, there are marked differences
in these three films. *Electra* is in black and white, the other two in
colour; *The Trojan Women* is in English, the other two in modern
Greek; Clytemnestra is played by two different actresses, Aleka
Catselli in *Electra,* Irene Papas in *Iphigenia*. Most crucially, there
is no developing philosophical question easily detectable in these
films, as there is in Ingmar Bergman's trilogy, *Through a Glass
Darkly* (1961), *Winter Light* (1962) and *The Silence* (1963), whose
questioning of God's relations, if any, with humankind provides a
link between films which have scarcely any narrative or character
links.

The three films will be treated in the present study in the order
of their making. The points of similarity ought to become obvious
in this way, so that certain strategies should emerge as commonly
underlying Cacoyannis's approach to his material, but there will be
little attempt to question further the credibility or otherwise of the
claim for a trilogy. The important thing may be that he has made
three films on the Trojan cycle of myth, all based on the same
playwright's originals, with an apparently broad similarity of treatment and of priorities in the adaptation. Much more attention
will be directed to the question of whether or not these films are
'Euripidean'. Cacoyannis has chosen the same playwright each time;
therefore, the comparison with his Euripidean originals is almost
obligatory. Consideration of the differences in treatment between
Euripides and Cacoyannis ought to permit some weighing of the
claim that two at least of the Cacoyannis trilogy — *Electra* and
Iphigenia — are 'by far the best films yet made out of Greek
tragedy'.[13]

Electra (1961)

Cacoyannis sets his film's action in the world of actuality, using the
ancient site of Mycenae itself for his prologue and shooting the rest
of the action in the countryside off the road between Athens and

Sounion. By taking the film outside the world of the theatre entirely (unlike Philip Saville later) and by refusing to use studio sets at any point (unlike Tzavellas in the same year), he has made the film in one sense 'realistic', but at the same time this realism is not to be confused with 'naturalism', since the film is often highly stylised.

This is particularly true of the prologue, created from some materials within but largely outside the Greek original, where a wordless montage of incidents, reminiscent of Eisenstein (*Ivan the Terrible* [1942–46] particularly suggests itself here), transmits information about Agamemnon's murder by Clytemnestra (Aleka Catselli) and Aegisthus (Phoebus Rhaziz) and the birth of Electra's (Irene Papas) passion for revenge. Clytemnestra is from the beginning reduced to a jewelled arm, so that her appearance just before her own slaughter in heavy make-up and richly-patterned robes is less of a surprise. She is the same vain, superficial woman that she always was. In the opening sequences, Cacoyannis establishes his method as synecdochic, allusive, metaphorical.

Even in the countryside, the Chorus is in several senses retained. A choir singing a modern song (composed by Mikis Theodorakis) fills the hillside as the peasant passes with Electra. The women of the countryside also sing in chorus but, even when they simply talk or listen, the formations which they adopt are stylised, often symmetrical and usually patterned in some fashion, to mark them out from the men and women who sometimes look on at key moments (at the wine festival, for example, where Aegisthus is encountered by Orestes (Yannis Fertis) and Pylades, after the matricide). These are Electra's confidantes, to be trusted totally, even when Orestes talks of murder.

Natural sights and sounds are rendered less so in the film. Thunder is heard when Agamemnon dies, while a sudden windstorm blows up at the time of Clytemnestra's murder. The light of dawn after Aegisthus' execution is merely an extension of the light of freedom signalled by the torches lit in the darkness of the night. There is, then, no attempt to hide the formality of ancient tragedy, but rather to soften it occasionally. It is not difficult for a modern audience to accept workers' songs in the fields. The ritual of the murders calls for a ritualised response, just as the rites in honour of Bacchus 'explain' the artificial groupings and dances at the wine festival. Even then, there are moments when the authentic countryside and the semi-authentic countrywomen Chorus together produce jarring effects. The protection of Electra by her rustic friends is by means of a moving formation that brings to mind a version of a rugby scrum. (Incidentally, it is interesting that the original play does not demand such stylisation. There, the women simply scatter at the approach of the strangers.[14]) The absence of a life for the country-women other than fetching water or song and dance, the way that they function as a group, despite the individualisation attempted through the use of the close-up, and as a group whose sole aim seems to be the expression of support for Electra, is harder to accommodate in a film which establishes its countryside as credible enough to be ploughed and planted.

Despite some problems, Cacoyannis's film seems a highly accept-able rendering of Greek tragedy to many critics, especially those who have formed a generic notion of tragedy in Aristotelian terms. On the evidence of the film, Euripides' play is as formal as any other tragedy, unified by probability and necessity to produce an emotional climax in the audience — an organic whole designed for the achievement of catharsis. The paradox is that Cacoyannis seems to have made Euripides' puzzling play far more obviously tragic than the original could have been, and to have made a film which resembles ancient Greek tragedy far more than Euripides' *Electra* may have done.

The first production of Euripides' *Electra* must have opened startlingly. The *skene* façade traditionally associated with palace fronts and, even in the seashore setting of Sophocles' *Philoctetes,* with characters of noble rank, here represented a peasant's cottage on the borders of Argos. Moreover, the prologue, frequently uttered by a god or gods, is delivered by the peasant owner. While the information communicated by him has the prologue's traditional objectivity, the fact that he is the speaker must surely serve to 'reduce' the events of Agamemnon's homecoming, his murder and the maltreatment of the royal children on Aegisthus' accession — a strategy which may indicate Euripides' wish to create a new category of drama before a name for it existed,[15] or to suggest that tragedy need not exclude experience of human realities.[16] By assigning the bulk of the informational role[17] not to the play's peasant but to the camera in Cacoyannis's opening sequences, the focus returns to royalty in its customary setting, and the fact that there is a period of transition from palace to cottage eliminates the sense of shock produced by the play.

The differences between the two *Electra*'s are more fundamental than this, though. Although the jarring, anti-heroic quality of the original is unusually marked, this has been almost completely suppressed in the film. That is, Electra's whining self-pity has been transformed by omission of such motives for her water-fetching as to show 'the gods the insolence of Aegisthus' (*El.* 57–8), by her unvarying tact with the peasant and by the insertion of an early scene in which Aegisthus' abuse of Agamemnon's grave, only *rumoured* in the original play (362 ff.), becomes an actuality perpetrated as direct insult to Electra. The atmosphere of neurotic anxiety, indicated in the play by, for example, the most perfunctory and joyless *anagnorisis* (recognition) ever penned, is dispelled by the length of time and the sense of release created for the *anagnorisis* by the film. The degradation of the murderers which is, indeed, suggested in their guilty departure into exile at the end of the film, is limited to the horror felt for matricide, however justified. In the play, Aegisthus is dealt a hideous blow in the middle of a sacrifice, to which he has kindly welcomed the strangers; in the film, he is cleanly executed off camera while he presides over a more licentious-seeming festival than that of the original. It is his head, not his corpse, which is brought back to Electra in the play.

Crucially, Cacoyannis selects a 'winner' in the *agon*, the debate between Electra and her mother, making Clytemnestra's ostensibly reasonable arguments appear shallow, and Electra's rhetoric of sexual jealousy seem restrained and rational. He has further softened her by making Electra cry out in warning, 'Mother!', so that what is plainly a callous, sarcastic remark in the play, 'Take care this smoky wall does not / dirty your dress' (*El.* 1139–40),[18] is uttered only to cover her near-betrayal of her purpose through daughterly concern. Significantly too, with the elimination of the play's *dei ex machina*, it seems as if the sad removal into exile is inspired by the characters' guilt (also experienced in the play, admittedly) and public opinion, rather than by purely external command from Apollo.

In his *Electra*, Euripides appears repeatedly to be offering a critique of the transmission, by such playwrights as Aeschylus, of heroic myth without sufficient regard to human personality or even human reality. Aeschylus' *Oresteia* treats the need for matricide as a moral problem, the last play indicating that, once pollution is cleansed and moral responsibility taken off Orestes' shoulders, no malaise remains. Euripides seems less interested in abstract questions of justice but asks his audience to contemplate the act, whether just or not, of killing a mother, to become aware of the physical realities involved in slaughter.[19] Furthermore, he makes his avengers so uninviting, and the victims so pathetic, that the empathy which Aristotle appears to consider as a prerequisite of the tragic experience is less capable of achievement. The audience cannot be diverted by questions of right and wrong, cannot evade the unpleasantness of the murders by calculating their justifiability. As part of his critique, Euripides parodies Aeschylus' use of tokens in the scene where grave offerings are discussed, making Electra object to the various signs of Orestes' return on logical grounds. In thus criticising Aeschylus with his conventionalised use of signs leading to *anagnorisis,* Euripides questions an entire tradition of tragic construction on grounds which might loosely be termed naturalistic or — the more common epithet in Euripidean scholarship — realistic. Cacoyannis's film is closer to Aeschylus' conception of tragedy than Euripides'.

Cacoyannis himself appears to claim fidelity to the original: 'My love of the text was the measure of my respect for it.'[20] His conviction that the function of all tragedy, Euripides' included, is to be discerned in terms suggested by Aristotle, as that of the inspiration of pity and fear leading to catharsis, appears to be implied in his statement: 'the basic purpose of Greek drama . . . is *to move.* To serve both the original author and his audience the director must eliminate the distance between them'.[21]

Against this Aristotelian attitude to tragedy, we may set Ekbert Faas' thesis (pp. 39-40) that Euripides displays anti- and sometimes post-tragic attitudes in his writing. Whether or not the original is 'tragic' (largely) by Faas' understanding of the term, there are many obstacles to the uncritical submersion of the audience within the world of the play, the kinds of obstacles that provide the very distance which Cacoyannis seeks to deny. Thus, the audience is jolted out of its comfortable relationship with the tragedy by the infighting which seems to be foregrounded at the point where Euripides ridicules the sorts of recognition tokens set up by Aeschylus in his version of the Electra story, *The Libation Bearers.* The appearance of the *dei ex machina* to pronounce on the fate of the survivors and to finish — but not end, in an Aristotelian sense — the dramatic action is another method of distancing the audience from the world of the play. Setting it in a peasant environment is yet another. Cacoyannis eliminates the gods of the epilogue, cuts out all references to the other playwright and makes the recognition smooth and traditional, eases the spectator gently into the countryside after establishing the atmosphere of high tragedy in the opening sequences. Electra and Orestes are made sympathetic, Clytemnestra insincere even when she appears to have a point in her favour, Aegisthus licentious even when he could be thought pious. The allegiances and sympathies of the spectator are directed in favour of certain characters and actions, against certain others. How successfully this can be maintained needs consideration, though. If Electra's attitudes to Clytemnestra are justified, why the guilty end? If the countryfolk and Tutor have egged Orestes and Electra on to matricide, why do they seem so repelled by them after the accomplishment of the matricide, especially as they are spared its repulsiveness, as is (largely) the audience?

According to John Ardagh, Professor Lloyd-Jones had nothing but praise for the Cacoyannis film: 'Removing the stagy prologue by the farmer, and the *deus ex machina* ending, are . . . improvements and so is the rearranging of the stiff passages of stichomythia.'[22] These 'improvements' are made at a cost, though. The very least we could ask is why Cacoyannis has chosen the Euripides rather than the Sophocles *Electra,* since his attitudes to tragedy and to this story in particular seem so much more Sophoclean than Euripidean.

The Trojan Women (1971)

Ten years, the traditional duration of the Trojan war, elapsed between the filming of *Electra* and of *The Trojan Women.* Cacoyannis must have been encouraged by the critical success which the earlier film enjoyed. Despite pessimism in advance of its making about the chances of such an enterprise within the Ministry of Arts and Theatre, for example, Cacoyannis was honoured with the award for best screen adaptation at Cannes, and the film was given the Best Picture Award at the 1962 Salonica Film Festival, and an Academy Award nomination.[23] Still, *The Trojan Women* was not included in his original plan for a Euripidean trilogy. For this project, it must have been the success of his staging of the play that encouraged him to film it. He first presided over what has been described as a 'semi-improvised'[24] production of *The Trojan Women* at the 1963 Spoleto Festival, and he then re-staged it at the Circle-in-the-Square Theatre, New York. 'Never before, at least to my knowledge,' Cacoyannis has said, 'had a Greek tragedy run commercially [there were over 650 performances] . . . people always considered them as museum pieces. . . . And if you can do it on stage, I don't see why you shouldn't do it on the screen.'[25]

There were also political factors which made the filming of this particular play an especially attractive proposition in the early 1970s.

The Colonels were in power in Greece, but more crucially the Vietnam war made the play's concern with the victims of war seem timely. The fact that these victims are female must also have been appealing at a time when feminist ideas were impinging on popular consciousness with unprecedented success. (All the more extraordinary, then, is the wording of the dedication in the film — 'We who have made this film dedicate it to all those who fearlessly oppose the oppression of man by man'!) Genevieve Bujold, the French-Canadian actress who plays Cassandra in the film, seemed to touch on both aspects in an interview: *'The Trojan Women . . .* is a universal gathering of people saying no to war, to injustice. [The actresses are all] very modern, very involved and aware of what's going on, and all with strong political ideas.'[26]

Critics of the film sensed that there was an attempt to explain its making in terms of contemporary relevance, or — a less controversial way of suggesting the same thing — timelessness. Cacoyannis claimed that the play was born from Euripides' outrage at his compatriots' crime (against Melos) during the Peloponnesian war — a likely, but not certain inference. He proceeded to generalise this application when talking of the film. In interview, for example, he related the clubbing of rebellious women in his film to events in Chicago: 'Chicago, Paris. I mean you can take your choice.'[27] Unimpressed with this generalised argument for applicability and with the possible relevance of Vietnam or 'women's lib', Molly Haskell headed her review of the film with the question, 'Why are we in Troy?'[28]

As with *Electra,* the director opted for actual locations rather than studio reconstructions. But, instead of Greece, Cacoyannis chose the deserted walls and rocks of Atienza in Spain as the setting for his film. Because Atienza is already a ruin, however, the burning of the city which provides a climactic moment in the play becomes redundant in the film. 'Why would anyone bother to burn the ruins and how would stone catch fire?', John Simon asks, not unreasonably.[29]

The setting of tragic action within a natural location, which causes the occasional problem in *Electra,* is more controversial in *The Trojan Women.* Pauline Kael believes that it is *stage* space in which the film's drama is played out. She finds that space claustrophobic and confusingly employed, since the film lacks motivating entrances and no certainty exists about the spatial relation of one person to another within a sequence.[30] These complaints would not be damning if the film were conceived in theatrical, anti-realist terms, but because Cacoyannis's attempt is to involve his audience, to permit easy identification, they have some force. The critic continues that the devices of the freeze frame, whirling camera, 'fast cuts', are the 'attempts of a man without a film sense to make a drama cinematic'.[31] Yet, she feels enthusiasm for the film, precisely because it is a film of Greek tragedy, which, she claims, 'has a purity that you *can't get from anything else'* [her italics]. 'That's a very good reason,' she continues, 'to make a movie — to bring people the emotions that only a few in our time have experienced in the theatre.'[32]

The film of *The Trojan Women* is considerably closer to the play on which it is based than *Electra* or *Iphigenia,* though there are omissions and additions. Thus, for example, the characters of Cassandra (Genevieve Bujold) and Andromache (Vanessa Redgrave) (like that of Electra in the 1961 film) are rendered more appealing to twentieth-century sensibilities. While Cassandra's passion and sense of truth are vividly presented in Genevieve Bujold's performance, those lines in which she is specially vindictive about the Greeks or sarcastic to Talthybius[33] are cut. So too are the disapproving remarks of the Chorus during her prophecy.[34] Instead, the Chorus is given a patriotic ode to sing. Again, Andromache's advertising of her model-wife conduct, more appropriate to Periclean Athens than to heroic Greece, expressed in such self-congratulatory and complacent terms that it may well have puzzled even the fifth-century BC audience as to its 'seriousness', has been removed.

Cuts must be made in the original dialogue. Nevertheless, the choice of these particular cuts is interesting. While these women are softened, the portrait of Helen as whore and hypocrite is rendered more clear-cut. In an 'imported' sequence, the naked Helen (Irene Papas), prowling behind bars like a dangerous caged beast, is granted the water refused to the women of Troy pleading in the noonday heat and, in their sight, uses it to bathe. Their violence against her necessitates the summoning of Menelaus (Patrick Magee), who attempts to judge her arguments that her life should be spared against those of Hecuba (Katharine Hepburn), championing the Trojan women's view that she should die. While Helen's speech is roughly similar to the Euripidean Helen's, the camera indicates the insincerity of her delivery and draws attention to her bare back, her attempts to use her physical charms to blind Menelaus to truth. Hecuba's response in the film is almost too rational, too easily a refutation of the flimsy pretexts and tale-spinning of her adversary, and she 'loses' only because of Menelaus' weakness and Helen's fake suicide attempt (another importation). The sense of injustice engendered in the audience when Menelaus does not kill Helen on the spot is augmented by the film's visual vouchsafing of the information that despite advice against so doing he permits her to share his ship on the return voyage.

The *agon* between Helen and Hecuba appears much more finely balanced in the play, however. The most recent consideration of the Helen/Hecuba debate concludes, after an unusually careful review of the arguments and their validity in context, with the following verdict: 'In this agon . . . it is not made clear whose version of events is correct: both characters make good points, and both accounts of what happened are possible'[35] and 'it would be as mistaken to suppose that Helen must be right because her views are traditional as it would be to assume that Hecuba must be right because her views are advanced. Menelaus agrees with Hecuba (1036–9), but this is not decisive: he has no special knowledge, and he does not convincingly justify his decision.'[36] The callousness and narcissism of the water-consumption scene being absent, we are uncertain whether feeling against Helen is justified or yet another exemplar of the brutalisation of both victors and victims. Helen's arguments, particularly that in which she shifts blame onto Aphrodite, would not seem as false in a heroic context as they are made to appear by Hecuba, whose rationalising of the gods as projections by human beings is startlingly anachronistic in that setting and might well have shocked those in the audience to whom Aristophanes addresses his manifold jokes about Euripides' impieties. Moreover, the irrationality of blaming Helen for all the suffering of the war because her seduction began the war vitiates Hecuba's case. Euripides' sympathies are of less certain identity than Cacoyannis's, it would appear. Furthermore, the motive for war which, as in the latter's *Iphigenia* (see below, pp. 85-91), is said to be desire for material gain is not so described in the play, where it is only to Helen — by her adversary, Hecuba — that this motive is attributed.

Most crucially, the Euripidean prologue is absent from the film — or rather the essential information in the prologue, that the victors are soon to die themselves, is provided by an impersonal voice-over. The effect of this alteration may seem slight — the information about the Greeks' own destinies is no less 'true' in the Euripidean prologue than it is with the device of the omniscient narrator uttering during frame-freezes in Cacoyannis's prologue. However, in the play, it is Athene and Poseidon who decide on their doom, thanks to the goddess's 'somewhat casual' (*Tro.* 67)[37] change of affection consequent on the insult to her sanctuary in Troy. The Homeric quality of the play's prologue, with petty-minded deities blithely arranging to wipe out thousands of mortals, functions in at least two ways. It removes any questions of justice which may be implied from consideration of merely human intention and it creates further uncertainty about the literal credibility of the narrative, in that Hecuba's rationalisation of human belief in deities is highly problematic in a play which opens thus. If in Euripides the prologues and the frequent appearances of a *deus ex machina* have a different dramatic status from the action bracketed by them, they are still vitally part of his drama. The problem has been removed by the film. Its prologue seems to suggest ultimate justice in the Greek deaths and thus to offer consolation to the audience listening to Hecuba's complaints about the Greeks. In the play, on the other hand, the carnage dictated by the deities for the particular offence at Troy — not, notably, for the maltreatment of the Trojan women — is yet another example of the injustice perpetrated at every level by the victors, and arguably by Hecuba herself in her treatment of Helen.

Once again, as in *Electra,* Cacoyannis has made identification a much easier matter for his audience, thanks to his different emphases. The anger which the already outraged women of Troy feel against Helen may be shared by a latter-day audience, given the depiction of Helen's self-absorption and indifference to the suffering of all less powerful than she. As emotion against Helen is strengthened, so sympathy with Hecuba is augmented. In this film, she is the voice of reason, attempting to denounce Helen to a man who will not be guided by such reason. The less disposed he is to be swayed by her authoritative views, the more powerful is the Chorus's engagement with Hecuba and, through the Chorus, a modern audience's. The sense that injustice reigns is threatening to such audience implication, is threatening, many would argue, to tragedy itself, in that it has been discerned as 'purposive' (p. 33). Hecuba's dogged optimism in the earlier part of the play is no less cruelly mocked in the film, but the framework of the Trojan women's suffering is different in play and film. To whomever the voice of the prologue belongs, it is a voice of quiet authority, akin to God's in Hollywood epics. It promises that there is, unbelievable as it may from time to time seem in the face of such suffering and injustice, an order in the universe. The Greeks who lord it over these innocent women in the film will, after the film is over, suffer for their *hubris*. This promise permits a greater empathy in the film audience than could ever have been possible with the play, where there is no such voice of detached authority, only the shriller tones of utterly partial, and petty, deities deciding on life and death with as much concern for their *amour propre* as the Helen of the film. Helen's strength in the film has been discerned by Pauline Kael,[38] leading her to believe that she embodies the very spirit of war. This spirit of war splits Olympus at the very opening of the play. If the gods themselves are gods of war, the play could be read as saying how idiotic are the hopes of a Hecuba that there should be any prospect of betterment for war's victims.

Pity and fear are much more likely to be inspired by the film than the original play. Freed from its Euripidean uncertainties and its unrelieved pessimism, the dramatic action can be powerfully moving. Cacoyannis has provided a disturbing emotional experience. The performances of these actresses from Greece, Canada, Britain and the USA provide sufficient reason in themselves for the film to be seen. Despite a tendency to undercut their readings with camera techniques that draw attention away from the actresses at the ends of their 'big scenes', there is a generous attention accorded to their histrionic powers. The suffering inflicted on woman and child by man has seldom been presented to more unrelieved and appalling effect than in Cacoyannis's film.

Iphigenia (1976)

Cacoyannis produced Euripides' *Iphigenia in Aulis* on the New York stage in 1968. He wrote a screenplay based on the play and directed the film of it eight years later, using as his location Haidari, near Athens, with the mountains of Euboea visible across the straits.

In choosing the *Iphigenia in Aulis* as the basis of the third film in his trilogy, Cacoyannis was taking on a difficult assignment. The text of the *Iphigenia in Aulis* is so problematic that it has been concluded that the play may have been put together after Euripides' death by his son, using rough drafts.[39] Two versions of the same short speech would suggest that we are dealing with an uncorrected draft; the prologue contains structural anomalies; the verse of the last part of the messenger speech is faulty; the catalogue of ships is sometimes taken to have been composed by another hand; and the end of the play is particularly defective. While, then, the classical scholar may resort to textual criticism and argue over the authenticity or credibility of certain passages as they stand, the play producer or film-maker must face the difficulties of a much disputed text, either taking it on, interpolations and errors notwithstanding, or heavily adapting it, to make sense, as it were, of the confusions.

Moreover, there are problems of interpretation even within the certainly Euripidean parts of the play. Faas, surprisingly, thinks of the *Iphigenia in Aulis* as a 'traditional tragedy';[40] partly, it appears, because it was singled out by Hegel as embodying the conflict between 'ethical life in its social universality and the family as the natural ground of moral relations'.[41] Nevertheless, there are several factors which make this tragedy far from 'traditional'. For a start, the language is quite un-Aeschylean. Within its conventions, the diction chosen by Euripides for his characters is, as often in his work, unsuited to heroic figures in heroic situations, but closer to the conversational and quotidian. A major problem in the play, breaching Aristotle's wishful 'rule' of beginning–middle–end linked organically by probability or necessity, is Iphigenia's sudden change of heart. That she should launch into an unswervingly patriotic justification of the war, and unflinchingly go to her death, is at least curious, given the sordid manipulation of events to ensure her sacrifice and her own arguments at the point where she is terrified by her fate. This is just one question reasonably to be asked of the play as it stands. Bernard Knox believes that several are raised by it: Who knows whether Iphigenia's death will make the winds blow? What would have resulted from the two kings' silencing of Calchas and Odysseus, their appealing to the better nature of the army, or from their flight to Mycenae?[42] There is much appeal in Knox's conclusion that the play's effect on its audience seems to remind us of Brechtian theory and practice. He feels that the probing action of the play is possible only if the spectator remains detached, emotionally uninvolved with the characters.[43] And yet, he notes, the play 'takes the spectator by the throat' from the beginning and forces his/her identification not only with the wronged mother and threatened girl but even with the cowardly royal father.[44] Knox's diagnosis of the tension between two divergent practices in Euripides' play, so that the action seems to 'alienate' the viewer while the viewer is at the same time drawn into it through the processes of identification, is broadly in line with Faas' analysis of Euripides. Faas argues for anti-tragic and post-tragic elements within Euripides, not as a consistent position but as tendencies within his tragedy. This makes production of his plays, whether as plays or films, unusually demanding.

Published statements about the reasons for the choice of this play are, as usual with Cacoyannis, fairly unhelpful. David Wilson justly considers that Cacoyannis's explanation of the modern relevance of Euripides' theme in *Iphigenia* is platitudinous.[45] 'Aren't people's lives being sacrificed every day?', Cacoyannis asks. 'When I'm provoked by something [as he had been by the Turkish invasion of Cyprus in 1974], then I feel the urge to make a film, to scream.' Irene Papas, who plays Clytemnestra, is even more passionate, but even more opaque, in her verbose defence of the decision to make a film of this particular play:

> It wouldn't have been made if I thought there was no relevance. I believe that ideas are immortal and that the problems of the human race are still the same . . . we still go to war, we still fight for money, we are still politically minded, and with more than any other century I think the twentieth century is closer to the bone of the Greek problems: the problems of death and survival . . . Greek drama dealt with genuine crises and the problems that are vital to human beings. And now in this century with the threat of a nuclear war, and Vietnam just ended — it is just the same.[46]

The point of the play in the late fifth century BC, towards the end of the Peloponnesian war, must have been far more specific than these generalisations would permit us to believe. A likely reference to recent events from within the play may be detected in Iphigenia's jingoistic, anti-barbarian speech. This example of Hellenic chauvinism could well be a response to the sophist Gorgias' proposal, in his speech at Olympia, that the Greeks should set aside their differences and unite to fight the barbarian Persians. While some have seen in her speech a parody of the proposal, others have taken it to be a reinforcement of Gorgias' ideas, since Persian subsidies were keeping the war going and each side had to court Persia for aid.[47] The confusion about the tone of the speech — satirical or sincere, to put it simply — may be productive, as it reinforces the likelihood that Euripides offers an idea, or set of ideas, in his *agones,* which the individual spectator is free to accept or reject.

Cacoyannis's film has to find a point in the original play which transcends the peculiar circumstances in which Athens found herself

towards the close of her war with Sparta, and additionally to deal
with a play which seems sufficiently incoherent at times as to produce
a *Verfremdungseffekt* in its audience. What it accomplishes ought
now to be considered in more detail.

The play opens with a nocturnal dialogue between Agamemnon
(Costa Kazakos) and his old slave, a dialogue which is delayed
considerably in the Cacoyannis *Iphigenia*. The opening sequences
of the latter detail a number of events which are alluded to in
Agamemnon's speech or later in the play, while still others are
invented to offer specific illustrations of general commentary within
the play. Thus, the original catalogue of ships sung by the Chorus
(*I.A.* 235 ff.) becomes a daringly accelerating tracking shot along a
line of beached vessels, followed by shots of hundreds of idle soldiers
on the beach. The army's discontent is indicated by the cry of
'WHEN?', Agamemnon's customary attitude towards it by his only
momentarily being discomfited by a soldier fainting in his path. The
evidence of suffering on the part of the Greeks due to the absence
of a sailing wind and of sufficient fresh food is followed by an
explanation of Artemis' demand for the sacrifice of Iphigenia which
is nowhere discoverable in the Euripidean version. White-robed
men of sacerdotal appearance are unable to prevent the soldiers'
slaughter of their sheep and of a deer (obviously in the context
sacred), at whose death Calchas steps forward menacingly. Calchas
then brings word 'from Artemis' to Agamemnon, in the company
of Menelaus (Costa Carras) and Odysseus (Christos Tsangos), that
his daughter's life must be offered to her in order to secure a wind.
As Agamemnon attempts to set his face firmly against the demand,
he is assailed by the cheers of his army and its song about the
glorious expedition to Troy.

The depiction of incident and character in these film sequences is
highly illuminating. The principal difference between film and play
in this area is that inconsistency and ambiguity seem to be eliminated
in the film's account of events. That is, the camera's eye lends an
air of objectivity and veracity to what are no more than possible
interpretations within Euripides. For example, the film makes it
clear that Agamemnon refuses to countenance the sacrifice of his
daughter until the army's enthusiasm for him forces him to think
again. In the play, the army's real attitude and particularly Agamemnon's psychology are more elusive. According to Agamemnon himself, he first ordered the disbanding of the army and it was only
through Menelaus' arguments that he was induced to agree to the

sacrifice (*I.A.* 94–8). However, Menelaus in the later argument between the brothers offers a different account, one in which the Greeks wished to disband the fleet and waste no more sweat at Aulis, while Agamemnon, fearful of the loss of glory, was pleased when Calchas brought word from Artemis (*I.A.* 350–62). In his reply, Agamemnon evades further comment on his decision, except to say that he has now changed his mind (*I.A.* 396).

While in the film the overwhelming pressure of the Greek hosts is powerfully suggested both visually and aurally, subjection to the will of the soldiers is used by Agamemnon himself in the play as an excuse, in the curiously abrupt *volte-face* by the brothers (Menelaus pleads for Iphigenia, while Agamemnon claims that her fate is sealed). Immediately after Agamemnon has asserted that they are in 'Fate's grip' (511),[48] a statement which Menelaus finds obscure (513), this is equated with pressure from the army (514). Each time in this crucial stichomythia that Menelaus attempts to extricate Agamemnon from his sense of impotence in the matter, the latter raises some new objection — that Calchas will tell the army if he sends her back; that the demagogic Odysseus will assemble the Argives and inform them of his retraction. With mounting paranoia, he claims fear of retribution even in Argos:

> Even if I escape to Argos, they'll come after me,
> Capture the town, Cyclopian walls and all, and make
> The land a ruin. Such is my pit of misery,
> The blind despair in which the gods now have me trapped.
> (533–7)

If all this is true, why did he not feel so trapped by Destiny when he wrote to Iphigenia warning her off in the first place? How can he logically identify pressure from other human beings with 'Fate's grip'? Most significantly, why is Menelaus unable to follow his argument, Agamemnon so eager not to be rescued by Menelaus? Either Agamemnon was aware of all these pressures when he wrote the letter and did so in blind optimism, or they are convenient pretexts now for inaction. In both play and film, the reason why Agamemnon gives up his attempt to allow Iphigenia to escape the moment he knows she is arriving remains unclear. The first time that, in the play's terms, there is some objective evidence of the army's demands that she be sacrificed is late in the play (1346–8) and this occurs, significantly, only shortly after a note of panhellenic righteousness has been struck for the first time (1264–6), a note which helps to establish the credibility of Iphigenia's imminent change of heart, by which she readily assents to her sacrifice.

Cacoyannis has thus supplied a convincing explanation of Agamemnon's sense of powerlessness in the ubiquity and scale of the army's presence, an army consistently dedicated in the film to the Trojan enterprise for the sake of material gain. The killing of the deer,[49] and particularly the suggestion of stage-managing by Calchas, remove some of the enigma attaching to Artemis' command in the play. A 'subjective' tracking shot as the deer flees in vain which is later paralleled by an exactly similar track as Iphigenia (Tatania Papamoskou) becomes a hopeless fugitive, and the final confrontation of Iphigenia with priests in clothes worn by the presumably sacred herdsmen of the deer sequence, are importations with their own ambiguity, possibly suggesting a destiny latent in the secular machinations of the priest.[50]

As the film proceeds, the most striking alterations until the dénouement itself must be in the characters of Clytemnestra and Achilles. The latter has been vastly changed from a tactless Homeric warrior and, worse, a long-winded sophist, to a fulfilment of the handmaidens' romantic dreams. After the allure of his mysterious introduction, naked on the sand with a white stallion nearby, he turns up again immediately after the girls have expressed delight in the heroes and, although his mistaken assumptions about Clytemnestra's warmth to him and his embarrassment are as comic as in the play, instead of the dull pedant who produces 55 lines of frigid rhetoric in crisis, we are presented with a fair-minded, dashing young man who succinctly puts justice and concern for the army first. When Iphigenia first encounters the man to whom she was to be wed, there is a precisely symmetrical turning of the young people's heads and bodies towards each other, a sense of magical spontaneous attraction between them oddly reminiscent of Tony's first glimpse of Maria in Robert Wise's *West Side Story* (1961)! Clytemnestra, the model mother of the opening sequences, sheds the matter-of-fact shrewishness and self-absorption of Euripides' version. The prescience with which she detects something amiss in Agamemnon's bearing and in his wedding arrangements seems absent from the play. The sequences in which Iphigenia listens appalled to discussion of her death and makes a vain attempt at flight and where Odysseus harangues the army are entirely new.

At the climax of the play, when Iphigenia suddenly decides to die willingly, she gives her reasons as devotion to Greece, together with the less obviously 'sympathetic' elements of revulsion at barbarians and her belief that women are relatively worthless beings in any case. These problematic reasons are excised in the film. Cacoyannis's heroine claims a victory in choosing *how* she will die and asks, 'Why should my life count for more than others'? Then, too, Achilles' love for her seems to give her the requisite strength and serenity; one recalls this time the possibly doomed heroine of Agnès Varda's *Cléo de cinq à sept* (1961) resigning herself to her fate when a soldier meets and falls in love with her.

The probably un-Euripidean ending of the play, with Artemis substituting a hind for Iphigenia on the altar, is scarcely suggested but not ruled out by Agamemnon's amazed stare as he watches the sacrifice. The mounting wind as Iphigenia climbs the steps to the altar in the film makes the status of Calchas' pronouncement questionable. Does the fact that neither army nor priests discontinue the preparations for Iphigenia's death despite the rising wind indicate a purblind desire for bloodshed at any price, or signal that Artemis is indeed appeased in her certain knowledge that the maiden is determined to die? Or, more probably in this context, that the wind coincides conveniently with the decision? In this respect at least, Cacoyannis's version achieves a characteristically Euripidean open-endedness regarding deity.

It is interesting to view the 'trilogy' as a whole after these analyses of the individual films, particularly in relation to the Euripidean originals.

For one thing, the progression from *Electra* to *Iphigenia* is largely that from relative formalism to relative 'realism', even within a broadly realistic context. That is, while Cacoyannis has chosen convincing pre-existing locations for all three films, and authenticates their action, to some extent, by use of these, he dwells less and less on the formal aspects of the original plays. The countrywomen of *Electra* unmistakably behave as a Chorus at certain points. Their movements and their songs are not those of rustics, but of a dignified, sympathetic band of observers. Their function is to attend to Electra rather than to express themselves and their own special concerns. In *The Trojan Women*, the Chorus's sympathy and attention to Hecuba is motivated by the drama itself, in that these women witness their former queen's desolation and still look to her for advice in their present calamity. Yet, Cacoyannis attempts to photograph them individually. When they take formal postures on the rocks, the camera still moves searchingly from one face to another, as if seeking an individuality that the group utterance of the stasima masks. By *Iphigenia*, the original stasima have become songs sung by individuals at 'credible' moments in the drama, or else when excited chattering handmaids pour out the thoughts of the original Chorus in a manner that raises no obstacles for a modern audience, once it has accepted the customary heroic relation of royalty and slaves. The symbolism at certain moments of the first film has made way for the less allusive, more naturalistic, depiction of incident in *Iphigenia*. If Cacoyannis' definition of the function of tragedy is that it should move its audience, he creates more emotional involvement each time, progressing from the more problematic revenge theme of the first film, through a harrowing depiction of suffering in the second, to a 'rattling good yarn' of youthful idealism (and possibly young love) which is readily appreciated by an audience with little notion of Greek tragedy's conventions, although its power is not lost on those with detailed knowledge.

Part of his strategy to ensure identification and audience implication is his consistent focus upon human beings, not gods, providence or chance, as the fount of good or evil. Most effectively, above all in *Iphigenia*, Cacoyannis permits us to experience the tremendous secular and human pressures of the mass upon the apparently isolated noble figures who appear on the tragic stage, using the panorama of beached ships and idle men to remind us of the enormity of Agamemnon's power and, therefore, political/military responsibility. The Trojan war, stripped of all Homeric glamour and religious sanctions, is reduced to an imperialist venture, with the single incentive of material gain, all else being convenient pretext. In *The Trojan Women*, it becomes more specific, seeming at times to stand for America's conflict in Vietnam.

Even more noteworthy is his concentration upon the contrast of power politics in the masculine domain with the relative victimisation of women, as excluded from and abused by politics. The brief scene in *Iphigenia* of Argive women brutally beaten back shows the subjection of a sex to the insensitivity of men, a theme illuminated by all of *The Trojan Women* and by his conception of Electra in the 1961 film. His relatively simple and schematic division of men and women into the potent and insensitive on the one hand, the impotent and suffering on the other, is made particularly interesting in his use of the Trojan women as a sort of physical barrier of ineffectuality as against the barrier of force represented by the men at the point where Andromache attempts to allow her son to escape. Astyanax runs along the line of sympathetic women who, despite their agony of fellow feeling, can conceive of no form of action which will help, and who thus act as a fence no more penetrable than the soldiers. Hence, perhaps, the director's fondness for whirling, bird-like women at moments of crisis, mirrored in the vertiginous camera turns, Electra on her back on Agamemnon's grave, Clytemnestra dashing hysterically around the compound where the royal family is penned in by the army, Cassandra supine in the wagon bearing her away to slavery, her head lolling over the edge. While men decide, women give vent to prolonged, animal-like cries of rage or anguish, as what (considerable) debating skills they possess are rendered irrelevant by Menelaus' lust, the Greeks' vengefulness, or Agamemnon's ambition.

Then, too, there is the fascination which the players exert, the presence of Irene Papas in all three films, the ensemble playing of such a multinational cast as American *grande dame* Katharine Hepburn, French-Canadian Genevieve Bujold, British Vanessa Redgrave and Brian Blessed in the only English-language film, *The Trojan Women*.

A number of points may legitimately be concluded as a result of the comparison of these films with the ancient plays on which they are based, all the same. In every case, the narrative has been almost completely secularised so that questions about divine interference raised by the characters themselves, and the puzzling use of deities to start or end Euripidean plays, are avoided. Furthermore, it has largely been freed of inconsistencies or any sense of the characters' subjective vision as a factor obfuscating truth. It should be stressed that this last is an aesthetic choice, since cinema is eminently capable of suggesting various levels of credibility or subjectivity. (Indeed, in Pier Paolo Pasolini's version of Euripides' *Medea*, Jason sees Chiron sometimes as a centaur, sometimes as ordinary man, and after his expedition to Colchis encounters both versions side by side. In the same film, two accounts of the deaths of Glauce and her father are offered, one after the other, the first taking the Euripidean account more literally than the second, which offers the audience the possibility of auto-suggestion as the explanation for their deaths.)

The possibility of identification with Cacoyannis's heroines is considerably increased by the excision of those elements in their characters which rendered them less amenable to straightforward empathy in the originals — the pathological vindictiveness of Electra, the consciousness of her wifely merits in Andromache, the national and sexual chauvinism of Iphigenia — and by augmentation of their oppressors' evil.

Paradoxically, Cacoyannis has achieved the curious feat of making Euripides remarkably like Aeschylus, his antithesis in Aristophanes' *Frogs* — a playwright more interested in establishing the ultimate justice of the universe than we can credibly discern Euripides to have been. Cacoyannis's Iphigenia, on the other hand, in being brought to the realisation of the inevitability of her death and then accepting it with dignity, is essentially Sophoclean, even the strength she seems to derive from Achilles being reminiscent of Antigone, beloved of Haemon.

Whatever the attractions of his vision, Cacoyannis has, in choosing Greek tragedy as vehicle for it, re-heroised the world of Euripides and suggested to the non-specialist viewer and even to the unwary specialist the ossification of a dramatic mode which was in reality undergoing its most radical and disturbing alteration at the hands of a playwright who was in his own time recognised to be challenging religious, moral and dramatic orthodoxies at every turn.

Notes

1. John Coleman, *New Statesman*, 5 July 1968.
2. John Russell Taylor, *The Times*, 1 July 1968.
3. Michael Armstrong, 'Oedipus the King', *Films and Filming*, vol. 14, no. 11, August 1968.
4. 'Oedipus the King', *Monthly Film Bulletin*, vol. 35, no. 415, August 1968, pp. 112–13.
5. As, for example, P. Oakes, *Sunday Telegraph*, 17 March 1963.
6. *The Times*, 15 February 1963.
7. N. Albert, *Saturday Review*, 22 September 1962.
8. Oakes, see note 5 above.
9. Penelope Gilliatt, *Observer*, 17 March 1963.
10. Dilys Powell, *Sunday Times*, 14 April 1963.
11. See note 9.
12. Roger Manvell, 'Electra', *Films and Filming*, vol. 9, no. 8, May 1963.
13. Oliver Taplin, 'The Delphic idea and after', *The Times Literary Supplement*, no. 4085, p. 812.
14. *El.* 218–19.
15. This wish may be still more persuasively discerned in, for example, his *Helen* or *Ion*.
16. Thus, he makes Ion include sweeping of the temple steps among his sacred duties, while Electra has to tend the cottage, fetch water from the spring and concern herself about suitable fare for her guests' meal. Arthur Miller appears to be directly

in agreement with this (assumed) line of thought when he makes a salesman or stevedore the central figure of his tragedies.

17. Part, at least, of the information is certainly given by the peasant onlookers as Electra and her 'bridegroom' ride past on their way from the Argive palace.

18. Quotations from the play are as they appear in Euripides, *Medea and Other Plays*, tr. Philip Vellacott (Penguin Classics, 1963, 1976).

19. Alfred Hitchcock invites his audience in *The Torn Curtain* (1966) to consider the practical difficulties of killing a man in a protracted sequence in the first half of the film. The sequence may be the most memorable of the entire film and demonstrates the particular point outlined. Cacoyannis, however, omits the killing almost entirely when the play seems to call out for the resources of cinema to make its point. The brutality of Aegisthus' death is entirely suppressed earlier in Cacoyannis's *Electra*, too.

20. Michael Cacoyannis, 'The producer talks about "Electra"' (Lopert Pictures Corporation, 1962).

21. Cacoyannis, see note 24.

22. *Observer*, 14 April 1963.

23. See Athena Dallas, 'Michael Cacoyannis', *Film Comment*, vol. 1, no. 6, Fall 1963.

24. Fred Robbins, 'Director Michael Cacoyannis and his Trojan Women', *Show*, vol. 2, no. 8, October 1971, p. 30.

25. Ibid., p. 30.

26. Ibid., p. 32.

27. Ibid., p. 32.

28. Molly Haskell, 'Why are we in Troy?', *Village Voice*, 7 October 1971.

29. John Simon, *The New Leader*, 27 December 1971.

30. Pauline Kael, *New Yorker*, 16 October 1971.

31. Ibid.

32. Ibid.

33. For example:

> 'Servant'! You hear this servant? He's a herald. What
> Are heralds, then, but creatures universally loathed —
> Lackeys and menials to governments and kings?

Euripides, *The Bacchae and Other Plays*, tr. Philip Vellacott (Penguin Classics, 1954, 1974), p. 104.

34.   You speak of the extinction of your family
          With a bland smile! And as for your prophetic muse,
          You've little truth to show for all this eloquence.

Ibid., p. 103.

35. Michael Lloyd, 'The Helen scene in Euripides' *Troades*', *Classical Quarterly*, 34, 1984, p. 312.

36. Ibid., p. 313.

37. Euripides, *The Bacchae and Other Plays*, p. 91.

38. Kael, see note 30 above.

39. Bernard Knox, *Word and Action* (Johns Hopkins University Press, 1979), p. 345.

40. Ekbert Faas, *Tragedy and After: Euripides, Shakespeare, Goethe* (McGill-Queen's University Press, 1984), p. 24.

41. Hegel, quoted in ibid p. 44.

42. Bernard Knox, *Word and Action*, p. 349.

43. Ibid., pp. 350–1.

44. Ibid., p. 351.

45. David Wilson, 'Faces of Michael Cacoyannis', *Monthly Film Bulletin,* January 1979.

46. Irene Papas, quoted in James Cameron Wilson, *What's On In London,* 17 March 1978.

47. See Knox, *Word and Action,* pp. 348–9.

48. Euripides, *Orestes and Other Plays,* tr. Philip Vellacott (Penguin Classics, 1972, 1980), p. 385.

49. This motif is presumably suggested by Euripides' *Iphigenia among the Tauri* which adapts it from the *Cypria* tale of Agamemnon boasting after shooting a deer that Artemis herself could not have shot better.

50. Calchas' psychology is as uncertain as Agamemnon's or the army's in the play. Both Atreidae loathe prophets, not unnaturally in this context, and Agamemnon calls them 'power-thirsty' (Euripides, *Orestes and Other Plays,* p. 385), but there is no clear suggestion in the play that Artemis is a convenient fiction by which Calchas protects Odysseus' interests.

6   FILMS IN THE FILMIC MODE

At the outset of this chapter, it should be stated that these films do not provide for, say, the student of classical drama a way into the plays on which they appear to be based. There is no possibility of confusion between drama and film in any of these cases, so that to dismiss the films as betrayals of their originals seems to miss the point. None of them purports to *be* the original in transposed form. The Cacoyannis films, and the Tzavellas *Antigone*, seem much more likely to raise problems for those who believe that they are watching a relatively faithful transcription of the original play. Even with *The Trojan Women*, in which much of the dialogue and the basic situations of the original play are retained, such apparently insignificant choices as the 'objective' prologue in place of the play's squabbling over damaged (though divine) egos can cast a light on the central sections which is not particuarly Euripidean.

What each of them seems to do is to take certain elements of the myth and to use these in a new manner. Some might object that this is unhelpful for our understanding of Greek tragedy. In an obvious sense, this objection would be correct. In another, it is too confident a claim. These film-makers are true to the spirit of Greek tragedy in a less obvious sense: Aeschylus, Sophocles, Euripides and, presumably, their fellow tragedians, took heroic myths and explored and inevitably altered them in the re-telling, as they added psychological nuances to actions and choices, for example, or invested them with religious, or socio-political, significance that was of special relevance to fifth-century BC Athens, their own (unheroic) age, Dassin, Cavani, Ferris and Jancsó do something very similar in transposing the Greek heroic myths to other times and other societies and reinterpreting them for a modern age. Just as there are disputes, even in his own time, about Euripides' wisdom in tampering to such an extent with the concepts of deity, so the dressing-up of ancient tales in (literally) new clothes can seem automatically to damn these cinematic works. Yet, it seems as presumptuous now to deny Jancsó his right to reinterpret the Electra story in terms of political allegory with some relation to Hungarian history as it would have been to denounce Euripides in his time for casting

97

doubt, through the *Trojan Women* speech, on the heroic conception
of Aphrodite. Euripides was indeed attacked, to judge by the number
and import of the jokes about him in Aristophanes' comedies, for
this sort of questioning, but the hostility to him seems to have had
an anti-intellectual basis and to have been popular rather than
scholarly.

This is not to say that Cavani is on a par with Sophocles, or, for
that matter, that there cannot be different sorts and degrees of
achievement in these four film-makers. The first judgement would
be vitiated in any case by the comparison of unlikes, since Cavani
is a twentieth-century film-maker more interested in making points
relevant to post-1968 Italy (or Western Europe) than in creating
Greek tragedy. To denounce Cavani because she is not Sophocles,
for example, seems as helpful as a denunciation of Sophocles because
he is not Homer.

Phaedra (Director: Jules Dassin, 1961)

A clue as to the tactics adopted by Dassin in his filming of the
Phaedra/Hippolytus story can be found in an almost contemporary
Dassin movie, *Never on Sunday* (1960). The tart with heart in this
comedy is played by Melina Mercouri who, not incidentally perhaps,
plays the title role in *Phaedra*. She encounters an American pedant
(Dassin himself) who, as is traditional in such encounters when
portrayed in popular media, is as out of touch with the world of
mundane actuality and of human feeling as she is in touch. During
a conversation concerning Greek tragedy, which the heroine claims
to love, Dassin's character is horrified to find that she reinterprets
the endings so that they may be comfortable, reassuring to a
sentimental creature of her sort. The Dassin character attempts
to impose upon her some appreciation of the original, far from
comfortable, endings of such tragedies as *Medea*, but the Mercouri
character resists the knowledge. It is obvious that she is, in context,
meant to be far more representative of popular attitudes to ancient
drama than the more correct professor, and that her emotional
responses to it indicate that strict interpretation has nothing to do
with cathartic experience of tragedy in performance. Her reinterpretation of it moves and delights her as a scholarly reconstruction
never could.

When in her biography Melina Mercouri considers the film *Phae-*

dra and its claimed failure, she says more about it than she is perhaps aware. 'Our judgement of the film was that we had failed. It was an honest attempt, but finally it became more a bourgeois drama than a tragedy.'[1] To judge it as a tragedy seems contrary, when so much of the film seems to demand that it be classified with that supreme genre of bourgeois drama, the melodrama. That Mercouri thought she was in a failed tragedy is obvious now, but the screenplay produced by the joint efforts of Dassin and the Greek novelist and playwright Margarita Liberaki seems to represent a 'melodramatisation' of the tragedy, all the more obviously in the light of the debate presented in *Never On Sunday*.

The impulse towards 'bourgeois drama' is evident even in Cacoyannis, especially in the *Iphigenia*. True, his characters are largely of royal or slave status, but in his bid to ensure pity and fear in the audience Cacoyannis replaces political chauvinism with hints of romantic love. The chief characters may belong to a royal family, but in the film it is first of all to a family. The heroine of the film, being only just pubescent and played by an actress of very tender years (just twelve years old when Cacoyannis first met her and decided that she would make a good Iphigenia), largely obscures thoughts of social difference in the interests of 'universal', 'human' emotions.

Geoffrey Nowell-Smith, in his account of the history of melodrama, shows that it involved from the start a new equality of address, from one bourgeois to another, concerning matters of crucial importance to the bourgeoisie, particularly questions of legitimacy and family.[2] The largely royal personages of tragedy make way for bourgeois protagonists. There is, he might have gone on to consider, a vast social gulf between haut-bourgeois and petit-bourgeois, a gulf that is particularly evident in such modern television series as *Dynasty* and *Dallas*, but the values which permeate melodrama are broadly those of the bourgeoisie. Concerns of state and of Olympus-sanctioned justice as they affect the individuals in a family, in tragedy, are replaced in melodrama with concerns of high finance and of bourgeois decency as they affect the individuals in a family. The principal form in which a popular audience is seriously addressed today is that of melodrama. From the beginnings of narrative cinema, melodrama has been the dominant genre.[3] Tragedy is, broadly speaking, a coterie event in cinema circles. A director who wishes to reach a wide, international audience must find a way of turning tragic material into the stuff of melodrama.

A director who has hired the American film star, Anthony Perkins, for his Hippolytus, the Italian star, Raf Vallone, for his Theseus, and the woman who has recently penetrated the American market with *Never on Sunday* for his Phaedra, has powerful reasons to turn from tragedy to melodrama.

When Mercouri describes the evolution of the screenplay, she makes the various decisions about equivalences seem logical and innocent enough. Since the tragedies of the Greeks and of Shakespeare were taken to be devoted to the consideration of the 'theme of the mighty fallen',[4] Margarita Liberaki had, she says, to consider who the mighty were in our times, who the kings and gods of the twentieth century might be. The mighty, it was decided, were those who had an empire, today a financial empire. The particular empire chosen for *Phaedra*'s setting was that of the Greek shipowners, who, Mercouri believes, have power but also glamour, to be both kings and gods therefore. The logic is persuasive enough, but the premise, that only a modernisation in terms of twentieth-century capitalist society is thinkable, is not examined or even enunciated.

In view of modern attitudes, even those of scholars of the classics, it seems impossible to capture a large audience, or, in Cacoyannis's case, to be nominated for an Academy Award, unless the spectator is emotionally involved with the spectacle. No matter that Euripides' tragedies are as likely to distance as to implicate their audiences, a twentieth-century adaptation must eliminate the distance as far as possible. As ought to be evident from Chapter 5 above, the manifold alterations of emphasis from Euripidean original to modern film in Cacoyannis's 'trilogy' are largely explicable in terms of audience implication. In order for this implication to be effective, it seems as if even the less Aristotelian tragedies' methods must be replaced with those of melodrama.

Phaedra has obvious antecedents in European drama. Although no earlier dramatist's name appears in the film's credits, the Hippolytus story was tackled by such tragedians as Euripides, Seneca and Racine. Robin Bean, usefully for the present consideration, shows how the allure of popularity accounts for certain changes to the original — if that be equated with Euripides' version — treatment:

> the myth of Phaedra and her infatuation with her stepson has undergone various treatments since Euripides' *Hippolytus*. . . . It became the basis of Seneca's *Phaedra* and Racine's *Phèdre*, but both authors evidently decided it lacked 'commercial appeal' and

developed incidents for dramatic effect. . . . Seneca contrived a situation whereby Phaedra's love for Theseus is unfulfilled, and she is attracted by his 'young, beautiful, virginal' son. . . . Racine went further and brought in a young princess with whom Hippolytus falls in love, so providing Phaedra with the additional motive of jealousy.[5]

George Steiner, in noticing the change made by Racine whereby the 'cold, pure hunter' of Euripides, Seneca and even Garnier becomes a 'shy but passionate lover', suggests that the image of a royal prince fleeing the approach of women would seem ridiculous to a contemporary audience.[6] Even within a tragic tradition, then, it should be noted, there is a famous precedent for Hippolytus no longer being so ascetic as to remain aloof from the carnal expression of love. Oliver Taplin discounts Dassin's *Phaedra*, as unworthy of comment, because it 'does not begin to grapple with Hippolytus' asceticism, his rejection of carnality for the purity of the "uncut meadow"'.[7] The whole of the relation of *Phaedra* to Euripides' *Hippolytus* need not be deemed out of consideration because in one area it prefers to follow Raccine rather than the Greek playwright; and, in any case, if the film does not 'grapple with' Hippolytus' rejection of carnality, it does, as will be argued below, at least 'begin to grapple with' it.

That there is a relationship between modern story and Greek treatment seems to be suggested in various ways. Two of the characters, Phaedra and Thanos (Raf Vallone), are Greek, while the third important character, Alexis (Anthony Perkins), is half Greek. Much of the action is shot on location in Hydra. The credits of the film appear against a background of Greek sculpture, and immediately after there is a cut to the modern Greek flag. When Alexis is first seen by the audience, in London, he is painting details of the Elgin marbles in the British Museum. When Phaedra tries to persuade Alexis to return home, she talks of the necessity of sacrifice in ancient Greece when something was specially wished for, and throws an expensive ring into the Thames. In the Greek sequences, the doings of the shipping magnate set are watched and laconically judged by the peasantry, acting like a tragic Chorus. There is a sequence where the Greek Chorus is recalled with particular force. After news of the sinking of the SS *Phaedra* has reached them, black-garbed peasant women crowd Thanos' office, wailing at the loss of their male relations. Phaedra is marked off from the Chorus by her white clothes. She elbows her way through them, apparently uncaring of their reproaches and curses. Theirs is a communal grief, hers a private, personal agony. Chorus and actors are once more differentiated as in 'the good old days' to which Alexis alludes before he meets his death, speeding along suicidally in his sports car.

All of these elements could be swept aside as window-dressing, indicating nothing of the relationship of the 1961 film to the Euripidean original. One could be equally dismissive of the moments where allusion is made, briefly, to details of the ancient dramatic treatment as, for example, when Thanos refers to himself as a bull, and Phaedra as 'my queen'; or the joke earlier in the film about 'the old sea monster' that Andreas (Andreas Philippides), one of the shipping magnates and father of Ercy (Elizabeth Ercy) to whom Alexis will be engaged once he is back in Greece, has become; or old Christos' (Jules Dassin) remark, after he has described Alexis' car in its crate as like a coffin, about horses (rather than horse power).

The only test as to whether or not these references are simply diversions intended to blind the audience to the film's abandonment of all Euripidean elements in the tale is an examination of how, if at all, the film adapts certain components vital to the Euripidean handling of the story.

At the opening of the ancient play, Aphrodite appears to inform the audience of her intention of punishing Hippolytus, the devotee of Artemis, for his neglect of her. To achieve this punishment she will use Phaedra and inspire her with desire for Hippolytus. The principal aim of the goddess is, then, to bring about the downfall of Artemis' worshipper and Phaedra is merely an instrument whose fate is of no vital concern to Aphrodite. Hippolytus' unswerving devotion to chastity is part of his outstanding piety to Artemis in this play; Phaedra's passion is inspired by means beyond her power to resist. Two key elements, then, are Hippolytus' dedication to Artemis and Phaedra's innocence in at least her love for her stepson.

In the film, the gods are only statuary, and are not overtly mentioned. This does not mean that Aphrodite and Artemis are absent, however. It is easy enough to see Phaedra's falling in love with Alexis, infidelity to her husband and subsequent secretiveness and destructive jealousy over the engagement to Ercy, as signs of her falling victim to Aphrodite, if the goddess is taken to stand for overpowering desire. Perkins' nervousness and passivity are well exploited here. In the famous love scene in Paris, where we see the first lovemaking between Phaedra and Alexis through tear-like rain, Phaedra is the aggressor, adopting dominant positions physically and being the first to declare her love. While he is not a complete stranger to Aphrodite as conceived in this film, he manages to extricate himself from her sway once back in Greece, when a sense of duty returns to him.

Is Artemis absent, then? If Aphrodite is purely a psychological force in Phaedra's character in the film, we should look, if at all, for Artemis as a psychological component of Alexis' character. Since Aphrodite is recognised by Hecuba in *The Trojan Women* to be a name for a human tendency, other deities must presumably have been open in Euripides to such rationalisation. It is difficult to see Artemis as a force in nature, since virginity is not a noticeable instinct in the animal world. Yet it is, if we recognise that there are breeding seasons and, conversely, seasons in which sexual activity is at least unproductive. In still wider terms, spring and summer might be the seasons of Aphrodite, autumn and especially winter those of Artemis. In human nature, the denial of carnality, or more broadly self-fulfilment through pleasure, the choice of duty or career in place of love (a classic choice in melodrama later) could be thought to be represented by devotion to Artemis. If this is fair surmise, then Alexis does have a relatively ascetic attitude. His devotion to painting threatens to ruin his career at the London School of Economics and therefore as a future inheritor of his father's shipping empire. While this could be read elsewhere as devotion to self-indulgence rather than career, such a reading here would be false to the context. When we first meet the shipping magnates, they are celebrating a launch. The association of wealth is from the beginning with luxury and self-pampering. People dance, drink champagne, kiss, and Phaedra receives the expensive ring which she later — relevantly to this interpretation — sacrifices. Therefore, it could plausibly be argued that Alexis' love of art is an austere choice, liable to prevent him later from enjoying himself with his father's money. When he does become a good enough son to be engaged to Ercy, it is filial devotion rather than his eye to profit that is stressed. In the London sequences near the beginning of the film, Alexis expressly denies carnality, although his devotion is to a glittering status symbol rather than to a more austere ideal. He tells Phaedra that he wants to introduce her to his best girl. This turns out to be an Aston Martin in a car showroom. It is this car that he rubs his face against rather than any woman. If this is his

best girl, presumably Alexis is a virgin when he is seduced by
Phaedra, a point that he underlines by sighing, 'My first love', at
that moment. This innocence of sexual pleasure is remarkable in
the context, which is insistently created, of luxury living and London
student life of the early 1960s. While it is difficult to see Alexis'
devotion to a car as a sign of asceticism, it is evident that it is the
speed of the car and its 'sporting' possibilities that attract him rather
than the obvious potential of it as a status symbol. His shyness and
hesitancy are Racinian, but his ignorance of the ways of Aphrodite
and his inability to stay under her sway once back in Greece make
him approach the Euripidean conception of the character in the
vastly different social setting of the film.

As for destiny, which is often — probably erroneously — claimed
to underlie the action of all Greek tragedy, that too has been
detected. Thanos has been identified as the incarnation of destiny.[8]
It is Thanos who obliges Phaedra to leave for London, he who
persuades Alexis to return to Greece. The sports car which kills
Alexis is the bait held out by Thanos to ensure his return, too. The
sense that each of the characters is not only responsible for the
catastrophe at the film's end, whereby Alexis is killed in his car and
Phaedra is permitted by her maid and confidante Anna (Olympia
Papadouka) to die by an overdose of sleeping pills, but also domi-
nated by impulses beyond human understanding and resistance, is
in Dassin as much as in Euripides.

Nevertheless, this is not a Euripidean tragedy, but modern, cinematic, Greek melodrama. The description is offered purely *as* description, not with the intention to downgrade the film. Fundamental to
melodrama is the tension between self-fulfilment through love and
through the family. True to the spirit of melodrama is the film's
treatment of this tension as being a problem for the woman more
than the man. It is Phaedra's inability to remain a good wife or a
suitable mother to Alexis, her potential threat to the new family of
Alexis and Ercy, that mark her out for doom. The way that her
devotion to extramarital love is seen as a force of destruction to
others and then to herself could be paralleled easily in the melo-
dramas of Douglas Sirk and Vincente Minnelli. So too could the
'failure of patriarchal ideology', whereby the woman in love with
an unapproved object cannot find a place within the fabric of the
legitimised pattern of relationships and must therefore be eliminated.
Alexis seems to die more by reason of his father's curse than because
he has hurt Phaedra. He could, after all, have thought of his relations

with his father as at an end and chosen Phaedra, but this choice is almost unthinkable in the world of this film, as of most melodrama. Before he dies, he tells Phaedra that he wishes her dead. Their love is an act of betrayal to his father and must therefore be rejected. It is also an affront to the family as an ideal. The lovers can be united only in death in the face of such breaches of social rules. What was discoverable in Euripides is inevitable in the context of melodrama. Ultimately, it is with reference to melodrama's workings that the success or failure of *Phaedra* should be judged.

The Cannibals (Director: Liliana Cavani, 1970)

George Eliot rightly insisted that *Antigone* is not so much about burying corpses as about the conflicts of loyalty to family and to state. Liliana Cavani's film *I Cannibali . . .* did not take this point. The streets of Milan are littered with the corpses of rebels against the regime. Antigone . . . insists on burying heaps of them. She is helped by a silent Christ–hippy figure going under the name of Tiresias.[9]

If George Eliot is right, she is right about Sophocles' *Antigone*. If the film does not take her point, it may be because it is not to be confused with Sophocles' *Antigone*, even if the credits claim that the screenplay (by Cavani and Italo Moscati) is based on the celebrated tragedy. The new title alone would suggest that the spectator should beware of expecting a 'faithful' rendering of the original, in the manner of Cacoyannis. Yet, Cavani, who announces her intentions by such means, has been severely ticked off for not reproducing Sophocles, while Cacoyannis, who claims to be offering a Euripidean experience to cinema audiences, is never blamed for not reproducing Euripides with sufficient fidelity. 'Such distortion is unforgivable,' Derek Elley writes of *The Cannibals*, once he has offered a short, and by no means exhaustive, list of changes from the original play, 'and Cavani, who has a degree in Classics, should have known better. *The Cannibals,* because of its severe shifts of emphasis, cannot even claim to be a reinterpretation: merely a flagrant rip-off of another playright's work.'[10] What does this heated rebuke amount to? If Cavani has a degree in Classics, she may well have known what she was doing with Sophocles' play. If the shifts of emphasis are 'severe', presumably they are obvious. 'Obvious' is a less emotive term than 'flagrant', and no less useful. What exactly is a 'rip-off of another playwright's work'? If it is flagrant, then it is not concealed in the manner of most rip-offs. At what point does a film with severe shifts of emphasis cease to be a reinterpretation and become, instead, a rip-off?

It cannot be said often enough, apparently, that *The Cannibals* is not Sophocles' *Antigone*. Rather than contenting themselves with spotting the differences, critics of the film might ask why there is reference in the credits, in certain aspects of the situation, but particularly in the names of the chief characters, to the ancient play. The film cannot, Elley declares, claim to be a reinterpretation. It does not overtly make this claim, in fact, but it does affirm a relation between itself and the Sophoclean original. The nature of this relationship, and the fruitfulness or otherwise of it, might be explored before Cavani's shameful conduct as an ex-Classics student is denounced.

The differences between *Antigone* and *The Cannibals* go well beyond even what has been noted in British criticisms of the film. It may be rewarding to consider the number and 'severity' of the shifts of emphasis.

There are indeed heaps of corpses littering Milan — not just the streets, but decaying in coffee bars and underground stations. The single unburied corpse of Antigone's brother in Sophocles has become a mighty army of cadavers. Antigone's (Britt Ekland) concern with her unburied brother is retained in the modern-dress fable, but it graduates into a desire to bury as many of the dead as she can accommodate in her car. Having, with the help of Tiresias (Pierre Clémenti), spirited away her brother's corpse to the beach for symbolic burial, she returns with him to seize a second, then a third corpse and perform the same rites over these. This Antigone is as much an expression of the human impulse to freedom as the original,[11] but her narrow concern with kinship has been replaced with a broader concern for human dignity.

Tiresias is indeed a very different character from the blind seer of Thebes as portrayed in the play. The film begins with his being washed up on a beach. Noticeably, from the opening moments of the film, he is not blind. Communication is not so much enigmatic, though that it is to most characters apart from Antigone, as minimal. He speaks one word, 'Senna', which, according to Geoff Brown,[12] using the information provided by mental nurses within the film, is Ostrogothic. Tiresias also makes the sign of a fish when he enters a

coffee bar and is looked after by Antigone. This may be why he has
been labelled 'a Christ–hippy figure', though the director of the film
has stressed that the fish symbol is pre-Christian and is not intended
to have a Christian meaning in the film. It is, according to Cavani,
a pagan symbol signifying life. (Christ represented life to the Christians and so the symbol was adopted by them, she says.[13]) She would
concede that Tiresias, if not exactly a hippy, at least represents
young people, especially those of post-1968 Europe. His silence,
explicable at a more literal level by his inability to speak a language
accessible to Italians, indicates for her the need for a new language,
a sort of psychological Esperanto.[14] While these details are of
interest purely as providing information about the director's conceptions and intentions, not their execution or 'reading', it seems
appropriate that this film, taken by one French commentator at
least as 'bien un film d'après mai',[15] should draw attention to the
silence of its principal characters, by denying them the use of verbal
language. The events of May 1968 are intimately connected with
French students' knowledge of structuralism and of the way that
language (not only verbal) may be appropriated by a ruling class to
construct identities malleable by that ruling class. Since all language
could be viewed as 'tainted' by bourgeois ideology, it is apt that
Tiresias, the representative, thanks to the casting of Clémenti, of a
particular kind of middle-class rebel youth sub-culture, should more
or less abandon it. Following his lead, perhaps, Antigone confronts
Haemon's father (Francesco Leonetti) without using the eloquent
arguments given to her at that moment by Sophocles. There is no
pleading, not even an explanation. The silence that exists between
Tiresias and Antigone is communicative, while the silence between
Antigone and her parents, the police, the prime minister, represents
a loss of faith in the possibility of dialogue between her and these
parties. The abandonment of Sophoclean rhetoric for Cavani's
silence may be the most signal departure of all.

Only in the confrontation between Haemon (Tomas Milian) and
his father are echoes of the Sophoclean argument permitted to be
heard. (This, incidentally, is described as the 'most powerful, and
Sophoclean, scene in the film' by Oliver Taplin.[16]) Yet, it is important to place this scene in context. The result of the quarrel between
father and son is that the latter defies his father sufficiently to
become involved in the body-burying. The defiance, if not the action
itself, is Sophoclean enough, arguably, but the sequel to this act is
quite different, lapsing into irrationality. Imprisoned for breaking

his father's edict, the son claims before his father that he wishes to 'become an animal . . . mad . . . anarchistic . . . a rebel . . . anti-social . . . delinquent . . . homosexual'. His father's soberly delivered response is, 'Have you become an intellectual?'! 'If I leave here, I'll steal other bodies,' Haemon warns him, and then in his self-chosen madness he elects to stay within the institution. 'You are . . . my father and my master,' he avows, playing in the Italian language on the resemblance of 'padre' to 'padrone'. After his father leaves him, he adopts a foetal position, indicating the sort of wishful refusal of entry into the symbolic order which Tiresias and Antigone represent by their silence. When Haemon is last seen in the film, he crawls out of his cell on his belly to eat, like a beast, from a dish of food.

Ismene, Antigone's more conventionally-minded sister, is played in the film by Delia Boccardo. Derek Elley notes, with disapproval, that this Ismene is 'robbed' of even the wish to help Antigone.[17] Undoubtedly, she is more consistently averse to her sister's attitudes than the original Ismene, who underwent a change of heart. There is no change of attitude for her, as in Sophocles. From the beginning, her wish is to be acquiescent, to be like the others. 'Don't. Please, they're looking at us,' is her reaction to Antigone's even touching a corpse on the floor of the train on which the sisters are travelling. She is so much on the side of the military authority that she is provided in this version with a fiancé, a military policeman lover, whose future career is of far more concern than her sister's safety.

All these differences — the ostracising of Antigone and Tiresias, Haemon's collapse into a self-inflicted madness, Ismene's unbending rejection of all that Antigone stands for, the almost total absence of debate between oppressors and freedom fighters — may be explicable as originating from one particularly 'severe' shift of emphasis. Sophocles was specially honoured by the Athenians for his *Antigone*. Although the play is set in Thebes, it may be that the play was thought to be peculiarly Athenian in spirit, since contrasted with Creon's authoritarianism is the approval of the *demos*, as well as, Antigone presumes, of the gods. Haemon appeals to popular sentiment, and reproves his father for his violent rejection of the importance of the people's wishes. The play implicitly, by its out-come, lauds the democratic political system. Antigone may be alone in her defiance of the edict forbidding Polynices' burial, but there is a wave of sympathy for her in the *demos*, the ordinary people of Thebes. In the film, the populace offers no resistance to the authorities. It either behaves as if all were normal, or actively co-operates with the military government.

Although the public places of Milan are teeming with rotting corpses, the citizens of Milan do not glance at them, but pick their way through the heaps as if nothing were amiss. Liliana Cavani seems to be particularly impressed with the way that the bourgeoisie may accommodate horrors and anaesthetise itself to their reality. She recalls in an interview watching a man in a waiting-room reading a newspaper where photos advertising Marlboro cigarettes and of victims of the Biafran war appeared side by side. The man, she noted, seemed not to feel the impact of the latter.[18] Nobody, she claims in 1972, wants to look at photographs of Vietnam anymore. 'It's a matter of fashion,' is her conclusion.[19] What she cites as the most striking proof of people's indifference to the horror surrounding them is the fact that the reactions of the Milanese as recorded in the film are those of actual citizens of Milan who knew nothing of the circumstances explaining the presence of corpses in their city (though she does not go on to say they probably must have been aware that these were 'acted' corpses). Her conclusion from this observation, that after initial astonishment no further reaction was visible, is that the situation of the film was accepted in actuality.[20]

So all-pervasive is the indifference or acclimatisation of the bourgeoisie under bizarre conditions that Antigone's parents join in the general condemnation of their daughter for burying their son. Or, rather, their concern with their daughter's 'rudeness' leads to their fully co-operating with the police who have come to search the house for further evidence. Antigone's mother bids the maid to bring drinks for what would appear in her opinion to be guests. 'I can give you the addresses of her friends,' she says, and expresses the hope that Antigone will be taught 'some good manners'. What Antigone has to cast off in the film is the oppressive nature of the family. Small wonder that she must think beyond her brother and her kin to humanity itself. Parents in the film are tyrannical and supportive of a fascist government (Haemon's father, to an extent, *is* the government). Therefore, the family itself, standing for bourgeois society, has to be rejected. The sequences in which Tiresias and Antigone cast off their clothes to become a new Adam and Eve are, like those in which speech is impossible or when Haemon is reduced to the level of an unreasoning beast, indications of possible responses to the pervasive influence of an authority which has been assimilated by the good citizens of Milan.

These marked differences may be the very point of using Sophocles' play as an alleged basis. Cavani's explanation is different, though. She claims that she did not want to use the language of record (*la chronique*). Antigone, one of the great myths in our collective unconscious, was chosen as a point of departure. The subject is easy to communicate, she believes, 'précisément à travers le mythe: les mythes — toute la psychanalyse l'a montré — expriment l'inconscient de l'homme'.[21] Her belief is that certain myths, such as that of Antigone, are universal, that these great myths take us back to our origins in Greco-Latin culture, 'from Oedipus to Prometheus and Dionysus', and that Christianity has only been able to take them up again and to 'adapt' them, so to speak.[22]

If we accept her reasoning, the point of basing *The Cannnibals* on *Antigone* is not to create a deliberate or ignorant travesty of the original, but to tap the universality of the myth to add point and power to her modern-day fable. Taken as political manifesto, the film seems too naïve to be discussed seriously, despite the cheers with which Molly Haskell tells us a New York Film Festival audience greeted certain speeches.[23] It seems instead to be better interpreted as a tale about political conviction and death. Haskell has made a good case for the argument that the theme of the film is the reconsecration of death and attempted resurrection. Death, she argues, has been secularised and made routine by its exposure in the media, just as in the film the presence of corpses on Milan's thoroughfares has been accepted as normal.[24] By this reasoning, Tiresias' importance — he is the first character introduced in the film — is that he represents not so much a new language as a forgetting of language, which results, it could be reasoned, in a defamiliarisation of the routine (so that the unburied corpses may once more be seen as an abomination) and a more mythical, pre-rational consciousness.

The cannibals of the film are not, as might be anticipated, the wielders of brutal power. A song performed near the beginning and at the end of the film, 'Call me a cannibal,/ I don't care', would suggest that there are some labelled savage, irrational, who gladly accept that labelling, since it marks them off from the corruption around them. Haemon goes to the limits in his savagery, reverting to animalistic behaviour. Antigone and Tiresias, however, act. Their attempts to bury the dead are manifestly absurd. There are far too many corpses for them to solve the problem, and citizens abound who are willing to denounce them as soon as they lay hands on a corpse. In such a repressive state, there is no chance of their escaping detection, and, once detected, little chance of their evading death or incarceration in a mental hospital. In terms of their individual destinies, their action seems as hopeless as Haemon's. Yet, it is less absurd than at first appears, much less nihilistic, to judge by its results, than Haemon's regression. At the end of the film, after Antigone has been executed and Tiresias is shot dead, the people who were classified as lunatics begin to gather up corpses, climbing up a hillside with the bodies in the same dogged, defiant manner with which the young people had done so.

Cavani's pessimism about bourgeois ideology hardly needs her interviews to establish it. Yet, she is not entirely negative about bourgeois potential. In the film Antigone is the well-brought-up daughter of bourgeois parents and yet she defies them to enlist the mysterious stranger's aid in burying bodies. Cavani defends her limiting of the film's revolt to the middle class by arguing that protest movements often come from the bourgeoisie, who have, unlike the working class, passed beyond an obvious need for consumer goods.[25] While there are bourgeois cannibals, this film seems to remind us, the state, even as repressive as it is represented to be here, is not beyond rescue. By entirely different routes, Sophocles' play and Cavani's film come together finally to offer a glimmer of hope through the resistance of the devout to secular and secularising authority.

Prometheus, Second Person Singular (Director: Costas Ferris, 1975)

It is understandable that little has been written about this film, and there are two obvious reasons for the dearth of information about it. The first is that, of all the films claiming a relationship with Greek tragedy, this one seems to owe the least to its ostensible source of inspiration, and appears the most determinedly 'modern'. While *The Cannibals* abandons Sophocles' dialogue, retaining some of Haemon's argument with his father as an isolated burst of rhetorical debate with a markedly un-Sophoclean aftermath, it does offer a coherent narrative with some relation with the original *Antigone* — usually a relation of antithesis, but a relation all the same. *Elektreia* uses dance, choreographed movement and song considerably more than either the Dassin or Cavani films, but again there is a discernible narrative, bearing a recognisable, though far from close, similarity to the Electra story as narrated by the tragedians of classical Athens. Ferris's film, which claims not only *Prometheus Bound* but also Hesiod's *Theogony* as its ancient antecedents, largely defies narrative analysis, working by repetition, colour filters, dance against a rock-music score, to create its own world and thus a film which is more self-referential than linked to that of fifth-century BC tragedy. Oliver Taplin calls the film 'a self-indulgent stream of whimsy', and thinks that it may represent 'a rejection of ancient Greece as a symbol of conservatism and pedantry'.[26] Mel Schuster labels it 'an outrage of directorial stunts' and 'most kindly described as "artsy" '. He talks of its 'sensual but repetitive camerawork', adding 'a slick sheen, partly disguising the egotistic shallowness of the whole'.[27] The film did win prizes, but for its musical score only, at the 1975 Thessaloniki Festival and the 1976 Cairo Festival.

The second is that, whatever one's opinion of the film — and the very little published about it is predominantly hostile in tone — it tends to be much more difficult to write about a film that works, if at all, by imagery and sound rather than narrative. Films of this sort remind us that writing on cinema shares the handicaps of writing on painting or music when that cinema is more closely allied with these art forms than the novel or play, that a vocabulary adequate to this sort of film is only in the making, because 'art movies' of this sort, in the peculiar sense of their dependence on, for instance, kinetic art, are so marginalised in the histories of cinema. Avant-garde practice in, say, French cinema of the 1920s and 1930s or American and British of the 1960s calls for different criteria of judgement and different descriptive tools in written accounts of that practice, but the painterly cinema is a tendency to which there has been a fierce resistance. (The rock video, interestingly, owes more, it would seem at a superficial viewing, to this tendency than to dominant, narrative cinema practice.)

Both Taplin and Schuster notice the prominence of the directorial self, or its representation, as a feature of the Ferris film. To the former, the film is 'self-indulgent', to the latter 'egotistic'. They are undoubtedly right in drawing our attention to the self-advertising qualities of the film, which involves an overt move away from the imagined objectivity, or at least impersonality, of Greek tragedy and most films based on it, towards a foregrounding of self. It is not only the self of the director which is foregrounded, however, but, as the title implies, the collective self of the audience. On further consideration, 'collective' is almost certainly an over-simplification.

It is the individual member of the audience who is specifically addressed on the soundtrack, the individual in his or her singularity. Whether the personalisation of that apparently most impersonal of narratives, heroic myth, here dealing largely with immortals, not human beings, is fairly described as 'shallow' or 'whimsical' ought at least to be questioned, as ought the assumptions behind such judgements.

An attempt, albeit hampered by the difficulties attendant on any venture to transmit the experience of a film in a category separate from not only the others in this book but of little statistical importance in most accounts of cinema history, at an account of the first 20 minutes of the film should give some idea of its effect. The opening, for example, is in darkness. The visual track is absent so that the soundtrack may draw attention to precisely that absence. A direct address is made to the individual listener (rather than spectator, at this point), an address in the second-person singular. 'Forget those around you . . . accept the darkness . . . recognise its value . . . remember why you came', the individual member of the audience is urged. As he or she is told that images will add nothing to this knowledge (of the reasons for coming), there are quick, almost subliminal, flashes of a man bound to a wooden, spoked wheel like that of a wagon. 'Accept these as if they were your images,' the soundtrack continues, adding that the film will last 1 hour 15 minutes, and that it will be shown on two projectors.

The conditions of the film's performance having been established and the demystification of that performance having been begun, the credits appear, against a dark-blue background, with the rock score sounding forth on the soundtrack. The audience is informed that any resemblance with the reality of today is not due to coincidence.

A character wearing a mask that looks African is photographed in the foreground, while a troupe of dancers wearing white bird masks can be seen in the background. The spectator is informed that Zeus has just been seen. 'Zeus is you, spectator.' (The English translation alters all Greek deity names to the Roman form — thus, here it is, 'Jupiter is you, spectator' — but, since the original Greek text offers Greek names and since these are less confusing in any case, it is the Greek version that will be offered in this account.) The dominant colour, the filter through which Zeus and the background Chorus are filmed, is sepia.

Next, the colour changes to blue. A limping, black-robed figure is seen dragging chains over the landscape. 'He who comes from the depth is . . . Hephaestus . . . loyal, devoted . . . Hephaestus is you, spectator', we hear.

The bird-masked Chorus is filmed, then the sea through a red filter. Oceanus, the go-between, is shown ('Oceanus is you, spectator').

The bird Chorus is filmed in sepia, the beach in blue. Prometheus is now seen chained to a 'rock' represented by two writhing human figures. Io is introduced: 'Io . . . with no country or home. Io is you, spectator', as she gesticulates beside the agonised Prometheus.

Once again, the bird Chorus is filmed on the rocks through a sepia filter. Bouzouki music plays, while an athletic actor performs cartwheels and walks on his hands. 'Zeus' servant — Aeschylus called him Hermes — is you, spectator.' Back to the sepia-coloured Chorus.

A naked actress is filmed in negative, apparently 'floating in space' in a foetal position by the wheel. The camera moves down to a mask; then the female disappears, to be replaced by trees in full colour (without the usual filter). The earth is viewed upside down, and Hermes walking on his hands past two black-robed figures. He sits on a hill. The two figures approach him while a masked figure (Zeus?) watches. 'The two castrated children — Kratos and Bia — live in harmony with all masters', the audience is told.

Hephaestus is ordered in a whisper on the soundtrack to carry out Zeus' orders. There is a reference to Prometheus' offence, the theft of fire, and a shot of the chain being dragged along. Shots of Kratos and Bia in masks are intercut with others of Prometheus without mask. As chains are thrown round him, we hear a chant about his binding, and there are intercut shots of the bird-masked Chorus. Once Prometheus is gagged and chained, Kratos and Bia remove their masks. The Chorus dances to rock music.

As a girl with long hair falling back from her head is shown, the voice tells us, 'About twenty minutes have passed'.

Scenes from the original play are obviously alluded to and sometimes half acted-out in the film, as are incidents from the myths of Uranus, Cronus and the Titans. The characters are those of the myths which form the background to the play. Yet, the film is determinedly not an attempt at tragedy or even remotely at a faithful transcription of the original source material. Costas Ferris seems to have taken Liliana Cavani's stated belief in the Greek myths as elements of the collective unconscious to a greater extreme than she seemed to conceive, by stressing the unconscious, and turning this set of myths at least into a dream experience, or an experience that defies rational analysis and whose appeal must be anticipated to be to the unconscious. As the dreamer in 'life' is normally solitary, or rather the dream is an individual, solitary experience taken by psychoanalysts to reveal possibly important illuminations of the individual psyche, so it is the individual spectator who is addressed overtly by the film. Particularly at the beginning, it is suggested that the film is being summoned up by, not just for, the individual spectator, just as the creatures of myth are projections of individual desire ('Zeus is you, spectator').

The oneiric quality of cinema has long been claimed. The viewer is normally isolated in a darkened venue, encouraged by the absence of the physical reality of the people filmed to enter an intimate relation with them, a relation involving identification and loss of self-awarness. French surrealist cinema, modest as that may have been in sheer quantity of film, attempted to utilise the irrationalism and oneirism of the cinematic experience. Ferris seems to be broadly in line with its sort of thinking when he directs this film; only broadly, however. The direct address to the spectator demands a consciousness that might be suppressed in, say, the Buñuel/Dali films. And the tenuous, but certainly detectable, narrative strand of the film is quite different from the anti-logical construction of, say, *Un Chien andalou* (1928). Ferris's interest in foregrounding the materiality of film is closer to the American avant-garde's interests, as is his use of colour filters, shooting in negative, etc. When he breaks into his already fragmented narrative to remind the spectator of the time that has passed in watching the film, or the time that remains for it, or draws attention to the separateness of visual and aural tracks by completely suppressing the former at the outset of the film, or to the use of alternate projectors, the strategy is Brechtian/Godardian. But these tactics, coupled with the constant drawing of the viewer's attention to the properties of celluloid, to the abilities of the camera as a piece of machinery, are particularly reminiscent of those of the American avant-garde.

The film's version of the Prometheus tale vacillates between a realist and strikingly anti-realist version. The unfiltered Eastman Colour suggests — but only suggests — an unmediated world, as does Prometheus' wheel when set on the cliffs, but for every unmediated-looking segment there is at least one alternative version. When it is expected that the rock will collapse on him, the two players who have represented his rock cover him from sight, for example. The spectator is deliberately disoriented until attempts at sorting out 'real' as opposed to 'symbolic' moments are so thoroughly frustrated that the attempts are abandoned. Identification of characters is uncertain, as in a dream, and even when certain is often delayed, as in a dream. One character, thanks to the devices of masks and stylised costume, begins to resemble another, a character that seemed dead is suddenly alive again. In such a cyclical work as this, nothing is certain, or at least nothing is established as within its place in a chain of cause and effect. Thus, Prometheus bound is unbound just before the final sequence in which he is 'eternally bound' on his wheel. Argus (it may be) is despatched by a blow, but then returns to life, functioning without impairment in the way that he functioned before the lethal attack. Zeus at his most tyrannical is juxtaposed at his most tender with Io. Past, present and future are destabilised, as they are in prophecy as well as dream. What Prometheus foretells may be filmed as having already occurred (Zeus' release of Io, Prometheus' own salvation) before an event which, in the play, 'happens' rather than 'is prophesied'. To talk of flashbacks and flash-forwards seems against the spirit of the film's design, which appears to impede such logical analysis even by those with detailed knowledge of the myths and dramatic work which form its basis. Schuster talks about 'repetitive camerawork' as if he had discovered a fault. The time of the film's consumption may be 'real time', as the voice on the soundtrack assumes, but while that time's reality is asserted by the attention drawn to it, the time of the film's events becomes ever more unreal, as pre-rational as the world of the Prometheus story. The 'Aeschylean' play is sometimes described as 'static' in that, once Prometheus is pinioned to the rock, there is little narrative thrust forwards until the cataclysm of the very end of the play. Still, the action unfolds in a recognisable chronological framework, with past and future opposed and seen from the point of view of the present. Ferris relativises time itself, and by undermining the traditional coherence of even an unusual Greek tragedy, he draws attention back to ways of seeing, ways of making sense of elements in film. If myth is a product of the unconscious, then the film outlaws the cognitive processes or at least their 'invisible' working, as far as that is manageable.

Prometheus, Second Person Singular is intended, it would seem, to confound even those with specialist knowledge of play and mythological foundations of play, as it certainly must those without prior knowledge. It seems to be an experimental film, foregrounding the processes by which we make sense of narrative and especially cinematic narrative. Its merits or demerits will depend, like the film's experience, according to the soundtrack, on the individual response. An audience which is unaccustomed to the work of, say, Michael Snow will find the film intolerably pretentious, just as audiences of Snow's work who are ignorant of the context in which it appears condemn such films as *Wavelength* (1967) as intolerably pretentious. If the film does nothing else, it would still be valuable if it raises for further consideration the question of the assumptions behind the negative judgement of 'pretentiousness'.

Elektreia (Director: Miklós Jancsó, 1975)

There are at least two factors which discourage the expectation that Jancsó's film has taken upon itself the task of 'faithfully' rendering any of the ancient Electra tragedies (and three are extant — Aeschylus' *The Libation Bearers*, and Euripides' and Sophocles' *Electra*s): one is that the film is avowed to be based on the play, *Szerelmem Elektra*, by László Gyurkó; the other is that this looks strikingly like so many other Jancsó films, although the director has never tackled an overtly mythological subject before *Elektreia*.

Gyurkó wrote his play intending some relation with the events of 1956.[28] At the time that the film based on it appeared, the play had proved so popular that it had been running continuously in Budapest for five years.[29] The interpretation of the play within Hungary appears to have been that it both celebrates the death of Stalin by means of the deposition of the play's tyrant Aegisthus,[30] and also defends and explains the 'liberalisation' undertaken by Janos Kadár in the early 1960s.[31] A more specific allusion has been detected in the character of Aegisthus to Rákosi, dictator of Hungary until 1956.[32]

The setting for the film is, as so often in Jancsó's films, the Hungarian plain. It is as much a Puszta film as, say, *Agnus Dei* (1970) or *Red Psalm* (1971). Horsemen ride over the plain through mist, smoking flares of different colours are made to surround sections of those involved in the action, whitewashed buildings, men cracking whips, girls in white dresses and boots, constant undressing and re-dressing; all feature prominently in the *mise en scène*. Tony Rayns, in his review of the film, talks of 'motifs such as nudity, smoke-screens and animals' as 'established in earlier films' so that they become 'elements of controlled or calculated redundancy' which can now be taken for granted.[33] When David Robinson describes predominant elements in the film, he could be describing a number of other Jancsó works: 'Men and girls and children dance . . . round the white-washed walls of a group of barbaric buildings isolated on the plain. Behind the dancers horsemen pass and repass monotonously. The costumes seem symbolic (cloaks and whips for the tyrants, white tunics for the victims), the constant undressing is ritualistic.'[34]

Above all, the technique of long takes, the camera tracking ceaselessly back and fore over the terrain, established as an essential component in Jancsó's technical repertory as early as *The Round-Up* (1965), is taken to a new extreme in *Elektreia*: 'As for the "technique of long sequences", well, "Elektreia" probably represents that technique carried to an extreme: the whole picture consists of no more than ten sequences.'[35]

If the film is composed of visual elements and shot in a method which immediately marks it out as the work of Jancsó — although it might be fairer to see it as the result of a collaboration of the director with his favourite script-writer, Gyula Hernádi and cameraman, János Kende — the resemblances go deeper. Tony Rayns argues for a development in Jancsó's work, from the earlier anti-Stalinist 'chronicle of oppression' to 'the more positively Trotskyite accounts of revolutionary dialectics in action (almost everything since *The Confrontation* [1968])'.[36] Rayns links the 1975 film, the first Hungarian work after Jancsó's return from his three-year stay in Italy, with, in particular, *Rome Wants Another Caesar* (1974). The tendency to see *Elektreia* as having a more immediately evident relationship with the corpus of work produced by the Hungarian director than with any ancient Greek tragedy is not simply a mark of auteurism's dominance in discussions of 'art' cinema. The stylistics and thematics of the film are utterly consistent with Jancsó's preceding work.

Curiously, if there is a cinematic reference beyond the world of Jancsó's own films, it is to the western genre, which incidentally could be discerned as a likely context for remade Greek tragedy (even if it has never to my knowledge been so used), thanks to the frequency of the revenge theme in it. The finale of the film has the hero and heroine riding away, not on white horses but in a red helicopter, their work of cleaning up the town at an end. It should be mentioned that, unlike the western hero, they suddenly return whence they left, but, lest the link with the western be dismissed as sheer fantasy, it is worth remarking that there is in *Elektreia* a theme song composed by a young Hungarian folk singer, making specific reference to the star of many westerns, Lee Van Cleef,[37] and using the rhythms of the music traditionally associated with westerns.

Still, the play on which the film is based, by its title and the names of its characters, appears to claim a relationship with the world of heroic myth as reinterpreted by the Greek tragedians. It is true that the kinship conflicts which are a crucial part of the story as told by the ancient playwrights are more or less abandoned in favour of socio-political points. Thus, Clytemnestra is dead ten years before the sole ruler is despatched in the central section of at least the film. Orestes' (and to an extent Electra's) involvement in matricide was either at the centre of the tragedians' treatment of the tale or at least an important part of the story. Sophocles' version of the story comes closest to minimising the importance of Clytemnestra's murder by making Aegisthus' murder happen second, thus becoming a climax which is not even accomplished within the action of the play. That it is Sophocles' *Electra* which particularly inspires Gyurkó is suggested by this. More suggestive still is the fact that Chrysothemis, who appears only in Sophocles' version, is an important part of the Hungarian play and film. Electra's sense of isolation is, again, Sophoclean. However, the marriage of Electra to a dwarf at Aegisthus' insistence seems an echo of the peculiarly Euripidean marrying of Electra to a humble peasant.

Yet, while areas of the film (and play) bear some relationship to areas of the ancient dramatic versions of the Electra story, there are striking alterations from those versions. One is the extraordinary moment, after Orestes has appeared in the disguise of a messenger proclaiming Orestes' death, where Electra stabs him to death. Another is the even more extraordinary moment when the revivified Orestes and Electra, towards the end, perform a kind of suicide ritual. (Their resurrection after their convincing 'deaths' seems to have no place in the world of Greek drama, needless to say.) Yet another remarkable change of emphasis is the way that the people, who form a Chorus which is largely detached from the action proper, view Aegisthus as their liberator from the intolerable burden of freedom imposed on them by Agamemnon. So, on this, the fifteenth anniversary of Agamemnon's murder, not only does Aegisthus represent himself as the people's benefactor, but they, in celebrating the Feast of Justice, seem willingly to accept this representation. Jancsó's (and, originally, Gyurkó's) pessimism about popular resistance to tyranny is, interestingly, similar to that of Cavani, who, in *The Cannibals*, has the people totally acquiescent to authority and reluctant to side with such rebellious acts as Antigone's (see pp. 108-9). In *Elektreia*, the heroine may embody love of freedom and opposition to despotism, but Chrysothemis appears far more in touch with popular sentiment than she. In keeping with the play's shift of emphasis from private, kinship matters to public, ideological matters, the film ends with an innovative epilogue, not even found in the Hungarian play. Electra is concerned not primarily with revenge for her father's assassination, but with re-establishing a just society. After she and Orestes have entered the red helicopter, Electra's voice-over tells the tale of the fire-bird. This creature was born of freedom as father, happiness as mother. Each day, it flies from east to west, giving strength to men until its wings grow weary. At evening, the bird dies, but it is reborn with the first rays of sunrise. After the allegorical tale, Electra goes on to prophesy the end of social divisions: 'Blessed be your name, Revolution,' she pronounces finally. Unlike even the Sophoclean Electra, this Electra sees the killing of Aegisthus as just one significant action in a chain of events which will ensure the survival of revolution, a perpetual revolution, whose leaders must perish and be reborn like the fire-bird.

The fire-bird story is the most overt summation of what would appear to be the philosophical core of this film, as of so many others from Jancsó's *œuvre*: a view of history itself as a matter of constant flux, cyclical in nature, whether the cycle be one of repression, as in *The Round-Up*, or, as here, of repression/death/rebirth in freedom. The idiosyncratic *mise en scène* of the film, with its apparently endless circling and panning over crowds of people themselves circling and regrouping, seems highly appropriate to the theme of perpetual revolution. Nigel Andrews plausibly spots a play upon the term 'revolution' in the depiction of the deposed tyrant Aegisthus precariously balancing on a gigantic ball which is made by the people to keep rolling and revolving,[38] a symbol entirely in keeping with Jancsó's technique elsewhere in *Elektreia*, as in those scenes, for example, where characters wade through a pool which seems to symbolise the bath where Agamemnon met his death 15 years earlier. The introduction of a hopeful ending, though Jancsó claims it is intended to be more ambiguously hopeful than the subtitles accompanying the fire-bird tale allow to be seen, is a rewriting of the play's ending. The play seems to preach amnesty for former supporters of the tyrant (former Stalinists in Hungary's government), and to advise the limit of the slaying to Aegisthus himself. The film depicts deaths other than the tyrant's, though. A courtier of his, for example, is made to dance naked and is put to death. Yet, the deaths of Electra and Orestes, followed by a miraculous resurrection, their ascent into the helicopter to proclaim the firebird tale, and the return, against generic expectations, of the liberating couple to the land which it had left so recently and so colourfully, all suggest rebirth, progress, light after dark. It is noteworthy, also, that the film, which begins in fog, ends in sunlight. The final sequences represent a dream for the director, but 'un rêve raisonnable'.[39]

Where is it possible to detect a particular relation, if any, to Greek tragedy? What is basically a revenge tale has been invested with a new political, and specifically East European political, significance by the play, and that in turn has been converted into a parable about the necessity of perpetual revolution by the film. Curiously, the film takes to an extreme the timelessness of Greek tragedy, where (in Aeschylus' *The Eumenides*) such recent historic developments as the curtailment of the powers of the Areopagus may without jarring intrude upon the heroic scene, and Athene, Apollo and the ancient goddesses, the Erinyes, may all appear in that contemporary Athenian court. What is already of indeterminate period in the classical Greek context is made all the more non-specific and universal in the film. Thus, the characters and the basic moves of the tale come from fifth-century BC Attic tragedy, but the costumes could be dated to the sixteenth century. There are pistols, but there is also a guitar and, in the final sequences, the unmistakably twentieth-century element of a helicopter, and the essentially twentieth-century rhythms of music fit for a western on the soundtrack. The culture of the film's characters was conceived by co-scriptwriter Gyula Hernádi to be 'vaguely nomad–agricultural–mystic', not historically (or for that matter geographically) defined.[40]

Where the film most clearly indicates a relationship with tragedy is in its (albeit highly individual) choreography. Jancsó conceived of the people of the play as a Chorus, which does not intervene in the struggle ('j'ai réduit le peuple à une sorte de chœur'[41]). Moreover, when talking of the film as a whole, it is on the dance elements that he most concentrates:

the drama is simplified to concentrate on the problem of tyranny. .... It is first and foremost a series of spectacles, a happening, a pantomime, even a ballet. It contains meticulously choreographed dance productions. The whole corps de ballet — more than two hundred dancers — were drafted from professional dance groups.'[42]

The most striking achievement of the film, as far as it relates to Greek tragedy, is in its triumphant demonstration of the power of choreographed movement to be the focus of the spectator's attention. The plot is reduced to a number of brief episodes — the failure to persuade Electra (Mari Töröcsik) to acquiesce in tyranny, the false story of Orestes' (György Czerhalmi) death, Chrysothemis' (Gabi Jobba) attempt to placate her sister, the marriage of Electra to a dwarf, the fatal stabbing and resurrection of the disguised Orestes, Aegisthus' (Jozsef Madaras) death at Orestes' hands, the ascent in the helicopter, and the telling of the fire-bird story — treated as bursts of action which punctuate an all-encompassing ritual. Sometimes, the principals are part of the grouping and regrouping and participate to an extent in the people's festival, sometimes they are separated, with their special concerns, but whatever their position within the frame or the importance of the action with which they are concerned, the audience is never unaware of the presence of a mass of people regimented into patterns or more freely dancing and interweaving.

The role of dance and song, and above all of spectacle involving dance and song, is crucial in *Elektreia*. While the vast Chorus on the Hungarian plain is in nearly every respect different from a Greek tragic Chorus, performing songs and movements that are inconceivable in the fifth-century BC Theatre of Dionysus, for example, this is a choral work of a sort that has not been attempted by any other film-maker choosing a tragic subject. The awkwardness of the Chorus in Cacoyannis's 'trilogy' is such that he seems to be forced to abandon attempts at stylisation (in *Electra*) until the Chorus is almost invisible in *Iphigenia*. The obvious problem is that, in a basically 'realist' approach to the filming of tragedy, such a stubbornly anti-realist component of the drama as the Chorus must represent a source of difficulty. There are sequences in some of the 'realistic-mode' films where the chorus is clearly identifiable, and there are moments in all of these films and in those of this chapter where people behave 'like a Chorus'. Yet, there is no other film which not only retains the Chorus but gives it the central place which the architecture of the ancient Greek theatres suggests the Chorus may have held in ancient drama. The conventions are new and seem personal to Jancsó (or his team of creators), but they establish the possibility of filming choral drama with none of the embarrassment that seems to beset Cacoyannis, Dassin or even Cavani. *Prometheus, Second Person Singular*, though shot in largely anti-realist manner, is not a choral film in the way that *Elektreia* is. It gives a place to movement and music that is seldom accorded to them in the films of Greek tragedy, but the movement and music are more likely to be performed by individuals asserting their individuality than by a group. The bird-masked Chorus does perform at several points in Costas Ferris's film, but it does not perform incessantly, almost unheedingly — so that the dramatic action of the principals sometimes seems of little moment to it — as the people of *Elektreia* do. Perhaps it is appropriate that the Greek Chorus, a vestige of pre-democratic, religious ritual in all probability, should rediscover a home in a communist state, in a film whose message seems to be that leaders are, if not interchangeable, at least expendable, and that the crucial matter is the survival, through constant destruction and rebirth, of the ideals of revolution, giving the people a permanence and centrality that is denied to the individuals of a governing family.

The four films of this chapter represent attempts to create a form of tragic experience which is different from, but in some interesting relation to, that available to spectators of ancient Greek drama. *Phaedra* chooses to concern itself with the arousal of pity and fear and must perform a sort of bourgeoisification of the Euripidean situation so that there can be greater possibility of identification. The film, opting for sufficient 'realism' to facilitate audience implication, takes tendencies discoverable in Cacoyannis to a more obvious extreme, so that it becomes a melodrama, the popular form most likely to encourage audience catharsis today. *The Cannibals, Prometheus, Second Person Singular* and *Elektreia*, to differing extents, abandon 'realism' and audience implication. The latter two films effect the distancing of the audience by the creation of a world peculiar to each of the two, offering a more intellectually challenging experience than Dassin's film attempts, but working through stylisation of movement, symbolism and the use of music. Cavani's film shares some of these interests. The Milan of the film is not to be simply identified with the city of that name, although it gains credibility by obviously being, in some senses, that city. A fictive world is created out of the streets and buildings of Milan, together with the Italian seashore. Antigone's rebellion is designed to be more exemplary than moving (in the manner of, say, Phaedra's and Alexis' suicides in the Dassin movie), to invite the resistance of a new generation to authoritarianism.

As suggested at the opening of this chapter, these film-makers have taken to themselves the freedom that the playwrights of Athens appear to have considered theirs when dealing with heroic myth. Their films bear only a tenuous resemblance, often none at all, to any individual Greek tragedy or generally to that dramatic genre as practised in fifth-century BC Athens. Like the Attic tragedians, they seem more attracted to the possibility of experimentation with heroic myth than to any notion of rendering a dramatic original, and to be working towards a number of different answers to the implicit problem in attempting to make a film which bears some relation to theatrical tragedy.

In earlier chapters we have looked at films which seem to declare themselves to be films *of* pre-existing tragedies. These four films seem to *be* filmic tragedies, conceived for the cinema, and choosing to concentrate on only a limited number of links with Greek tragedy as likely to have been performed.

Notes

1. Melina Mercouri, *I Was Born Greek* (Doubleday, 1971), p. 158.

2. Geoffrey Nowell-Smith, 'Minnelli and melodrama', *Screen*, vol. 18, no. 2, Summer 1977, esp. pp. 114–15.

3. See Michael Walker, 'Melodrama and the American cinema', *Movie*, double issue 29/30.

4. Mercouri, *I Was Born Greek*, p. 151.

5. Robin Bean, 'Phaedra', *Films and Filming*, January 1963.

6. George Steiner, *The Death of Tragedy* (Faber & Faber, 1961), p. 85.

7. Oliver Taplin, 'The Delphic idea and after', *The Times Literary Supplement*, 17 July 1981, p. 812.

8. Claude-Marie Trémois, 'Les tragédies antiques, scénarios de films?', *Télérama* 1 October 1961.

9. Taplin, 'Delphic Idea', p. 811.

10. Derek Elley, 'The Cannibals', *Films and Filming*, vol. 22, no. 4, January 1974, p. 35.

11. See Tristan Renaud, 'I Cannibali', *Cinéma 72*, no. 167, June 1972, p. 145.

12. Geoff Brown, 'I Cannibali', *Monthly Film Bulletin* (42), no. 503, December 1975, p. 258.
13. 'Entretien avec Liliana Cavani', *Jeune Cinéma*, no. 63, May–June 1972, p. 22.
14. Ibid., p. 21.
15. Andrée Tournès, 'Liliana Cavani', *Jeune Cinéma*, no. 63, May–June 1972.
16. Taplin, Delphic Idea, p. 811.
17. Elley, 'The Cannibals', p. 35.
18. 'Entretien avec Liliana Cavani', p. 23.
19. Ibid., p. 24.
20. 'Propos de Liliana Cavani', *Ecran*, no. 6, June 1972, p. 69.
21. 'Entretien avec Liliana Cavani', p. 22.
22. 'Propos de Liliana Cavani', p. 69.
23. Molly Haskell, 'New York Film Festival', *Village Voice*, 10 January 1971.
24. Ibid.
25. 'Entretien avec Liliana Cavani', p. 24.
26. Taplin, Delphic Idea, p. 812.
27. Mel Schuster, *The Contemporary Greek Cinema* (Scarecrow, 1979), p. 177.
28. 'Entretien avec Jancsó', *Jeune Cinéma*, no. 90, November 1975, p. 13.
29. Virginia Dignam, 'Elektreia', *Morning Star*, 28 November 1975.
30. Mari Kuttna, 'The Budapest connection', *Film* (BFFS), no. 24, March 1975, p. 5.
31. Graham Petrie, 'Style as subject: Jancsó's "Electra" ', *Film Comment*, vol. 11, no. 5, September–October 1975, p. 50.
32. Kuttna, 'The Budapest connection'.
33. Tony Rayns, 'Elektreia', *Monthly Film Bulletin*, January 1976.
34. David Robinson, 'Elektreia', *The Times*, 28 November 1975.
35. Miklós Jancsó, quoted in John Gillett, 'Elektreia', *Academy Cinema Two* notes.
36. Rayns, 'Elektreia'.
37. See Gideon Bachmann, 'Jancsó Plain', *Sight and Sound*, vol. 43, no. 4, Autumn 1974, p. 220.
38. Nigel Andrews, *Financial Times*, 28 November 1975.
39. 'Entretien avec Jancsó', p. 14.
40. Bachmann, 'Jancsó Plain', p. 220.
41. 'Entretien avec Jancsó', p. 14.
42. Miklós Jancsó, quoted in Gillett, 'Elektreia'.

META-TRAGEDY

None of the categories suggested by Jorgens (p. 19) adequately covers the films in this chapter, or at least three of the four films discussed here. Pier Paolo Pasolini's *Oedipus Rex* and *Medea*, and Jules Dassin's *A Dream of Passion* are not 'theatrical' films, although the last does include scenes from a modern production of *Medea* in an ancient theatre. They are not 'realistic' films *of* tragedy. Neither are they 'filmic' in Jorgens' sense, since they are not free-wheeling modern adaptations with a traceable relation to heroic myth. Each of these three films is *about* Greek tragedy in a broad sense.

Oedipus Rex includes a section which, by its 'fidelity' to Sophocles' famous play, has the curious effect of making that play seem strange and jarring, out of alignment with the previous and final sections. *Medea*'s second half is clearly an enactment of Euripides' extant play just as it is equally clearly no longer just an enactment but a commentary upon it. *A Dream of Passion* overtly questions the relation of both the drama and also its modern performance to contemporary life. These three films, then, share a concern with Greek tragedy, interrogating its place in modern culture and even, in Pasolini's case, its place in ancient Greek culture. *Notes for an African Oresteia* is included in this chapter largely as evidence of Pasolini's attitudes to tragedy, to show that, had Pasolini's plans to film Aeschylus' *Oresteia* come off, his approach would have been similar to that adopted in relation to Sophocles' *Oedipus Rex* or Euripides' *Medea*.

The title for this chapter has been chosen in the belief that these films constitute attempts at modern tragedies while being simultaneously meditations on the significance of the ancient traged- ies to which the films claim a relation.

Oedipus Rex (Director: Pier Paolo Pasolini, 1967)

It is impossible to enter into a debate about this film on the basis of even a detailed knowledge of Sophocles' play alone. Therefore, a summary of the film's action is offered so that the subsequent analysis of it may be more comprehensible. Pasolini himself thought of the film as definable in terms of four sections or movements.[1] These would be identifiable as: 1. the prologue, set in 1930s Italy; 2. the apparently ahistorical, a-geographical world of the myth, covering the legendary Oedipus' story, from exposure as a baby to his marriage with Jocasta and the outbreak of plague in Thebes; 3. Sophocles' play, from the appeal by the people to their king, Oedipus, to his departure, blinded, from Thebes; 4. the epilogue, with the blinded Oedipus in 1960s Italy, returning to the meadow of his childhood.

Section 1

As crickets chirp on the soundtrack, the film's credits appear, then the music of a brass band. After an almost subliminal flash of a milestone indicating the way to Thebes and of an ancient-looking city, we find ourselves looking at an Italian square. In an upper room, a baby boy is being delivered. Then the scene shifts to a sun-filled meadow, where girls are laughing and playing. The baby lies on a rug watching the girls in their ankle-length skirts. As we look from the baby's point of view, we see his mother (Silvana Mangano) framed against poplar trees as she holds the baby to her breast serenely, then begins to look troubled. The baby looks at the treetops and scans the sky and leafage rapidly.

At a country house, the mother leaves her baby with a young uniformed man. The baby rises from his lying position to look at this man, obviously his father. Fear registers in the father's face as we read intertitles indicating his anxiety that his place will be taken by his son and that his possessions will be stolen by him. 'You will steal the woman I love', we read, and then the thought that he has already stolen her.

The officer and his wife embrace in their bedroom and leave to join costumed revellers at a dance. The baby wakes and cries, gets out of bed and runs out on the balcony to look at the dancers, and sees his mother being kissed. As fireworks burst in the sky, he cries loudly. Later, the baby is in his cot asleep. The parents tiptoe into their bedroom and begin to make love. The baby wakens, with anxiety on his face. As the husband mounts his wife, there is a shot of the meadow now empty at night. The couple lie back after copulation. Reedy pipe music is heard on the soundtrack as the father comes in to look at his son. He lifts his legs by the ankles, squeezing them hard.

Section 2

Reed pipes and a drum can be heard, accompanying a panning shot over a desert area. The baby is being carried along with ankles bound to a pole borne by a servant in a coolie hat. The dangers of exposure are briefly shown by shots of birds and a snake. Another man in the desert hears the baby's sobs. The first man cannot bear to kill the baby. As he leaves him and passes the other concerned wayfarer, a look passes between them, and the exposer of the baby smiles. (It is as if they already know their roles in the story.) 'What swollen feet you have,' the rescuer exclaims, adding another familiar element to the story, the derivation of Oedipus' name.

At a walled city (Corinth), with flocks of sheep surrounding it, Polybus is offered the baby found on Mount Cithaeron. He is taken joyfully by mule to the queen, Merope. Laughing women cry, 'The king! The king!' as they behold Oedipus.

Wreaths of flowers are plaited by female hands. Young men are engaged in throwing a stone discus. Oedipus, now a man (Franco Citti), employs deception to win, and demands to be crowned. The defeated youth, resentful of his cheating, calls him 'child of fortune' and a foundling. Disturbed by a bad dream, Oedipus tells his parents that he wishes to go to Delphi unescorted. When he leaves, Merope (Alida Valli) weeps, as if she too knew the story, and expected not to see him again.

Flute music plays as he passes the sign for Corinth. A North African crowd wait at a respectful distance from a tree under which a masked witch-like priestess and her acolytes sit. Priests bring bowls of rice to her, from which she eats, to prophesy. When she pronounces Oedipus' doom, she laughs wildly. 'Do not contaminate these people with your presence,' she bids him. As he leaves the priestess, the visuals sometimes indicate the 'subjective' impression that he walks alone, then, immediately after, that he is walking through the earlier crowd waiting to consult the oracle. His eyes mist over, as he runs in the opposite direction from Corinth, and sobs alone in a green field. Next, he is in the desert crying. 'Whither goes my life, my youth?', intertitles ask. Faced with a choice of two roads, he puts his hands over his eyes and whirls round. By this random method, he chooses the direction of Thebes. On his way, he witnesses a joyous wedding celebration as he sits eating alone. At another crossroads, he again uses the random method and 'chooses' the direction of Thebes. He is lured by a child and whirling priest to go into an enclosure of honeycombed walls. When he finds a bare-breasted woman awaiting him, he shows agitation and anxiety.

Again, a Thebes sign. A wagon approaches. The herdsman who had exposed him as a baby is there, looking troubled at sight of Oedipus. Laius orders him out of the way. A combat ensues, of protracted duration and some ferocity, as well as some anti-climactic-seeming respites from sheer exhaustion. Oedipus kills all the guards and returns to the wagon. He mocks the king, even when he puts on his gold crown, stabs him twice and takes a helmet from one of the young slaughtered.

After passing a long line of black-robed figures, Oedipus is told by a messenger (Ninetto Davoli) why so many are leaving the city. He is also shown the blind, flute-playing prophet, Tiresias (Julian Beck). 'How I would like to be you,' is Oedipus' thought, according to the intertitles. He approaches an African-looking figure, identified by the messenger as the Sphinx who had caused the exodus. 'There is an enigma in your life,' the Sphinx tells him. 'I don't want to know,' Oedipus retorts, forcing the Sphinx back into the rocks from which she emerged. 'The abyss into which you thrust me is within you,' she calls back to him. Nevertheless, the citizens rejoice at the Sphinx's death. Jocasta, the queen (Silvano Mangano), is wheeled out to Oedipus on a decorated wheelbarrow. She has an Oriental look about her, a porcelain, doll-like face with eyebrows completely shaved off.

In a bedroom which looks remarkably like that in the first section, Oedipus makes love to Jocasta. Immediately after comes a sequence in which sore-ridden corpses lie on the ground, prey to carrion birds, while there is the sound of weeping from the buildings.

Section 3

Oedipus is at the gates of the town wearing the ornamental beard and crown which Laius had worn at the murderous encounter with him. The first lines of Sophocles' play are spoken by Pasolini himself, in the role of priest. Creon has been sent to Delphi, Oedipus informs him, while Jocasta watches from her chamber high above. When Creon returns, he brings a cheerful message that the trouble will clear up if the guilty man responsible for the plague is exiled or put to death. Jocasta's face is photographed as she listens to the information about Laius' death. Oedipus issues a proclamation asking for information about the murder of the previous king, about whom he speaks 'as though he were my own father'.

Together in their bedroom, Jocasta expresses fear. Oedipus kisses her fiercely. This is followed by funeral processions bewailing fresh dead. Oedipus, back at the town gate in his ceremonial garb, addresses Tiresias. 'I have summoned you, and from you will know all.' Tiresias pronounces the truth about Oedipus, only to arouse his fury. Jocasta hears as he denounces the prophet for his imagined treachery; the people are shocked to see him throwing Tiresias out of his presence. Despite Tiresias' parting speech about Oedipus' fate and his incest, Jocasta is seen smiling, laughing with her women. Oedipus comes to her, seizes her and kisses her, twice. She returns his kiss. As they move to the bed, sobs are heard, and then we see a procession of priests in blue raiment.

A public quarrel between Oedipus and Creon is overheard by Jocasta. Alone together in a field, Oedipus tells her of his suspicions about Tiresias and Creon while, to reassure him, Jocasta informs him of what she takes to be the false prophecy about the danger to Laius of having a child. Later, he presses her for more information about Laius' death. At night, she reassures him about the incest prophecy: 'Many men have done the same in dreams.' In their bedroom, he shouts about his parentage and the oracle. She tries to stop him, but he carries on with his plaints, realising, it seems, that he killed Laius. 'Mother!' he exclaims, as she holds him.

Oedipus is alone when the man who rescued him as a baby arrives to tell him of Polybus' death and his succession as ruler of Corinth. In the fields, Oedipus and this Corinthian messenger head a procession dedicated to finding out the truth of his birth. Under threats, the servant who had exposed the baby confesses his part, and claims that he spared the baby 'out of pity'. Jocasta is at this moment at play with her women, but her anxious face is held in close-up as this final piece of information stuns Oedipus.

Back in their bedroom, Oedipus finds Jocasta hanged. He pulls her robe from her, crying out thrice. He stares silently at her nakedness, than pulls brooches from her robe and stabs at his eyes, yelling, 'In darkness I shall no longer see what I should not.' 'I should have pierced my eardrums too,' he adds.

Outside, he walks through the city elders to the gate. The messenger sees him and holds out a flute to him. Together, they leave the appalled Thebans.

Section 4:

Angelo (the messenger of Sections 2 and 3, played by Ninetto Davoli) whistles and feeds the birds as Oedipus, in modern clothes, plays his flute on the steps of a church in Bologna. People go about their business heedless of him. He calls Angelo three times, and they then go to a factory outside which he plays the flute. Men cycle past him on the way home from their workplace. He calls Angelo again.

Back in the same town square as Section 1, they walk past the same country house. They return to the meadow of Oedipus' infancy. The shots of tree leafage and sky are repeated. A brass band can be heard. 'I have arrived. For life ends where it begins.'

This synopsis of the film should make it abundantly clear that its action is not comprehensible simply in terms of a transcription of Sophocles' play, even though Pasolini prided himself on the faithfulness of his adaptation of Section 3. The manifold alterations and shifts of emphasis even within the 'ancient' or at least most 'legendary' central sections, the addition in Section 3 of the clear suggestion that Oedipus and Jocasta go on committing incest even when they have become aware of their true blood relationship, have disturbed critics who demand of Pasolini a Sophoclean story-line. The prologue and epilogue to the film are most disturbing of all, perhaps, since they apparently have the effrontery to recast Sophocles' Oedipus as an inhabitant of the mid-twentieth century or, more impudently still, as Pasolini himself!

It may be chastening to recall, at this juncture, how radically the import of the Oedipus story may have been altered by fifth-century tragedy. As Homer recounts the tale, Oedipus continues to reign when his unconscious guilt is revealed and he is finally buried with proper royal honour. This could suggest the credibility of Dodds' claim that the tragic need for catharsis was reflected in the growth, at the time of tragedy, of professional *cathartai* or purifiers, whose function was to provide literal catharsis, or, in other words, ritual purification from pollution.[2] It may be wondered whether fear of pollution, unfamiliar in the heroic tales as presented in Homer, becomes a major factor in tragedy because the democracy experiences a measure of insecurity at the same time as it appears to enjoy outward success. George Thomson would identify this malaise as a product of the perplexity attendant on social or political change.[3]

This is an appealing idea, that the dread underlying *Oedipus Rex* is explicable as anxiety at watching the ideals of democracy being betrayed by Athens herself, but it is unprovable since the play makes no overt allusion to contemporary history. Francis Fergusson sums up the theme of Sophocles' play in broader terms. For him, it is 'the perennial tragic quest of well-being, in the perennial terms of myth and ritual. The familiar moral, religious, or philosophical interpretations are all relevant but partial: Sophocles "preserves the ultimate mystery by focusing upon the tragic human at a level beneath or prior to any rationalisation whatsoever".'[4]

If Sophocles demonstrably alters the significance of the Oedipus tale as it was transmitted to and by Homer, Pasolini could be reckoned to be attempting a similar analysis of the relevance of the story to his times. Moreover, if Sophocles himself focuses on the human being 'beneath or prior to rationalisation', this is exactly what some commentators claim for Pasolini's Oedipus: that he is a product of a pre-rational society and confronts his fate without benefit of fifth-century Athenian systems of thought.

In re-exploring the Oedipus myth, Pasolini is in any case following a practice that has become relatively uncontroversial. One of the foremost scholars concerned with the (structuralist) analysis of myth to arrive at a definition of its implicit conceptual content, Lévi-Strauss, tackled the Oedipus story in 1955. His analysis led him to claim that the 'meaning' of the tale was reducible to two pairs of polar oppositions: over-rating of blood relations/under-rating of blood relations; denial of autochthonous nature of man/persistence of autochthonous nature of man.[5] This claimed basis to the myth may be contested by classical scholars concerned with overt content or even by structuralists who might contest these particular identifications. The point of allusion to the Lévi-Strauss approach is, though, to offer a reminder that the study of myth frequently involves a search beyond 'common sense' or surface significance, and that a film-maker may be such a researcher. One explanation of the film has been, for example, that it functions as a rigorous reading of the levels of meaning that the myth generates, from one particular reading (that of Sophocles) to readings of this reading, from Aristotle to Freud and Marx by way of Hölderlin, Nietzsche, etc.[6] Whether all these thinkers figure recognisably in the film is not the particular point of citing this comment. It is rather to draw attention to the possibility that the film may be actively concerned with the examination of the myth's (and play's) meaning as constructed by a variety of interpreters, and to the certainty that Sophocles' play is but one (albeit crucially important) reading of the Oedipus tale.

Freud claimed in 1900 that his discovery, the Oedipus complex, was 'confirmed by a legend . . . whose profound and universal power to move can only be understood if the hypothesis I have put forward in regard to the psychology of children has an equally universal validity.'[7] The confidence of Freud's claim is probably excessive. Neither the Oedipus complex itself, nor his particular interpretation of the basis for the play's 'power to move', can be assumed to have 'universal validity'. His re-identification of 'destiny' with the fate of all mankind — and it does seem to be man, not woman, who engages his attention in his creation of the Oedipus complex — and his explanation of the play's 'power to move' on the basis of its appeal to the spectators' own secret knowledge of their subjection to similar forces are interesting, but not unchallengeable, readings. Their principal value may be in their assertion of significance as buried, recondite, disguised beneath the surface meaning of a tale.

Freud's confidence about the 'universal power to move' of the Oedipus legend should not blind us to the fact, already noted above, that it is only in the tragedians that the Oedipus tale seems to involve profound anxiety about even unwitting incest and parricide. According to Ekbert Faas, Aeschylus' Oedipus is the first to blind himself, thus taking to himself the guilt and horror that all around him know are not truly his.[8]

Whatever problems there are in Freud's attempt to establish the Oedipus complex by reference to the Oedipus story, it seems cavalier to push Freud right out of the reckoning on the grounds that Jean-Paul Vernant has 'proved' that Freud has no light to shed on Sophocles' play.[9] Barthélemy Amengual believes that myth constitutes a disguised confession, which says the unsayable or unknowable without sometimes even knowing that it says it.[10] For Amengual, therefore, though Sophocles talks only of fate and the unpitying character of the gods in his play, he 'knows' that the son wishes to possess his mother carnally, that he must therefore be put in opposition by this desire to his father, and thus to his mother too, and consequently to the whole of his society. Though he 'knows', he carefully avoids saying so. The hatred which Freud aroused is used by Amengual to explain why Sophocles' 'knowledge' must be hidden for so long, only to emerge fitfully in such reinterpretations of Sophocles as Pasolini's film, as at the moment when Oedipus cries 'Mother!' to the woman he loves.[11]

Amengual's argument follows too closely the lines of Freud's own argument to be spared the objections that might be raised against the original assertion. However, while the fact that self-loathing is not evidenced in the Oedipus story's treatment before the tragedians undermines claims about 'universal validity', this does not alter the distinct possibility that the 'Oedipus complex' could make sense in a fifth-century context and that disguising of the unsayable could operate within it. Muller, for example, while allowing that 'Sophocles was of course not making a study of the Oedipus complex', is impressed by the fact that the Oedipal dream alluded to by Jocasta in Sophocles' play is reported by such other writers as Herodotus and Plato.[12] Therefore, he concludes reasonably, it was not uncommon for Greek men to dream of marrying their mothers. He also notes the legends involving the murder of the father. 'They hung on to the ghastly myth about Cronus, who castrated and killed his father, Uranus — a myth whose popularity is still more surprising if, as seems likely, the Greeks borrowed it from the Hittites. That the older god should be killed is a familiar idea in religious history, and readily understood on historical grounds of supersedence; but why must he be castrated? And Aphrodite born from the severed member?'[13] Dodds' conclusion, on the evidence of such myths, was that deep resentment of the father was one of the tensions which gave rise to Greek tragedy. In a patriarchal society, the assertion of sons' rights, he feels, can produce the profound anxiety that would result in the sorts of disguised horror which *Oedipus Rex* touches on. Sophocles was not necessarily conscious of this anxiety, it is argued, and the conflict of fathers and sons is only one element in his tragedy,[14] but at least the possibility of the role of such tensions in the evolution of the Sophoclean drama could be allowed as an area of investigation.

Amengual believes that Pasolini's Jocasta 'knows', though, like the equally 'knowing' Sophocles, she does not directly express that 'knowledge'. As in the play, she attempts in the film to deny evidence. Her enigmatic smile at moments of crisis may be interpreted, he argues, as superior, showing her silent awareness of the truth as she listens to verbal evidence drifting up to her chamber.[15] Raymond Durgnat concurs with the view that Jocasta senses, in the film, the truth before Oedipus. Her reference to the 'Oedipal dream' (which, incidentally, Oedipus should dream about Merope, not Jocasta!) is one of the means by which she will continue to hold Oedipus in thrall in the film, and her suicide, Durgnat argues, results more from the loss of his love than from any remorse on her part.[16]

Whatever Vernant may or may not have proved about Freud's relevance to Sophocles' play, the vital point may be that many have been impressed by Freud's argument to the extent that they impute disguised 'knowledge' to Sophocles. The evidence for this imputation is not negligible, but, even if it were, a film of *Oedipus Rex* which ignores twentieth-century belief about the meaning of the play could be thought irresponsible. In other words, even if Freud should shed no light at all on Sophocles' play, he sheds a great deal on modern readings of the play.

The prologue to the film seems like an exact, detailed illustration of Freud.[17] Long before Sophocles' play begins within the film, even before the legend of Oedipus begins, the child is caught up in an 'Oedipal' conflict, the father being regarded as a hostile intruder into the quiet intimacy of mother and child. Yet, it is too simple to see Pasolini's *Oedipus* in purely Freudian terms. The director himself claimed that he had lost interest in the researches of Marx and Freud, and was no longer seriously involved in the academic bog which turns Oedipus into a whipping post (the mixed metaphor is his) for Freudian or Marxist theories.[18] His opinion is that Freud carries no more weight in the film than an amateur would have given him. For Pasolini, Freud triumphs at the very end of the film, and in the Sphinx encounter which he altered vastly to supply an audio-visual case of 'displacement'.[19]

In interview with Pasolini, Oswald Stack goes so far as to describe his interpretation of the Oedipus myth as 'basically anti-Freudian', in that much more emphasis is given in the film to the parricide than to the incest.[20] Pasolini seems surprised by the suggestion and replies that the two are complementary, and that they have equal importance in Sophocles' text too. He does concede that there could be a psychological reason for the claimed priority of the parricide in his inhibitions in representing his love for mother. Stack continues by pointing out, 'In the Prologue you made a very deliberate choice of having a scene where the father says to the baby: "You're stealing my wife's love." This is a bit outside the usual Freudian concept of the myth. In fact you're setting up good reasons for the baby to hate his father.'[21] Pasolini, in reply, concedes that he is not simply confronting the problem of psychoanalytic theory's relation to the myth, but also states that such elements as Stack picks out are not 'outside psycho-analysis, because psycho-analysis talks about the super-ego represented by the father repressing the child.'[22]

All the same, the Freudian components of the film are never purely illustrations of Freudian conceptions of the myth. If the 'Sophoclean' Oedipus has been Freudianised by the contiguity of the central sections with the textbook Freud prologue, it is also true that the Freudian child has been made in some sense into Pasolini himself. Therefore, the Sophoclean–Freudian Oedipus is always at the same time Pasolinian![23]

If Pasolini confronts the relation of psychoanalysis to the Oedipus story, he is as likely to do so in Jungian as Freudian terms. Stephen Snyder points out that interviews with Pasolini show his familiarity with Jung's concepts of psychology. Snyder believes that, throughout his films, Pasolini develops the notion of human personality as involving a dynamic interaction of male and female principles, akin to Jungian ideas.[24] Enzo Siciliano believes that both *Oedipus Rex* and *Medea* in their film versions include the notion that 'the whole human succession of events could be contained . . . in the archetypal symbols';[25] a judgement close to Robert J. White's belief that Pasolini's conception of cinema is 'unmistakably close to Jung's notion of the Collective Unconscious', so that it is particularly well adapted to the transmission of dreams and symbolic patterns 'which because transpersonal we call myths'.[26] White, in this connection, makes the interesting suggestion that Pasolini's Sphinx, in not propounding a riddle but trying to force Oedipus to look into himself, 'is more Jungian analyst than Terrible Mother'.[27]

The film is, then, both Freudian and Jungian, while never being explicable simply in these terms. Extensive knowledge of Pasolini's personal history results in the belief that *Oedipus Rex* is demonstrably a 'Marxist' film also. White makes a case for Pasolini's demonstration through his film that the emergence of the petit bourgeoisie and therefore of its moral code is 'decidely historical and temporal', replacing the transcendental reality of the soul with the shadowy social conventions of the conscience.[28] This demonstration is largely by the absence of bourgeois morality, by the location of Oedipus in a mythic, subproletarian world.[29] Although the relationship with Marxist teaching seems undeniable in certain parts of the film, particularly the epilogue, Pasolini seems to be looking at Marx in a detached manner, believing himself no longer to be involved with Marxism.[30]

If a case can be made for *Oedipus Rex* being Freudian, Jungian or Marxist, it is hardly surprising, since Sophocles was evidently none of these, that Pasolini's film is un– or even anti-Sophoclean. Marc Gervais believes that, at a time when even the heroes of westerns are robbed of their mythic stature, Pasolini cannot retain the glorious aspects of Sophocles' heroes' struggles with the gods or the language appropriate to these heroes' lofty position. Thus, he argues, the film-maker substitutes 'exterior' action and more realistic dialogue.[31] White discovers a more persuasive aspect of Pasolini's endeavour to move *Oedipus Rex* away from Sophocles in his wish to place Oedipus outside history. White's contention is that Sophocles 'conceived of it [*Oedipus Rex*] in terms of contemporary circumstances and attitudes'.[32] Here, he seems to be overstating the case for the contemporary significance of Greek tragedy, because he follows Bernard Knox, who argues of the play, for example, that there are specific parallels between its incidents and recent Athenian history or resemblances between Oedipus and Pericles.[33] Although both Knox and White seem to overstate the case for placing Sophocles' Oedipus in such precise historical terms, there is little doubt that much may be said in support of the notion that Oedipus is placed by Pasolini outside history, not just fifth-century Athenian history, but the modes of thought governing Athenians' construction of the historical. He is of the twentieth century, thanks to the prologue and epilogue, while at the same time being pre-historical, inhabiting a world that is certainly not Greece in its physical aspect but not Morocco either, thinking in ways that show no relation with fifth-century thought, seeking external authority rather than inner understanding.

Pasolini's creation of a non-intellectual hero is probably the most startling departure from Sophocles' version. Whether or not Oedipus' intellectualism in the play is a reflection of the 'critical spirit and scientific outlook of fifth-century Athens',[34] his non-intellectuality as a protagonist renders him non-Greek for modern audiences, even if he has in actuality been rendered non-classical Greek. So crucial is this departure that Stephen Snyder concludes that the film deals with the problems of myth-oriented consciousness, that is, one which has surrendered personal identity to a world which has been endowed with anthropomorphic spirituality, and that Oedipus' crisis here is that of primitive man facing the emergence of rational thought.[35] The character's mindlessness is shown by various incidents — when he wants to be garlanded even if he has not won fairly at the discus; when he goes to the oracle and accepts its word without reflection; when he refuses to choose his path at crossroads rationally.

Much of the explanation for Pasolini's changes of points of detail in the Sophoclean treatment can be traced to this source. The lengthy, highly physical, struggle for dominance between Laius' retinue and Oedipus in the film is passed over in a few lines in the play. Father and son are not even provided with a persuasive psychological reason for their murderous battle. The insult to Oedipus, which in Sophocles helps to explain his reaction since he is of heroic stature there, is insufficient to account for the ferocity of the fighting and the pain which Pasolini's Oedipus inflicts on the young guards and then the king. Both father and son behave as if they are in the grip of forces which they cannot comprehend but which they must obey. What these forces may be is ambiguous, if not unknowable. The looks which pass between them are as noticeable as those that pass between baby exposer and baby rescuer or between Jocasta and Oedipus at their first meeting. It is as if people recognise each other because they already know the story. Predestination is then a matter of finding oneself caught up in a tale whose outcome is known in advance and against which there is no use in fighting. (The oneirism of the film, to which Pasolini and several critics refer, is made all the clearer when these knowing glances are exchanged.) What Pasolini regards as the most Freudian element in the film and the most un-Sophoclean, his treatment of the encounter with the Sphinx, becomes immediately explicable when we take her as an 'agent of precipitant rationality', and see Oedipus' attack on her as the repression of that force by a 'primitive mind afraid to understand itself '.[36]

It might be truer, though, to say that Oedipus in Pasolini's film vacillates between wanting to know and refusing knowledge. As in Sophocles, he is impelled to find out by visiting the Delphic oracle or pressing forward with his inquiry after the Corinthian messenger's arrival, and yet when knowledge is presented to him directly, in Tiresias' words or the Sphinx's message, he violently rejects the knowledge offered him. Pasolini has Oedipus see the blind Tiresias and wish to be in his place even before the encounter with the Sphinx. Since the prophet has knowledge, it is not straining the evidence to suggest that Oedipus yearns for his clarity of insight at the same time as he unconsciously refuses knowledge. Why else should he want to be Tiresias? The priest of Thebes, played by Pasolini himself, underlines the importance of wanting to know:

'What one doesn't want to know doesn't exist. What one wants to know does,' he tells Creon.[37] Oedipus seeks knowledge from external authorities, but when these require that he looks within himself, as the Sphinx in particular demands, he rejects this. That this reading of Oedipus' character is in the spirit of Pasolini's conception of the film seems to be proved by a note in the original script. In it, the evident hositility between Oedipus and Tiresias is explained as follows: 'Tiresias' aversion for Oedipus runs deep. His knowledge of the truth is enough. For his is the hatred of light for darkness, of truth for falsehood. And it is this which exasperates Oedipus, who is not aware that he himself is on the side of darkness and of falsehood.'[38]

There are other clearly un-Sophoclean elements in the film. Destiny, which seems beyond human control in Sophocles, appears to have a different application in Pasolini, above all because the Oedipus story has been linked to the prologue, where it is the child's psychological development which takes the form of a destiny, or necessity, governing adult man's actions. The Oedipus tale is told with a more contemporary application. In this film, he stands for the individual who lives imprisoned in the fetters of the family, above all, and of society and religion.[39]

The Sophoclean structure, which is so admired by Aristotle, has been undone, the classic detective story pattern unravelled, so that the incidents are told in strictly chronological order. Thus, the modern audience, even if unacquainted with the Sophocles play, knows all before Section 3 (the play itself) begins. This unravelling reinforces the points made above, that Pasolini's method is to take Oedipus out of a fifth-century context and to put him back into the world of heroic myth.

At the end of the play, the person on whom Oedipus will henceforth rely, and certainly his most devoted helper in *Oedipus at Colonus*, is his daughter, Antigone. Oedipus has no children in the film and it is immediately to Angelo, Tiresias' guide, that he turns in his blindness. Angelo and he made the transition together to modern Italy and together move back to the meadow where the baby Oedipus' life begins. The young man assumes an importance unthinkable in Sophocles for one outside Oedipus' kin.

Equally un-Sophoclean is the curious encounter with the naked woman, which appears to disturb Oedipus. She is clearly too young to represent any threat of being his mother. In the original script, the woman was to have been 'old and fat, her great breasts uncovered', and Oedipus was to have been 'struck by a feeling which he does not recognise'.[40] The feeling is made all the more mysterious by the substitution of a young, conventionally desirable woman, and could suggest that Oedipus knows he is destined to be reserved for a woman who could be a mother to him. Instead of being terrified of encountering her, he is 'unaccountably' averse to union with any other woman.

Echoes of the second extant Oedipus play of Sophocles, *Oedipus at Colonus*, are discernible in the epilogue, though. Oedipus in the play recognises that his journeys are over, that he has come home, when he reaches the Grove of the Eumenides at Colonus. In the film, Oedipus has literally arrived home when he passes the house in which he was born and returns to the peace of the meadow. The radical differences from Sophocles in Pasolini are more easily explicable when it is realised that the film may be taken to be as much about Pasolini himself as about Sophocles' hero. Pasolini claims that the little boy of the prologue is himself, the boy's father is his father, an infantry officer, and the mother his own mother. This is, according to his own testimony, the most autobiographical of his films.[41] Oedipus is born into the circumstances of Pasolini's childhood, with his parents' clothes in the film inspired by photographs of Pasolini's parents.[42] The first part of the epilogue is set in Bologna which has special resonance for Pasolini, being the headquarters of the Italian Communist Party, but also the city in which he spent his student days.[43]

This epilogue is more easily understood by reference to Pasolini's history than to *Oedipus at Colonus*. Guido Aristarco takes it as a form of confession,[44] one that is analysed in more detail by Dominique Noguez on the following lines: Angelo's games with the pigeons in front of the church, and the church itself at the foot of which Oedipus plays the flute, refer to the temptation of bourgeois ideologies, above all that of Christianity, which seems to be marked in *The Gospel According to St Matthew* (1964) and *Uccellacci Uccellini* (1965); the Milan factories sequence and especially the football game in the wasteland make one think of *Mamma Roma* (1962) and the appeal of 'social engagement'; while the last section makes one think of the self-analysis of *Theorem* (1968).[45]

Then, as if to ensure that the autobiographical aspects of the prologue and epilogue are not differentiated on that basis from the central sections, Pasolini plays the high priest of Thebes (though not, noticeably, Oedipus), while Silvana Mangano plays both the modern mother and Jocasta, the same actor plays Laius and the army officer father, and Ninetto Davoli is both the messenger of the pre-rational world and Angelo, Oedipus' guide, in the epilogue.

Some would see Pasolini's sexuality as a crucial 'autobiographical' element in his film. Guido Aristarco, for example, thinks of his films in general as being an expression of a homosexual sensibility.[46] Barthélemy Amengual is attracted by what he detects as a common element in another homosexual poet's treatment of the Oedipus story. Jean Cocteau's *La Machine Infernale* ends with Jocasta reappearing at the moment of Oedipus' departure from Thebes, dead and white. Importantly, Amengual says, she is no longer his wife but only his mother now. Oedipus' return to the meadow is, Amengual believes, a return to the Earth Mother, to the breast of his own mother. He argues, moreover, that Oedipus has replaced one mother with another, Angelo, an uncaring, unaware young man from whom he simply wants closeness and nurture.[47] He goes on to argue a particular fascination of homosexuals with the 'abnormal' or 'marginal' areas of society, the world of thugs and toughs, as well as of the exotic or primitive, because, he claims, they give promise of the possibility of a meeting with the Other — the Other conceived as a nature anterior to all culture. Eros thus becomes a sacred activity as opposed to eroticism, to be lived according to nature. Pasolini dreams, he claims, of a permissive society, agrarian and matriarchal, and is saddened that he was not an abandoned child.[48] This ascription of so many of Pasolini's private interests and obsessions to 'homosexuals' in general is unwarranted, but the carelessness of the attribution should not blind us to the appositeness of the analysis in relation to Pasolini himself, to judge at least from his films and what is known of his life. Certainly, the replacement of Antigone by Angelo, Oedipus' anxiety at the thought of union with the bare-breasted woman, and the childlessness of Oedipus all suggest, since all of these are un-Sophoclean, a possible rewriting of the tale to focus on a homosexual Oedipus.

On the other hand, it may be simplistic to assume that, because a film touches on elements that seem to have a direct relation with at least its director and writer, it is autobiographical, or *merely* autobiographical. Pasolini himself warns that, although this is the most autobiographical of his films, it is the one he views with most objectivity and detachment. Although he is recounting a personal experience, he says, it is an experience which is over and which is of almost no interest to him now.[49] He has also said, 'I have never

dreamt of making love with my mother. Never even dreamt it. . . .
Rather I have dreamt, if at all, of making love with my father . . .
and perhaps also, I think, with my brother, and with many women
of stone.'[50] Importantly, he does not play Oedipus himself, although
he appears in the film. He chose Franco Citti for the part because,
he says, he was so different from him.[51] This choice makes it obvious
that detachment and objectivity are crucial factors in Pasolini's
depiction of his 'personal experience' and that conclusions about
the place of his mother in the course of Pasolini's own sexual
development may be too facile for credibility.

To understand the stances from which Pasolini makes his 'objective' film of his experience, it may be worth while summarising his
intellectual development. The most popular account of Pasolini's
progress is that he passed from Marx to Freud to Lévi-Strauss,
from materialist reason to para-Catholic religiosity, then to 'la
pensée sauvage'.[52] He appears to have been most impressed by
Antonio Gramsci's Marxism, which analyses the cultural, as well as
the economic, forces of history.[53] Amengual writes that, from 1950,
he came into contact with Third World poverty in the suburbs of
Rome and became fascinated by the vitality of this world. The
result, he writes, was the creation of a philosophy of humanity as
Nature which excluded History but took refuge in myth.[54] Only
myth is realist for Pasolini because it recovers the unhierarchised
totality of the real. It is necessarily anti-dialectical, anti-Hegelian,
since everything coexists in nature.[55]

Oedipus Rex may be a personal film, but yet it is largely 'in the
third person', as we are reminded when intertitles allow us access
to first-person thoughts about the action. The curious relation of 'I'
in art to the 'I' outside such activity is far from limited to a few
films such as *Oedipus Rex*. Peter Wollen reminds us that the act of
writing about oneself [let alone filming one's preoccupations] produces puzzling results:

> I do not feel that I write in any particular style at all. . . . Nor
> do I write down the pre-existent reveries which run through my
> head. Indeed, the reveries only arise in and from the act of writing
> itself; they are reveries which are already written, which take the
> form of phrases, clauses and sentences as they arise. They are
> products of that strange situation — writing. . . . Nor do I
> necessarily recognise them as mine at all. They are like the
> solutions to a crossword set by someone else. They are dictated

by something quite separate from me, by their place in relation to each other, by their effect in combination, by their answering some question, some enigma, which has come to me from elsewhere.[56]

This may help to explain the paradox that Pasolini feels at his most detached and objective while making his most autobiographical film.

With this in mind, we can return to the film to re-examine the four sections in order:

Section 1

As already noted, the prologue is both the most straightforwardly autobiographical section and simultaneously the most Freudian, providing a textbook exemplar of the origins of Freud's Oedipus complex. Perhaps the confusion about the dating of this prologue arises from awareness of its relation to Pasolini's infancy. Although we have evidence that Pasolini wanted the solider to be wearing infantryman's uniform of the 1930s[57] and the woman's dresses suggest that decade, Raymond Durgnat believes that the story begins in the 1920s,[58] almost certainly because he knows that Pasolini was born in 1922.

The tendency to refuse knowledge, so discernible in the adult Oedipus, is repeatedly prefigured here by the baby's impulse to avoid seeing things that disturb him, covering his eyes to blot out the unacceptable realities in front of him.[59]

Sections 2 and 3

Oliver Taplin asks somewhat sceptically about the central portions whether Pasolini is making 'profound points' about cultural relativity.[60] The answer seems to be that much more than that is going on. Geoffrey Nowell-Smith detects an attempt at distanciation,[61] through the strangeness of the pre-historic world as represented here, producing a very different relationship between spectator and screen from that obtaining in the prologue. The passage is also detected by Nowell-Smith as from the personal to the universal, or, in Freudian terms, from the ontogenetic to the phylogenetic.[62]

Why is the central section shot in Morocco? Some feel unhappy about the choice of locale because it seems like the result of a wish for 'pure exoticism'. Obviously, though, the North African setting, with its particular architecture and landscapes, removes the action effectively from the world of Greece with its fifth-century, 'rationalist', civilised associations. Perhaps not entirely from the world of Greece, all the same. Amengual believes that it is chthonic Greece which is represented by Morocco.[63] The Moroccan landscape stands also, in turn, for the world of the Roman lumpen proletariat which so fascinates Pasolini.[64]

The central section's style has been criticised for being 'an uncomfortable mixture of frenzied realism . . . and straight baroque'.[65] An explanation has been suggested, in the constant balance between possession and loss of the world, between aggression and flight, seizing and letting go, a dialectic legitimised by its object, which is the suspension of the Greek world between two abysses, that of gods and heroes and, on the other hand, necessity.[66]

The general line on which Pasolini is attacked is for eclecticism. Pasolini is indeed eclectic, it should be conceded immediately. The costumes are inspired, it appears, by Aztec, Sumerian and black African cultures.[67] Asked by Oswald Stack about the music for the film, Pasolini replies:

> That is Rumanian folk-music. Initially I thought of shooting . . . in Rumania . . . but it was not suitable . . . in recompense I found some folk-tunes which I liked a lot because they are extremely ambiguous: they are half-way between Slav, Greek and Arab songs, they are indefinable: it is unlikely that anyone who didn't have a specialised knowledge could locate them; they are a bit outside history. As I wanted to make *Oedipus* a myth, I wanted music which was ahistorical, atemporal [and] . . . there is one bit of Japanese music, chosen for the same reason.[68]

(It might be added that a more identifiable piece of music is also used — Mozart's Quartet in C Major![69])

Raymond Durgnat points out that, while 'eclecticism' is not generally a word of positive value in our culture, eclecticism and scepticism bear a curious relationship to each other, and that eclecticism 'has a Protean or Dionysiac strain as in Jean Renoir'.[70] In any case, the eclecticism has the effect of creating a highly personal, 'unreal' world, like the landscape of a dream: 'I wanted to represent the myth as a dream,' Pasolini says, 'and I couldn't represent this dream except by aestheticising.'[71]

Section 4

A wide-angle lens is used for the abrupt transition from the dream world created in Morocco to the world of 1967 Italy, because a naturalist transition seemed impossible to Pasolini.[72] The transition represents, for Pasolini at least, a re-entry of the blinded Oedipus into society by means of sublimation. 'One of the forms of sublimation is poetry. He plays the pipe, which means, metaphorically, he is a poet.'[73] The poetry may be subdivided among the parts of the epilogue to suggest Oedipus as 'decadent poet', 'Marxist poet', then no poet at all, but merely somebody who is going to die.[74] Equally, the details of Pasolini's own history may be described in terms of his bourgeois youth, then his communist youth and finally his despairing maturity.[75] The flute music of the first part, outside the church in Bologna, is grotesquely funereal in an affluent city, where the bourgeoisie promenades looking at the sub-proletarian Oedipus in disgust. To Pasolini, Bologna is defined as 'communista e consumista'.[76]

On the surface, the epilogue appears to belong to Marx. Oedipus is a beggar expelled from the family, playing a Russian revolutionary air on his flute. At the very last moment, where Oedipus loses himself in the meadow where he was suckled as a child, it is as if Freud has ousted Marx, however. Yet, for Pasolini, it is *Oedipus at Colonus*, rather than Freud, which suggests the idea.[77]

The film has references beyond Sophocles, Marx and Freud. Pasolini's Oedipus seems related, for example, to Camus' absurd man. He cannot beleive in gods but, like him, feels defeated.[78] The visual style of the film has been compared with the pictorial traditions of the Renaissance practised by the Medici court's intellectual élite, when perspective was not yet subjected to rational regulation.[79] Amengual finds Poussin in Pasolini's countryside, Delacroix in the film's 'luminous moments', while Andrée Tournès has detected a relationship between Picasso's blue mothers and Silvana Mangano.[80] The struggle between Oedipus and Laius' retainers recalls, for Raymond Durgnat, Kabuki and Samurai traditions.[81]

Yet, despite — or arguably because of — the multiple cross-references in Pasolini's *Oedipus Rex*, and the complexity of its interrelation with Pasolini's own story, Freud, Marx and, not least, Sophocles, the film is not only a meditation on tragedy but, it has been claimed, tragic in its own right:

The ultimate point of arrival in Oedipus' search and blindness, one that is already implicit in the rest of Pasolini's work, is that human suffering is not fortuitous, not bound in its more intimate and burning aspects to this or that historical cause, but existential, inevitable, bound up with the blood and the destiny of blood, not historical but metahistorical, there where the great tragic myths have placed it.[82]

Medea (Director: Pier Paolo Pasolini, 1970)

The lessons of Pasolini's *Oedipux Rex* appear to have been absorbed by his critics and public by the time his version of *Medea* appeared. After the de-familiarisation of Sophocles' play by juxtaposing it with, on one side, a pre-rational universe inhabited by an inarticulate, resolutely unthinking Oedipus and, on the other, Italy in 1967, so that the most bizarre element in the film may be the verbal and intellectual sophistication suddenly introduced with Sophocles' text, the audience for *Medea* was prepared for similar strategies. The film's claim to be 'based on the play by Euripides' is, in the event, no more significant than its 'tragic' predecessor's claimed relationship with the Greek original. At least half its running time, for example, is given up to the detailing of Jason's early education by Chiron, as well as, more lengthily, Medea's place in Colchis' life. The conflict between Jason and Medea in Corinth, which constitutes the action of Euripides' *Medea*, with only allusions to Colchis, for example, occupies a more modest portion of the whole in Pasolini, being confined to the second part of the film, and seeming more elliptical and ambiguous than in Euripides' treatment.

The only 'theoretical' position of film scholarship popularised enough to be absorbed by reviewers in non-specialist contexts seems to be 'the auteur theory' — more an attitude, as has often been pointed out, than a theory. By the 1970s, it was becoming common practice to talk of Orson Welles' or Roman Polanski's *Macbeth* (1948 and 1971, respectively) rather than 'a film of Shakespeare's *Macbeth*', and it would be more likely that the Polanski *Macbeth* would be discussed in terms of such other works as *Rosemary's Baby* (1968) or *The Tenant* (1976) than with particular concern for its relation to the Bard's original. So entrenched had auteurism become as a basis for approaching the works of Pasolini, who seemed uncontroversially an 'auteur', that British reviewers, writing in newspapers, as well as film periodicals, expended far more energy in making links between his *Medea* and his earlier and subsequent films than on searching out 'infidelities' to Euripides. In any case, their experience of *Oedipus Rex* had probably warned them off what may have seemed a fruitless endeavour.

Thus, Derek Malcolm finds a link between Pasolini's *Medea* and *Oedipus Rex* in the way that the former harks back to the latter 'in his extraordinary physical re-creation of an ancient, barbarous but unsoiled world'.[83] Other critics make wider reference to Pasolini's work, however. Nigel Gearing talks of *Medea* as eschewing the allegorical complexities of *Theorem* and *Pigsty* (1969), just as it also eschews the 'evasive simplifications' of the films to follow.[84] Richard Combs talks of the film, all the same, as anticipating 'the whole milieu into which Pasolini plunged for the story-cycle trilogy, an investigation into the very roots of myth and a sort of pre-historical scene and landscape painting'.[85] In his book on directors, John Russell Taylor thinks of it likewise as looking forward 'with its picturesqueness and relative lack of intensity and internal complexity' to the cycle of 'entertainment films' based on medieval stories.[86] As if to validate the most prevalent habit of Pasolini critics by this time, the 'auteur' himself stated that in *Medea* he offered a reprise of all the themes in his other films, while, with regard to Euripides' play, he restricted himself to making some quotations from it.[87]

Few reviewers seemed specially troubled by such self-confinement to desultory quotations from the original tragedy. It is merely noted that Pasolini abandons the structure of the original, preferring instead to open it out in favour of accommodating a 'dream-like representation of the myth'.[88] Marc Gervais believes that tragic inspiration is more likely to come from Seneca's or Corneille's versions than Euripides'.[89] Pasolini himself cites Mircea Eliade, Frazer and Lévi-Bruhl as his sources of inspiration; since the *Medea*, for him, rests on a 'theoretical' foundation of the history of religions, it is works of modern ethnology and anthropology that are credited, rather than Euripides (or even Seneca).[90] The 'star' of the film, Maria Callas, was associated since 1953 with Medea, but Luigi Cherubini's Medea, not Euripides'.[91]

Morocco provided the city of Thebes and the surrounding countryside in *Oedipus Rex*. In *Medea*, Colchis is 'played' by Cappadocia in Turkey, particularly the region of Meteora near Goreme. Pasolini states that Medea's village is still inhabited and that at one time it had been Christians who had lived there and who took refuge in the caves when they suffered persecution. It was these Christians who built the little churches which Pasolini used for shots of the palace interior.[92] Corinth in the film is a composite. Much of it is provided by Alep in Syria, but the exterior of the palace is represented by the exterior of a large fortress in Pisa, much of the latter part of the film being shot beneath the walls of Pisa's Piazza dei Miracoli.[93]

Costumes and music are once again, as in *Oedipus Rex*, highly eclectic for presumably similar reasons (see above, p. 144). The clothes cover a variety of styles and periods.[94] Medea's costume is Andalusian, according to Pasolini, while the masks in certain Colchian sequences are Mexican.[95] Differing instruments (mandolins, the human voice, something which sounds like a bouzouki for the opening sequence of the film) from different cultures (Japanese, Indian, Arabic) provide the music for *Medea*.[96] As for the look of the film, this too may be linked with *Oedipus Rex*. What has been said about the proximity of the latter's visual style to the pictorial tradition of the Renaissance applies with even more force to the later film.[97]

Themes and motifs discoverable in *Oedipus Rex* are picked up by or developed in *Medea*. Pasolini claims, for example, that once again the Third World is addressed in this film, as it was in the central sections of his earlier film. For him, this story could be that of a Third World, specifically African, nation which has experienced the catastrophe of contact with materialist, Western civilisation.[98] It may be worth recalling that, by Pasolini's reasoning, the conflict at the heart of his *Medea* is thus linked with the sub-proletarian world of Rome's suburbs, since the marginalised in Italian society are, for the director, a sort of Third World of poverty and yet great energy in daily contact with the Western civilisation under which he categorises Corinth in the film.

His fascination with those regarded as abnormal or outside the mainstream of society seems to inform his construction of Medea, as of Oedipus. There is an important difference in the former character, however. Pasolini differentiates her by reason of her self-exclusion. She has achieved the maximum of integration at the point when she is deserted by Jason, he argues, and her exclusion from Corinthian society is self-imposed, as the result of a 'reverse conversion'. At the moment when she is traumatised by his rejection of her, she suddenly returns to the modes of thought that had been hers in Colchis. In the original shooting script, there had been instructions for a scene in which Medea has a 'regressive' dream, taking her back to her origins. It was to have been this dream which gave her the resolution to kill her own children.[99] Although the dream is not in the finished film as we have it, it simply makes more explicit what might be gathered from the progress of the filmic drama: the infanticide is a sort of propitiatory human sacrifice, of the sort habitually practised to ensure fertility in Colchis, as well as an act of vengeance against Jason, their father. Even the vengeance is explicable as an impulse arising from the savage Eros which possesses Medea in Colchis and on her flight with Jason therefrom, and which, after being deadened by her near absorption into 'civilisation', springs back into life as a result of her reconversion to the ways of Colchis.

Medea's marginality is related by Pasolini to his own profound sense of exclusion from which he has suffered in a way directly analogous, he claims, with the victims of racism.[100] He accepts the suggestion put to him by Jean Duflot, that his sense of marginality arises from his situation *vis-à-vis* his father and mother.[101] Thus, there are increasing reasons why the film's significance may be traced back to *Oedipus Rex*. Medea seems to live out, by the director's own argument, the results of Oedipus' estrangement, and thus Pasolini's *Medea* is as fairly (and as unfairly) capable of being described as 'autobiographical' as the earlier film. Yet, Medea does not merely bear the weight of representing a bourgeois-intellectual, homosexual poet. She is a woman, and her exclusion is representative, more simply, of what Pasolini takes to be woman's exclusion. (He would reject the charge of misogyny, arguing rather that he has a tendency to 'Raphaelise' woman, to express her angelic side.)[102]

If there are manifold reasons for seeing *Medea* in connection with *Oedipus Rex*, the later film is still an extension of the tale, not simply a repetition of it. Stephen Snyder thinks of these two films, together with *Theorem*, as offering a history of human consciousness, which is in Pasolini a process of radical transformations described by Snyder as 'quantum leaps'.[103] Thus, while *Oedipus Rex* portrays the confinement of primitive thought within an extra-historical limbo, *Medea* concerns a later stage, when mythological thought encounters modern, 'or specifically rational', consciousness.[104] While the summation of the conflict in these terms is largely persuasive, there are several other sites of conflict identifiable all the same. The clash of mythological thinking with modern or rational is

represented also by others: sacred/profane; ideal/real; tribalism/
individualism;[105] Dionysiac/Apollonian; Oriental/Greek; passion/
reason.[106]

These conflicts are embedded in the differences of portrayal in this
film of Colchis and Corinth. Colchis is introduced as a mysterious,
'magical' land of ritual, with, as its central symbol of magical power,
the Golden Fleece. It is a land of deeds without thoughts. As magical
significance is invested in a goatskin, so human blood, if shed to
ensure the fruitfulness of the new crops in springtime, is credited
with wondrous potency. There is a striking example of the deed
without thought in the sequence where Medea hacks up her brother
and parts of the severed body are collected by the pursuing soldiery.
No horror is registered on the faces of those watching the dismemberment or on Medea's face. The deed is presented as neutrally as it
would be in heroic myth, and the grotesque (to us, in our post-
rational world) heap of limbs brought back in a wagon to the royal
family of Colchis provokes maternal lamentation but no sense of
outrage or appalled reaction. (Pasolini is as true to the *sources* of
Euripides' tragedy here as he is to the spirit of the Bible's account
of the miracles in Jesus' life, in *The Gospel According to St Matthew*.
Deeds are done. Those to whom they have a relevance in the myth
express sorrow or joy. Those who are spectators at the time of
the deed's performance are no more than bystanders, uninvolved,
making no (visible) judgement of the deed witnessed.) Medea, the
priestess of Colchis, enjoying magical contact with the elemental in
her home, becomes nothing more than a sorceress in Corinth, just
as the Golden Fleece reverts to being a mere goatskin. The point is
underlined by Jason's (Giuseppe Gentile) remark that the fleece
means nothing outside its land. Corinth is impressive, expressing its
power in its fortress-like architecture, but it is free of the sense of
awe which the rites of spring suggest for Colchis. It is presented as
a place for settling down with a family, once new, 'respectable',
links with the ruling family of it have been forged by Jason. Corinth
denies Eros. Medea rediscovers it and, in establishing Colchis in
the alien territory of Greece, makes the land explode into a final
conflagration in which along with Jason's children she herself is
consumed. Jason, who has debased his 'civilised' self by seeking
success in materialistic, bourgeois terms, can only watch his children
burn. Though Medea is finally active, Jason passive, it is dificult to
argue that either victimises the other. Rather, each is unable to find
an accommodation with the other, since the more one cleaves to

bourgeois security, the more the other finds herself reverting to mythological modes of thought. Medea can no more help burning with her children than Jason can quench the flames. Although she reasserts her potency, restoring that sense of awe for magic which Corinth had denied it, her time and place have passed, and at the moment of greatest power she must destroy herself. Jason at his most powerless proves to be a survivor. If we see the painful survival of Corinth and the glorious eclipse of Colchis in these final moments, we may also be watching the emergence of rationalism from its intellectual inheritance, a disquieting and costly 'quantum leap' made at the heavy expense of loss of contact with the instinctive or magical, producing residual guilt without the possibility of an expiatory sacrificial ritual (although if the modern age is also in any sense a Christian world the notion of expiatory sacrifice is taken to a new pitch of intensity with the death of no less than God-as-man — yet, for Pasolini at least, the perception of Christ, as evidenced by *The Gospel*, is in as mythic terms as the Colchians' perception of the Golden Fleece).

Up till now, the description of the film's core of meaning has been in terms of binary oppositions, in classic structuralist manner. Many more could be added to the list — female/male, noticeably; immigrant/national; and so on — but far more rewarding than the compilation of lists of antitheses may be the observation that these oppositions coexist. And not just in the sense that they inhabit the same text, but that they inhabit the same individual. This is especially evident if we abandon the common sense division and give some regard to Pasolini's own view that Medea and Jason are one and the same character.[107] What he seems to be suggesting is that the film concerns conflicts within the individual psyche, as well as within human society. Thus, if the film chronicles the emergence of rational consciousness, it also celebrates the resilience of pre-rational, mythological consciousness. There is crucial evidence within the film that at least two modes of thought may coexist within a single psyche, especially Jason's.

For example, the centaur Chiron (Laurent Terzieff) oscillates between being the mythical creature, matter-of-factly presented visually, and being an ordinary man. The point of view in each case seems to be Jason's. Just as Oedipus, leaving the Delphic oracle, sometimes sees himself alone in the desert and sometimes surrounded by those who have assembled in large numbers to consult the oracle, from moment to moment changing his vision (and therefore ours), so Jason sees at one moment mythically, at another 'rationally'. Not only that, but Jason sees the two versions of Chiron side by side, within the same shot. The deconsecrated Chiron thus coexists with the mythical creature whom Jason not only saw as a child but on whose (horse's) back he rode. The multivalence of the symbols in the film is such that Pasolini offers another reading for the centaur, in terms of Freudianism: that it symbolises androgyny, the union of paternal power and of maternal nurture.[108] Thus, by this reading, gender dichotomising happens as a 'rationalist' habit alongside the magical fusion of male and female. The centaur's teaching to Jason involves a vision — literally, a vision — of nature which the adult Jason's perception denies but does not totally displace. Jason's infantile perception, under the tutelage of Chiron, results in his seeing Chiron as a centaur, a perception which he retains in his memory as a grown man. As long as the 'magical' perception remains a possibility, the sacred exists within Jason and so his sympathy with Medea is alive at the very moment when his rationality seems totally to discount it. The child is also thus father to the man and continues to live within him. Modern society, by analogy, retains a memory of the sacred, instinctual, irrational, beneath the surface of its rational consciousness. This is the memory which Pasolini, as a product of modern, 'Western' society, draws to the surface and exposes in many of his films, and most undisguisedly in his films of Greek tragedy.

If this interpretation of the film's core of meaning carries any weight, then the apparently puzzling double presentation of Glauce's death is highly appropriate. The fundamental difference between the two enactments seems to be that one death is magical or mystical, representing Medea's conception of her revenge, while the second is 'rational', a secularised version which accounts for the mysterious demise of Glauce in psychological terms, although that psychology is still bizarre, since her self-immolation is followed by the equally sudden death of her grief-stricken father.

It would be easy to misrepresent Pasolini's account of the place of the mythological, primitive, erotic consciousness in sentimental terms. Although the paltriness of Jason's attainments by his attempted marriage to Glauce is never disguised, *Medea* does not allow us to think of the pre-rational world as one of pure delight. While the horrors of human sacrifice and dismemberment are relativised, so that their function in an alien society may be comprehended and our awareness that horror itself is societally produced may be ensured, there is no unequivocally Romantic harking back to Colchis in the film. Medea cannot return. She may rediscover the Colchian in her, but only to perish through its power. What the world of Colchis excludes most obviously is progress. Stephen Snyder points out that the shapes which define Colchis in Pasolini's film are primarily curvilinear,[109] suggesting cyclical patterns of existence without movement forward. Medea, under the influence of Eros and by her contact with Jason, has broken out of the stasis characterising Colchian life. By her precipitate journey out of the enclosed circle which is Colchis in *Medea*, she has lost contact with it. It becomes as much a memory, with all the potency of vivid memory but a diminution of tangibility, for Medea as the centaur has become for Jason. Through her traumatising contact with the world of bourgeois materialism, she has passed beyond hope of return to her home. If Pasolini rediscovers the wonder of Eros, of the instinct, the irrational, latent in our modern consciousness, he has no illusions about the re-entry of modern humanity into a pre-rational world. His trilogy of medieval tale films is tied to the ages represented in the literary originals. When the post-Christian, rational world reverts to pre-rational habits of thought, it is the nightmarish world of *Salò* (1975) that seems to result, though once again Pasolini is true to his literary source (this time, de Sade) in having neither victims nor 'sadists' expressing perception of this world *as* nightmarish.

Eros, or, in one of its most recognisable manifestations, love, is far from a soothing or sentimental experience in this film. Medea is consumed by it, almost to the exclusion of knowledge of its object. Her consumption by fire simply renders explicit what underlies her every action in Colchis and then Corinth. Pasolini seems to recognise the inevitability and potency of love, but to be incapable of rationalis-ing it or of finding a place for it within 'civilised' society. It is always a threat to rational, Western society, destroying the sense of individuation which it depends upon, reducing — or, for that matter, exalting — lovers to pre-rational, mystical beings. The love may be for mother, or pigs, or involve the death of the loved object — as arguably even in *Salò*. It must perish if it is to be contained by rationality, or rationality must perish if Eros gains the upper hand.

What about *Medea* as tragedy, though, 'or as the concentrated portrayal of human suffering and its place in the multiverse?', Oliver Taplin asks.[110] 'His [Pasolini's] *Medea* touches upon anthropology but not on *anthropoi*; it dabbles with patterns of culture, but when it comes to personal relationships it is cold.' A similar unease seems to underlie Marc Gervais's complaint that aesthetic preoccupations are affirmed at the expense of conviction and passion.[111] Why must tragedy be 'hot', or passionate, though? Against Aristotle's demand for catharsis, we must set the anti-tragic tendencies in Euripides, which, by their ambiguity, render personal relationships 'cold', or the grand manner of Aeschylus, which seems to deny empathy, even in his contemporary audiences, to judge by the ancient Life of Aeschylus. (And Aeschylus does not seem to have been above similar 'dabbling' with patterns of culture.) Tragedy, to judge by Sophocles' *Oedipus Rex*, may also be about inevitability, about an uncomprehending passage towards catastrophe. While we can analyse the impulses driving Medea and Jason to their separate sufferings, we cannot solve the problem which the collision of their cultures generates. Pasolini seems to be saying, in both *Oedipus Rex* and *Medea*, that Western humanity's suffering is similarly analysable, but beyond remedy. His view of his own life and, when this life is 'universalised', therefore of human existence seems tragic by at least one definition of the term. *Anthropoi*, he seems to argue, are inseparable from anthropology in its widest sense.

Notes for an African Oresteia (Director: Pier Paolo Pasolini, 1970)

As the title suggests, this black-and-white film is a record of work in progress, 'notes' made by Pasolini on a journey to Tanzania and Uganda to look for both locations and players for his proposed film version of Aeschylus' *Oresteia*. Short as the film is, it presents difficulties for audiences who speak no French or Italian, since it has not been subtitled, and other difficulties for those who do, since so much of the film is given up to a recording of what Pasolini hoped would be a jazz–operatic performance intended to accompany the action of the film, and since the music on the soundtrack seems, even to jazz enthusiasts (especially to jazz enthusiasts?), derivative and ineptly performed.[112] The music that we hear throughout the film, interspersed with song from a Russian choir, is taken from a rehearsal for the Cassandra scene in the first play of Aeschylus' trilogy. It is performed by Gato Barbieri's trio, Barbieri being a black South American living in Rome, and sung by a black American, Yvonne Murray, giving what is justifiably described as 'an embarrassing, out-of-it performance'.[113] The point of this emphasis on black jazz musicians is suggested in Pasolini's claim on the soundtrack of the film that it is to be sung, rather than acted, in a jazz idiom, because, he claims, 20 million sub-proletarian black Americans are to be the forerunners of revolution in the Third World.

He detects a parallel between Athens at the time of the Aeschylean trilogy and certain African states, emerging around 1960 from their colonial past after the example of Ghana. For him, *The Oresteia* celebrates the passage of Athens from a feudal to a democratic state. However, Athens' democracy he sees as largely a formal matter, so that the parallelism between her experience and that of African democratic states is intensified. These states have a formal independence and a formal democracy, he believes, but the actuality is that there is socialisation with pro-Chinese tendencies while economic-political penetration by Western imperialism continues, and bloody wars are fought in such states as Angola and Mozambique. (In the film, the Trojan War was to have been represented by the Biafran conflict.)

In his search for players of the ancient characters, he claims that Electra is difficult to find, because young African girls seem to know nothing of hatred or pride. They laugh at life, he believes.[114] Orestes was to have been played by a young student of today. In casting, Pasolini's alleged guiding principle is that the characters must be intensely 'popular'. His film is to be a sort of folk epic. He imagines the Chorus chatting at petrol stations, for example, engaged in mundane activities, but ready to talk of politics. The people, he believes, will provide a mythic, ritualistic element. Factories and schools are included among the settings for his film.

As for the Furies, who are so crucial to the final play in the trilogy, crucial enough for the play to be named after them in their transformed role as guardians of Athens — *The Eumenides* — they are not to be depicted in human form at all, the film tells us. They are to be forces of nature, to be trees or animals, goddesses of the mind. In this film, he presents a montage of sinister-looking trees and of a wounded lioness to make his point. The taming of the Furies is to represent the domestication of primitive nature by agriculture. With their disappearance as fearful powers comes the disappearance of the world of the animal, he states, and so once again the progress of civilisation in Africa suggests itself as a parallel (for the naturalisation, this time, within Athens of the erstwhile Furies).

Although he thinks of Biafra when he considers the Trojan War, Pasolini also states that the wars in his film are to be metaphorical, representing the eternal reality of suffering.

In considering his setting for the new *Oresteia*, he decides to make Athens a composite city out of parts of Dar es Salaam and Kampala.

Pasolini never made his *Oresteia*. The 'notes' for it that are preserved in this film, made after *Oedipus Rex* and shortly before *Medea*, demonstrate what has already been discovered in these films: his fascination with the Third World, linked as it is to the sub-proletarian world of the USA as here, or in *Oedipus* to that of Rome, it appears; his determination to situate his versions of Greek tragedy outside any location that suggests the classical world; his hostility to 'realism', evidenced this time by his decision to make the drama operatic rather than spoken; his concern to situate the questions raised by ancient tragedy in a contemporary context. Pasolini's biographer, Enzo Siciliano, makes a curious link between this film and *Medea* which might well escape the casual observer: the Furies, he says, are the 'monstrous, anthropomorphic roots of the giant trees of the black continent', and 'Medea suggests these configurations by her load of gems and semi-precious stones, of black and bristling garments'.[115]

Pasolini's zeal for apparently exoticising the familiar, classical plays represents the execution of earlier suggestions by anthropologists, it may finally be remarked. Raymond Firth, for example, in 1958, discerns resemblances between Homeric culture and that of Polynesia and other non-literate cultures. For Firth, the value of studying Greek culture is not so much in comprehending the roots of our own culture as in providing a set of contrasts to contemporary Western culture.[116] Pasolini, a decade later, puts these ideas into practice and suggests also that the value of the study of 'Homeric' culture may be not only in providing a set of contrasts to Western culture but also in exposing what is hidden, but coexistent, within that culture.

A Dream of Passion (Director: Jules Dassin, 1978)

Dassin's film appears to be an attempt to explore the relevance of contemporary actuality to a modern production of Euripides' *Medea* and also, to an extent, the relevance of the ancient play to an understanding of contemporary actuality. According to the director, the germs of his idea for the film came from his experience at a trial in Italy of a woman who had murdered her children. He felt sympathy for the infanticide, but only when he saw Melina Mercouri play Medea did what he calls the 'click' come.[117]

In *A Dream of Passion*, a famous Greek actress, Maya (Melina Mercouri), returns to Athens to appear as Medea in a revival of the play. Friction is generated between her and her director (Andreas Voutsinas) when their opinions about the interpretation of the play lead them in different directions. Kostas, the director, believes that tragedy involves the fall of the mighty, whereas Maya looks for contemporary significance in it. It is enough for Kostas that the play involves heroic characters experiencing malign fates, but Maya is dissatisfied, feeling that the play and therefore her performance have not yet been anchored in a modern context. She agrees, in order to provide press coverage of the forthcoming theatre production, to meet the woman dubbed by the Greek newspapers 'the Medea of Glyfada', Brenda Collins (Ellen Burstyn), an American in prison for the murder of the three children born to her and her husband, Roy. The prison visit begins well enough, with Brenda behaving like a humble film fan. 'I sure never thought I'd get to meet a movie star,' she murmurs. Then, the door bursts open and photographers snap the meeting of the two Medeas to the intense annoyance of Brenda who swears at Maya, vowing that she will be punished for her part in this.

Fascinated and guilty because of her thoughtless exploitation of the modern Medea, Maya collects information about Brenda. She reads that her father left the family when she was a girl, leaving her to support her mother till the latter's death. She hears that Brenda was unable to learn Greek and could not fit in once Roy had brought her to Greece, that she had killed the children on Father's Day and had written a letter after the murders, mingling obscenities and quotations from the Bible while she ate a honey cake that she had baked earlier that day.

When Brenda consents to see her again, Maya listens as she reconstructs her feelings about the killings. She is determined not to be thought insane, because she wants her husband to feel her pain and not to take refuge in the thought that she is out of her mind. To prove her point, she tells Maya how she took back to the shop shoes that she had recently bought for her son, since they were as good as new — 'Would I have done that if I was crazy?'

As Maya's identification with Brenda grows, her performance is

more and more affected by it. She declares to the BBC television
team which is recording rehearsal scenes that, if Euripides' heroine
is mad, then we are captivated by her madness. After Brenda tells
of the quasi-religious ritual which she went through in committing
the killings, Maya is profoundly affected. Her playing of the Euripides' heroine in the theatre at Delphi is recorded in a montage
sequence where there is much cross-cutting between the play
rehearsal and Brenda's remembered 're-enactment' of the killings,
intended as her husband's penalty for beating her up and threatening
to leave her for another woman. In the final sequence of the
film, *Medea* is being performed before an audience at Delphi.
Identification between the actress playing Medea and the woman
who was labelled her modern equivalent is now so strong that Maya
and Brenda seem interchangeable, in the manner of the women of
Bergman's *Persona* (1966), a director and film which are expressly
given grateful recognition in the Dassin movie. The black-robed
Chorus stands in a semi-circle as Medea takes her place at the altar.
But it is Brenda who is praying, in her prison cell. The Chorus runs
to Maya as she promises that her children will die. She lifts the
knife. There is an immediate cut to Brenda's hands, clasped in
prayer. 'Go to your destiny,' the Chorus says as Medea walks away.
The Chorus's scream becomes Brenda's as she falls back on to the
floor of the cell. 'This happened here today,' the Chorus leader
pronounces at the end of the play. Brenda lies on the prison floor
in a foetal position.

There are other narrative strands in *A Dream of Passion*. Maya has
had a love affair with her director in the past. She takes a young
lover for one night of pleasure during the rehearsal period, before she
becomes intensely involved with Brenda. Her treachery to another
woman involved with the play production, Maria (Despo Diamanti-
dou), is recalled and exorcised in a sequence where the conviviality
of a late-night party becomes a series of confessions for the television
camera.

Nevertheless, the relation of actuality to a modern revival of the
ancient play seems a crucial question in the film. Critics of the
film seem bewildered by this element and, in their bewilderment,
oversimplify or unfairly import elements which have little to do with
the narrative as given.

Richard Schickel, having stated that 'nothing very vital is added
to anyone's understanding of that classic figure [Medea]', proceeds

to attack Mercouri's performance, as involving 'much eye-rolling, teeth-baring and anguished screeching'.[118] A number of assumptions could be questioned here. Perhaps the film does not attempt to provide further understanding of Medea, but to explore the relevance of the revivification of that heroine in a time where tragedy seems irrevocably of the past. A theatrical performance may well look intolerable when photographed as a documentary (by a TV crew, as here, for example). In any case, as her understanding of Brenda grows, Maya's performance becomes quieter, more understated and introspective. The eye-rolling, teeth-baring performance is much more likely to be that encouraged by Kostas in the belief that he is dealing with heroic myth and heroic characters. Schickel also complains of Maya's self-absorption. We are being shown, however, an actress contemplating her art, in a film which advertises its own relation with *Persona* and where conversations about Maya's ageing in relation to her performance in *Sweet Bird of Youth* or about improvisation in relation to Brando's performance in *Last Tango in Paris* crop up 'naturally'. The movie is as much about movie-making as it is about infanticide. Maya is self-absorbed as all the characters are, Brenda in her self-justification for infanticide, the cast and crew and TV documentarists in the progress of the play around which the action revolves.

Derek Malcolm condemns the film by claiming that 'what might have made a good simple melodrama is stuck with the trappings of fake tragedy'.[119] This seems a familiar technique in newspaper film reviews. If the critic doesn't appreciate the film as it stands, the assumption is that it ought to have been something else. *A Dream of Passion is* melodrama, whether good, simple or otherwise. It is also *about* tragedy, rather than stuck with its trappings. 'Fake' is puzzling. Presumably, Euripides' original is not fake. If not, then the film must be a fake tragedy. Why is Malcolm sure that it is a tragedy, fake or otherwise? If it is, why is it 'fake'?

Martyn Auty argues that 'Dassin's film fails to demonstrate how the parallel between a "real life" incident and the classical tragedy might illuminate Euripides' text for a modern audience.'[120] This alleged failure may be attributable to the certainty that it is Euripides' text which the film addresses. The characters Maya and Kostas certainly argue about that text and its modern interpretation. For Kostas, it stands as it always did: an undoubted tragedy dealing with heroic failure in a heroic setting. This view has already been cast in doubt in a filmic context with Pasolini's *Medea*. In the present

film, Maya is driven to find a reason for the play's performance.[121]
Auty is convinced that the film claims illumination of Euripides
through Maya's sense of identity, in her performance, with Brenda.
The ending of the film is far more open than this interpretation
would suggest, however. Brenda has explained all, as it were, but
nothing is explained. She has not been reconciled with herself,
despite the catharsis expected of her reliving of the murders. Is she
crazy? we may ask in the simple language that she herself uses.
Maya seems to believe that she is not, persuaded by Brenda's own
confidence in her rationality. Yet, Brenda's proofs of her sanity
seem to suggest the opposite, and her collapse in the last sequence
into an unreasoning foetus undermines much that seems to have
preceded. The play in its modern performance has become a catalyst
for Maya's psychological development (or regression, to press the
parallel with Brenda's psychology). It is possible that we are not
illuminated about the validity of Maya's rendering of Medea any
more than we are about the rationality or otherwise of Brenda's
thought processes in killing the children. The recognition of ancient
tragedy as a catalyst (as it is most obviously to Pasolini) should
make the film of interest, even to those who refuse to be absorbed
in what have been taken to be Mercouri's egotistical concerns.[122]
Auty talks of the cultural trap 'of updating the classics'.[123] Why
this should be a trap is left unexplored, but, if it is, it is a trap that
Maya falls into rather than Dassin's film.

A more generous critic claims that the film makes us suddenly
aware of something that the ancients knew well — that fate is
nothing else but the passion and despair which inhabit a person.
This is, it is claimed, what Jules Dassin makes Maya discover
gradually. In her contact with Brenda, she discovers the other, 'le
respect de l'autre, l'amour de l'autre'.[124]

If this sort of analysis has any validity, the film, while being
overtly about the place of tragedy in modern life, also considers the
moral education of an actress with a seriousness of tone that is not
out of place in melodrama and which suggests aspirations to modern
tragedy.

The Pasolini and Dassin films analysed in this chapter ask questions
whose answers are so often assumed by critics hostile to the project
of filming Greek tragedy in any form. Why bother resurrecting such
long-dead works? What relevance has ancient tragedy to modern

concerns? If a modern tragedy were realisable, what would it be like?

Pasolini suggests in *Oedipus Rex* and *Medea* that Greek tragedy in anything like its original context is indeed dead. The cultural history which is our modern heritage may, however, illuminate much that was absent from or latent in Greek drama. Thus, the familiar (for the educated) becomes bizarre and exotic, and particularly unfamiliar to the classically educated. His technique is both to defamiliarise the celebrated works of Sophocles and Euripides and also to return to the roots of these plays' narratives, to reinvestigate the significance of these with a freedom that the ancient tragedians themselves habitually enjoyed in their dramatisation of heroic myth. Dassin's film leaves the questions more open. The modern theatrical production within the film has a director which expects an audience to project itself backwards into fifth-century BC Athens, to respect the play's antiquity and to ask for no 'updating' of its concerns and conventions. It has a leading lady who wants psychological insight, contemporary relevance. What the Delphi audience for her interpretation experiences is as mysterious as Brenda's own experience of the drama in which she has taken a central part. All of these films ensure at least that questions go on being asked.

Modern tragedy, to judge by these films, is a complex matter. If *A Dream of Passion*, and such Cacoyannis films as *Iphigenia*, seem close to melodrama today, this may be because melodrama holds the place in cinema which tragedy once occupied in theatre. A modern film which is about tragedy may itself be a new kind of tragedy. Pasolini takes Oedipus' story and makes it his own, while also extending it to illuminate the helplessness of Western humanity at this point in its intellectual history. Dassin reminds us of the opacity of certain tragic drama. Against the view that tragedy crystallises and educates is the awareness that Euripidean drama, at least, involves its spectators in ambiguity, uncertainty, a sense of the futility of attempts at rational analysis of the human psyche. In tackling the same play, Pasolini liberates Medea from her alien rationalist setting and explores the story as an example of the impossibility of accommodation of the pre-rational to the rational.

On the evidence of these films, modern tragedy must be self-conscious, reflexive, confusing. In questioning the relevance of ancient tragedy to a contemporary setting, it inevitably questions its own existence, and makes these questions the nucleus of the new drama.

Notes

1. Marc Gervais, *Pier Paolo Pasolini*, Cinéma d'aujourdhui (Editions Seghers, 1973), p. 72.
2. Herbert J. Muller, *The Spirit of Tragedy* (Knopf, 1956), p. 56.
3. Ibid., p. 100.
4. Francis Fergusson, quoted ibid., pp. 89–90.
5. Clyde Kluckhorn, *Anthropology and the Classics* (Brown University Press, 1961), pp. 15–16.
6. 'Edipo Re', *Cahiers du Cinéma*, no. 195, November 1967, p. 28.
7. Sigmund Freud, quoted in Ekbert Faas, *Tragedy and After: Euripides, Shakespeare, Goethe* (McGill-Queen's University Press, 1984), p. 182.
8. Ibid., p. 183.
9. Oliver Taplin, 'The Delphic Idea and after', *The Times Literary Supplement*, 17 July 1981, p. 812.
10. Barthélemy Amengual, 'Quand le mythe console de l'histoire: *Oedipe Roi*', in Michel Estève (ed.), *Pier Paolo Pasolini: le mythe et le sacré* (Minard, 1976), p. 75.
11. Ibid., pp. 75–6.
12. Muller, *The Spirit of Tragedy*, p. 99.
13. Ibid., p. 99.
14. Ibid., p. 99.
15. Amengual, 'Quand le mythe console de l'histoire', p. 77.
16. Raymond Durgnat, *Sexual Alienation in the Cinema* (Studio Vista, 1972), p. 221.
17. Dominique Noguez, 'L'Oedipe de Pasolini', *ça*, October 1973, p. 103.
18. Pier Paolo Pasolini, *Oedipus Rex*, tr. John Mathews (Lorrimer Publishing, 1971), p. 8.
19. Ibid., p. 9.
20. Oswald Stack, *Pasolini on Pasolini* (Thames & Hudson/British Film Institute, 1969), p. 119.
21. Ibid., p. 120.
22. Ibid., p. 120.
23. Noguez, 'L'Oedipe de Pasolini', p. 103.
24. Stephen Snyder, *Pier Paolo Pasolini* (Twayne Publishers, 1980), p. 22.
25. Enzo Siciliano, *Pasolini: a biography*, tr. John Shepley (Random House, 1982), p. 305.
26. Robert J. White, 'Myth and *mise-en-scène*: Pasolini's *Edipo Re*', *Literature/Film Quarterly*, vol. 5, No. 1, Winter 1977, p. 31.
27. Ibid., p. 35.
28. Ibid., p. 35.
29. White's argument seems sound, except in a point of detail where he tries to establish Oedipus' amorality by pointing to the savage love scene following Tiresias' revelations, which, he says, is full of the 'excitement of sacrilege'. Although White is following Pasolini's lead in this interpretation, it is hard to square the 'excitement of sacrilege' with amorality rather than immorality (since this would demand that Oedipus had internalised enough bourgeois morality to recognise sacrilege, and therefore the excitement of it).
30. Siciliano, *Pasolini: a biography*, p. 305.
31. Gervais, *Pier Paolo Pasolini*, p. 71.
32. White, 'Pasolini's *Edipo Re*', p. 30.
33. Ibid., pp. 31–2.
34. Ibid., p. 34.
35. Snyder, *Pier Paolo Pasolini*, p. 87.
36. Ibid., p. 91.

37. Amengual, 'Quand le mythe console de l'histoire', p. 96.

38. Pasolini, *Oedipus Rex*, p. 69.

39. *'Oedipe-Roi'*, *Art et Essai*, no. 49, 30 October 1968, p. 20.

40. Pasolini, *Oedipus Rex*, p. 51.

41. Jean Narboni, 'Rencontre avec Pier Paolo Pasolini', *Cahiers du Cinéma*, no. 192, July–August 1967, p. 31.

42. Noguez, 'L'Oedipe de Pasolini', p. 99.

43. Ibid., p. 99.

44. Guido Aristarco, quoted in Gervais, *Pier Paolo Pasolini*, p. 79.

45. Noguez, 'L'Oedipe de Pasolini', p. 100.

46. Gervais, *Pier Paolo Pasolini*, p. 78.

47. Amengual, 'Quand le mythe console de l'histoire', pp. 78–9.

48. Ibid., pp. 91, 94.

49. Narboni, 'Rencontre avec Pier Paolo Pasolini', p. 31.

50. Siciliano, *Pasolini: a biography*, p. 305.

51. Pasolini, *Oedipux Rex*, p. 9.

52. Amengual, p. 90.

53. Snyder, *Pier Paolo Pasolini*, p. 21.

54. Amengual, 'Quand le mythe console de l'histoire', p. 91.

55. Ibid., p. 95.

56. Peter Wollen, *Readings and Writings: Semiotic Counter-Strategies* (Verso Editions and NLB, 1982), p. 136.

57. Pasolini, *Oedipux Rex*, p. 17.

58. Durgnat, *Sexual Alienation in the Cinema*, p. 220.

59. Snyder, *Pier Paolo Pasolini*, p. 88.

60. Taplin, 'Delphic Idea' p. 812.

61. Geoffrey Nowell-Smith, in Paul Willemen (ed.), *Pier Paolo Pasolini* (British Film Institute, 1977).

62. Ibid., p. 14.

63. Amengual, 'Quand le mythe console de l'histoire', p. 86.

64. Ibid., p. 89.

65. David Wilson, *Monthly Film Bulletin*, July 1969.

66. Amengual, 'Quand le mythe console de l'histoire', p. 80.

67. Gervais, *Pier Paolo Pasolini*, p. 73.

68. Stack, *Pasolini on Pasolini*, pp. 126–7.

69. Pasolini, *Oedipus Rex*, p. 14.

70. Durgnat, *Sexual Alienation in the Cinema*, p. 225.

71. Gervais, *Pier Paolo Pasolini*, p. 74.

72. Ibid., p. 74.

73. Stack, *Pasolini on Pasolini*, p. 129.

74. Gervais, *Pier Paolo Pasolini*, p. 74.

75. Amengual, 'Quand le mythe console de l'histoire', p. 97.

76. *Pasolini: Séminaire dirigé par Maria Antonietta Macciocchi* (Bernard Grasset, 1980), p. 137.

77. Pasolini, *Oedipus Rex*, p. 9.

78. Elie Maakaroun, 'Pasolini face au sacré ou l'exorciste possédé', in Michel Estève (ed.), *Pier Paolo Pasolini*, p. 44.

79. Durgnat, *Sexual Alienation in the Cinema*, p. 228.

80. Amengual, 'Quand le mythe console de l'histoire', p. 84.

81. Durgnat, *Sexual Alienation in the Cinema*, p. 228.

82. Guido Piovene, quoted in Siciliano, p. 306.

83. Derek Malcolm, *Guardian*, 24 April 1975; and compare John Russell Taylor, *Directors and Directions* (Eyre Methuen, 1975), p. 62, who describes *Medea* as a

retelling of classical myth on almost exactly the same lines as *Edipo Re*, except for the explicit drawing of a modern parallel in the latter.

84. Nigel Gearing, *Monthly Film Bulletin*, June 1975.

85. Richard Combs, *Financial Times*, 25 April 1975.

86. John Russell Taylor, p. 63.

87. Jean Duflot, *Entretiens avec Pier Paolo Pasolini* (Editions Pierre Belfond, 1970), p. 111.

88. Combs, (see Note 85).

89. Gervais, *Pier Paolo Pasolini*, p. 109.

90. Duflot, *Entretiens avec Pier Paolo Pasolini*, p. 111.

91. Siciliano, *Pasolini: a biography*, p. 332.

92. 'Entretien avec Pasolini', *Jeune Cinéma*, no. 45, March 1979, p. 20.

93. Siciliano, *Pasolini: a biography*, p. 332.

94. Gervais, *Pier Paolo Pasolini*, p. 111.

95. 'Entretien avec Pasolini', p. 20.

96. Gervais, *Pier Paolo Pasolini*, p. 111.

97. Durgnat, *Sexual Alienation in the Cinema*, p. 228.

98. Duflot, *Entretiens avec Pier Paolo Pasolini*, p. 112.

99. Ibid., p. 112.

100. Ibid., p. 113.

101. Ibid., p. 113.

102. Ibid., pp. 113–14.

103. Snyder, *Pier Paolo Pasolini*, p. 29.

104. Ibid., p. 95.

105. Derek Elley, 'Medea', *Films and Filming*, vol. 21, no. 10, July 1975, p. 45.

106. Gervais, *Pier Paolo Pasolini*, p. 109.

107. Snyder, *Pier Paolo Pasolini*, p. 95.

108. Duflot, *Entretiens avec Pier Paolo Pasolini*, p. 113.

109. Snyder, *Pier Paolo Pasolini*, p. 97.

110. Taplin, 'Delphic Idea', p. 812.

111. Gervais, *Pier Paolo Pasolini*, p. 111.

112. See 'Appunti Per Un'Orestiade Africana', *Variety*, 21 January 1981, p. 27.

113. Ibid.

114. Claude-Marie Trémois, 'Carnet de notes pour une Orestie africaine', *Télérama*, 6 November 1976.

115. Siciliano, *Pasolini: a biography*, p. 332.

116. Kluckhorn, *Anthropology and the Classics*, p. 15.

117. *Production Information* (Coline, Paris).

118. Richard Schickel, *Time*, 11 September 1976.

119. Derek Malcolm, *Guardian*, 1 February 1979.

120. Martyn Auty, '*A Dream of Passion*', *Monthly Film Bulletin*, vol. 46, no. 542, March 1979, p. 43.

121. We might recall that it is during a performance of *Electra* that the actress heroine of *Persona* is struck dumb.

122. See, for example, Patrick Gibbs, *Daily Telegraph*, 2 February 1979.

123. Auty, *A Dream of Passion*, p. 43.

124. Claude-Marie Trémois, 'Cri de femmes', *Télérama*, 16–22 September 1978, no. 1496, p. 79.

8 CONCLUSION

If Greek tragedy is dead and buried, as critics hostile to individual films from the selection of previous chapters occasionally insist, both theatre producers and film directors seem slow to accept its interment. A review of the films made in the 1960s and 1970s alone would seem to undermine the judgement. These have been relatively few in number, admittedly, but the commerical success of *Phaedra,* the involvement of such world-class 'auteurs' as Pasolini and Jancsó in the project of filming Greek tragedy, and the obvious fascination which that project holds for Cacoyannis, Pasolini and Dassin, in that they return to it after an initial attempt, combine to make the insistence on Greek tragedy's 'irrelevance' seem perverse.

What is clear, however, is that the notion of 'fidelity' to the originals is doomed, to judge by the range of tactics adopted by the film-makers. The evidence of the so-called theatrical film is that the staging of Greek tragedy largely involves a considerable reworking of the original material, not just in the obvious sense that the verbal element is translated into modern languages, including modern Greek. Against the Epidauros or Delphi productions preserved on film, which themselves depart significantly from what we would surmise the original productions to have been, we have to set an *Oedipus Rex* which renders strange the classical tragedy central to Aristotle's *Poetics* by using basically Hellenistic (later) techniques, or an *Electra* which substitutes intimacy for distance. These records of theatrical productions usefully remind us that tragedy is not only about the stimulation of pity and fear to encourage catharsis in the audience — Aristotle's opinion about the function of tragedy. For while it seems to apply admirably to Sophocles' *Oedipus Rex,* for example, it is difficult to believe that it could be seen as so persuasive in relation to Aeschylean tragedy or to the 'anti-tragic' areas of Euripides. Those films which seem to 'work', to implicate spectators emotionally, are thought by many reviewers to be most successful. Yet, Cacoyannis's Euripidean films seem less Euripidean than Sophoclean. If Euripides may plausibly be called 'anti-tragic' in his *Electra,* for example, Cacoyannis is 'anti-Euripidean' by virtue of being more 'tragic' than that writer. If a film encourages audience identification

165

by the conversion of tragedy into melodrama, especially modern-dress melodrama, critical approval is generally denied it. Dassin's *Phaedra* or, to a less obvious extent, his *A Dream of Passion,* do seem to make contact with the audience's emotions by emphasising interpersonal relationships and questions of love, in the sense of both ĕros and agapĕ, at the expense of destiny and heroic values. Their frankness about their methods does not endear them to reviewers, however. Cacoyannis's *Electra* has the advantage of looking like a Greek tragedy, while Dassin's *Phaedra* does not. That advantage is so important that even knowledgeable spectators seem less interested in 'fidelity', do not seem disposed even to search for it, provided the modern film at least looks like the real thing.

Most of the films in Chapters 6 and 7 have been attacked at one time or another for allegedly having little or nothing to do with the plays on which they are based. One aspect, however, that does link the film-makers with the tragedians who wrote the assumed or declared originals for these films is their attitude to heroic myth. The fifth-century tragedians seem to have invested heroic tales with significances and emphases that could not possibly have been theirs originally. Aeschylus uses the story of Orestes' killing of his mother and Aegisthus to settle the conflict of chthonic and democratic law, for example. 'Timeless' deities perform democratic functions within contemporary, Athenian institutions. Thus, Athena presides over Orestes' trial before a jury of Athenian citizens in the Court of the Areopagus. Euripides re-examines the tale of Orestes' revenge in a way that seems largely inconsistent with Aeschylus' *Oresteia,* and certainly inconsistent with the heroic myth. He emphasises the squalor of the motives — as of the setting in which Clytemnestra's murder takes place — and asserts the physicality of the matricide, more or less divesting it of moral or 'historical' significance of the sort which Aeschylus gives it. Euripides appears to invite his audience to think of what the physical act of mother-killing involves, how it affects its perpetrators psychologically, rather than ethically.

No modern or ancient commentator wastes his or her time complaining that the original story was not like that, when the commentator writes about *The Oresteia* or Euripides' *Electra.* Yet, those directors, often their own scriptwriters, who radically alter ancient tragedy in turn, are lacerated for so doing. At best, their practice may be condemned on the already noted ground that the material is mummified. Euripides' *Electra* not only rewrites the Orestes story but takes time to parody Aeschylus in the recognition scene. Yet, when Liliana Cavani gives Antigone an accomplice in Tiresias, or turns Sophocles' solitary, heroic act of brother-burial into an absurd but humanitarian impulse to bury as many rotting corpses as possible, it is pointed out that she thus betrays Sophocles, and little more is said. Having been caught out in her misconduct, she need not detain the critic further, it seems. When Pasolini declares, by making Sophocles' play only one part (less than half!) of his film, *Oedipus Rex,* that he is not simply making a film of the play, an extraordinary set of accusations are levelled against him, one of these being that this is not Sophocles' tragedy. Pasolini's conception of Oedipus could seem to be re-heroising him, if we take Homeric society in the way that anthropology might suggest that we do (see p. 156). Yet, in getting closer to heroic society, Pasolini runs the risk of castigation by classical scholars because he has largely abandoned Sophocles. In the new context, the snatches of Sophocles' dialogue heard in Section 3 of the film do admittedly seem as bizarre as the scenes from Shakespeare's *Hamlet* that suddenly irrupt into the world of Tom Stoppard's *Rosencrantz and Guildenstern are Dead.* Not more bizarre, though, than they might have seemed to a public that knew nothing of Oedipus but what the oral tradition had told them. Freud has nothing to offer in elucidation of Sophocles' play, we are assured, at the same time as we are told that Pasolini's film is manifestly not Sophocles' play. Freud may, though, have something to offer in elucidation of twentieth-century interpretations of Sophocles' play.

Cacoyannis's films are permitted some relevance to the 'tragic experience', but the so-called meta-tragedies, of Chapter 7, since they are meditations on the ancient plays, seem to be viewed as incapable of providing anything of the sort. Jancsó's *Elektreia* has changed the story of Electra by safely killing off Clytemnestra before Orestes' return. Therefore, it seems to be assumed, because this is not any of the Electra tragedies, it cannot provide a 'tragic experience' — a curious judgement, when the power of choreography, the role of instrumental music and choral song in drama, have seldom been more directly suggested.

This investigation of films of Greek tragedy has become also an investigation of their reception. The tenacity with which 'realism' has been privileged in attitudes to film has seldom been more clearly illustrated than in the enthusiasm for the theatrical- and realistic-mode films in sharp contrast to the distrust of and aversion to the filmic-mode works. This preference may be rationalised by appeals

to 'fidelity', but faithfulness to a source is viewed as of little consequence within a realist framework as is admirably demonstrated by
general attitudes to the Cacoyannis films. The privileging of 'realism'
is no surprise in itself. What is astonishing is that it should be so
privileged in the context of a genre which has so little to do with
realism as it is popularly understood today and whose formalism
has always raised obstacles to even the Aristotelian conception of
tragedy as mimetic.

Far from being a doomed enterprise, the filming of Greek tragedy
seems on the evidence of the films considered not only to be
'dramatically viable' but also to raise important general questions
about the relation of high to popular art, about the necessity or
otherwise of 'realism' as a mode of cinematic expression, and about
the problem of spectator/event relation in 'filmed theatre'.

Greek tragedy is a curious balance of the traditional, the personal
and the universal. As long as the heroic myths which provide the
basis of Greek tragedy may be interpreted on Jungian lines as
strands of our collective unconscious, as long as contemporary
authorial cinema follows the practice of making narrative sustain
the 'personal statement', inviting a complicit audience to detect
personal commentary in a broadly generic story, Greek tragedy may
continue to be filmed. If it does not, the films already made are
adequate testimony to the variety of interpretation and treatment
possible in the filming of Greek tragedy.

APPENDIX A: ANCIENT GREEK COMEDY INTO FILM

It is possible to argue, as David Wilson does, that ancient Greek comedy, 'with its audacious political satire, its bawdy, phallocentric jokes, its verbal and visual puns' is 'remarkably "modern"'.[1] It is also possible to see why Aristophanes, the only playwright from the tradition of Old Comedy (which is here described) to survive in bulk, resists modern production. The political satire is very much of its time, a sort of dramatised *Private Eye* of fifth-century BC Athens. Appreciation of Old Comedy's invective largely depends on knowledge of the personalities, whether politicians, poets or philosophers, inveighed against. The jokes are indeed bawdy. Their phallocentricity is well-motivated, in the sense that imitation *phalloi* are worn (some would argue carried) by the actors, and that Old Comedy may well be a development of phallic revels. In other words, the phallocentricity is based on an open acceptance of, or rather an open glorying in, the potency of the phallus, whereas in our society the phallus itself appears in symbolic, not normally actual, form in drama and film, while phallocentricity is frequently questioned or attacked for its socio-political consequences. For verbal and visual puns to work, knowledge of the original language or the original points of reference is highly desirable. Such puns are effective in modern production only if there is wholesale translation, not simply in the obvious linguistic terms but in terms of references, since Aristophanes' visual puns normally assume acquaintance with pesons or activities long ago defunct.

The problem with Menander, the principal surviving Greek exponent of New Comedy, is quite different. New Comedy which flourished from the last three decades of the fourth century BC onwards, abandons personal, topical lampoons and seems to avoid any direct commentary on contemporary society, preferring to entertain by virtue of its intrigues, the complications of plot as they affect a group of people who seem to become stock characters — the young man in love, the maiden whose birth and background are unknown at the play's beginning, the irascible old man, the quick-witted slave, for example. The world of New Comedy is only vaguely Greek (the setting is often outside Greece proper, being part of the Hellenised world of the Mediterranean), so that translation into other times and places is comparatively easy. The problem is that Menander is one of the earliest and most influential exponents of what today might be called situation comedy. In an age when slavery is a less common phenomenon and when the barriers to love's fulfilment are not so overly a matter of class, the situations of Menandrian comedy do not seem so interesting, let alone funny, because they appear more remote. Situation comedy strives for an appearance of 'normality' and 'credibility', within a very narrowly bounded understanding of these terms. Television situation comedy in Britain and the USA seems generally to centre on the middle-class nuclear family living in suburbia, although there have been notable ventures in other directions. Some of the aspects of daily existence which would seem 'normal' and 'credible' within the sub-genre of Greek New Comedy would be bizarre in modern sit-com. Menandrian comedy is at once too universalised and too localised to be easily capable of production today.

The National Film Theatre season, 'Greek Comedy: Ancient and Modern', which took place in March 1984, came up with only three films, all Greek, in which any relation with ancient comedy could be claimed. Two of these were based on Aristophanic comedy, while one has been argued to be derived from Menander's *Dyskolos*.

Lysistrata (Director: Yorgos Zervoulakos, 1972)

This film of what is today possibly Aristophanes' most celebrated comedy was made during the military junta of the Colonels; the original was produced at a time when Athenian confidence in the prosecution of the Peloponnesian War was likely to have been wavering. It seems to have represented a plea for peace, albeit in terms of fantasy, and for greater attention to be paid to women's viewpoints, achieved in the play by the withholding of sexual favours. The film attempts a 'realistic mode' of presentation of the ancient play. The action is shot underneath the Acropolis itself, often making use of the ancient-looking but clearly recently old streets of the Plaka district of Athens. The emphasis is on the notion of female emancipation as sheer good-natured fantasy, devoid of serious potential. In this, the film is following Aristophanes' lead, but it seems today not coincidental that the notion of sexual equality should be treated as amusing, devoid of credibility. 'Long live

Lysistrata! You have won!' the Chorus cries out near the end of the film. Her victory is celebrated with mass (but marital) copulation in the fields of Attica, and is immediately followed with an end-title, indicating that this was simply a fantasy that did not work: 'But no one listened to what the women in Athens did.'

The emphasis on 'escapism' is sustained throughout the film, in, for example, a blithe disregard for the precision of the time period, in both setting and costume. A car is seen moving along in the background during Lysistrata's first dance with the Chorus of women. The streets of Plaka have their modern blue street signs intact. The barricade erected to hold back the rebellious women from the Acropolis has an American flag on it, while some of the women have ban-the-bomb emblems on their panties. This eclecticism is reflected in the Latin-American rhythms heard in Stavros Xarchakos' music at the point where Lysistrata (Jenni Karezi) mentions Latin lovers. Lysistrata talks of 'the paper tiger of Male Imperialism'. Elsewhere, the question of Athenian imperialism is translated into questions of Greco–Athenian–Cretan culture.

The eclecticism of the time period for the action allows for some formal experiment within the film. For example, at one point where male and female Choruses confront each other, the men enter in single file exactly like shadow-play characters. This entrance is intercut with a real shadow play. Then, the women enter from the opposite side of the frame, again in shadow-play single file, making movements that are reminiscent of those in this form of entertainment. Song and dance are as important a part of this film comedy as they must have been originally. Soloist and Chorus are differentiated too, in a way broadly reminiscent of ancient comedy.

Lysistrata is conceived here as an entertainment which, despite its (in context) daringly irreverent references to American imperialism, for example, defuses any threat by foregrounding the fantasy elements of Old Comedy. The emancipation of women and the toppling of power structures within and without the Greek state are treated as amusing impossibilities. The charm of the film cancels out the potential in *Lysistrata* for questioning the way things are in the Colonels' Athens.

The Acharnians (Director: Mimis Kouyioumtzis, 1976)

While *Lysistrata* takes Aristophanes' comedy outside the theatre into the streets of Athens, this film is a record of Karolos Koun's production in the summer of 1976 of Aristophanes' *The Acharnians* at the ancient theatre of Epidauros. Aristophanes' play involves the comic exploration of a 'private peace' between the hero, Dikaiopolis, and the Spartans, with whom Athens has been prosecuting war for some years.

The film indicates the freedom and inventiveness of the stage production, including as it does verbal references to the Colonels and the to the CIA. A device frequently used in the production is, as in *Lysistrata*, visual reference to the shadow-play, whereby characters stand in profile in puppet-like positions behind a curtain through which their silhouettes may be seen, until the curtain is drawn back and further action may commence. The device suggests the tenuous relation of characters and issues to actuality. Masks are used, as in the ancient production, for the appearances of such groups as the Persians. Costumes are eclectic — parasols and pumpkins for the Chorus, patchwork clothes for the Persians, Homeric-style costume for Lamachos, for example. There are references to the ancient world of drama, in the way that Euripides is discovered on a crude version of the ancient crane (on which the *deus ex machina* is supposed to have entered), for example, or the location of Euripides' house on the *skene* roof.

The Virgin (Director: Dimis Dadiras, 1966)

The point of the title is partly lost in English translation. The Greek title for the film, *O Parthenos,* makes it clear, by the use of the masculine definite article, that the virgin is male. Although the object of female attention, any consummation of desire is blocked by the formidable opposition of the boy's (Alkis Yannakas) over-protective mother (Sappho Notara).

A pretty-looking entertainment, shot on the island of Naxos, the film seems to offer a rustic, Greek variant on the sit-com rather than to be recognisable in relation to Menander's *Dyskolos* from which it has, according to the credits, been freely adapted. The bad-tempered misanthrope of that ancient comedy has been turned into a shrewish mother. While the basic elements of love between young boy and girl being denied consummation by a domineering parent make their appearance here, these plot components have become so generalised in the intervening centuries that it would be well-nigh impossible to discern a relationship between this film and the Menander New Comedy unless it were pointed out. Even then, the claimed relationship seems extremely tenuous. The restoration of male supremacy at the film's end by the young hero's answering back to his mother and his slapping of his new bride, to her delight, seems to have more to do with Shakespeare's *Taming of the Shrew* or John Ford's *The Quiet Man* (1952) than Menander.

Note

1. David Wilson, 'Greek Comedy: Ancient and Modern', National Film Theatre programme notes, March 1984.

APPENDIX B: BRIEF SYNOPSES OF ANCIENT PLAYS ON WHICH FILMS HAVE BEEN BASED[1]

The Persians (Aeschylus, 472 BC)

This, along with Phrynichus' lost *Sack of Miletus,* seems to be a most exceptional fifth-century BC tragedy, in that it is based on recent history. The action takes place at the Persian court and centres on its reactions to what is presented as the almost exclusively Athenian victory of Salamis (480 BC). Principal characters are Atossa, the queen, and her son, Xerxes, but a notable appearance is also made by the ghost of Darius. '*The Persians* is perhaps the least dramatic of all Greek tragedies. There is no basic conflict, although the emotional tone intensifies as the play progresses. The plot is one of tragic discovery rather than tragic decision.'[2]

Prometheus Bound (date and author uncertain; popularly attributed to Aeschylus)

In the most obvious sense, this is a static drama in that its principal character is bound to a cliff on the remote corners of the world by Zeus' orders at the beginning of the play and remains there until the cataclysm which ends it. It is also episodic, in that it is made up of a number of encounters between Prometheus and other characters, or between Prometheus and the Chorus, during each of which Zeus' tyranny and sense of insecurity are brought out. Prometheus' pinioning to the rock is intended as a punishment for his theft of fire to help mortals. Hephaestus, the smith god, reluctantly carries out Zeus' demand that he be riveted there in the first episode of the play. Prometheus is accorded sympathy by the Chorus of daughters of Oceanus; is offered advice about the importance of recognising his limitations in relation to the supreme power, Zeus, by Oceanus; acts as comforter to Io when he prophesies her release from torment; and is finally admonished by Hermes, who urges him to bow to the will of Zeus. The play ends with Prometheus being cast into Tartarus for refusing to comply.

Oresteia (Aeschylus, 458 BC)

The three plays of this trilogy, the only trilogy to survive from classical times, are *Agamemnon, The Libation Bearers* and *The Eumenides*. The first play concerns the return of Agamemnon with his captive Cassandra to Argos after his victory at Troy. He is murdered by his wife Clytemnestra in league with her paramour, Aegisthus. In the second play, Orestes returns to take revenge on the murderous couple. In the first half of the play, he and his sister, Electra, invoke the shade of their slain father, while in the second half both Aegisthus and Clytemnestra are dispatched by Orestes, accompanied by his friend Pylades. The play ends with Orestes' growing unease as he becomes aware of the presence of the Furies. The final play deals with the Furies' demand for vengeance for the blood of Clytemnestra. Orestes has taken refuge at Delphi, but is sent to Athens where, before the Court of the Areopagus, the case against him is heard. Apollo defends Orestes, while Athena presides over the court. The human jurors' vote is indecisive and acquittal is decreed only on the basis of Athena's casting vote. The Furies, by the force of Athena's persuasion, relinquish their sense of grievance and agree to becoming the Eumenides, the kindly-disposed ones whose new role is to protect Athens and her institutions.

Antigone (Sophocles, *c.* 441 BC)

The play opens with a discussion between Antigone and her more conventionally-minded sister, Ismene, in which it is made obvious that the former is determined to disobey the decree of their uncle, Creon, the new ruler of Thebes, forbidding burial to Antigone's brother Polynices as punishment for bringing a foreign army against Thebes. Captured during her act of burial, Antigone argues her devotion to divine law against Creon's insistence on his demand for obedience to strengthen state security. Despite interventions by Ismene and Antigone's betrothed, Haemon, Creon's son, she is led off to perpetual captivity in a rock prison. Finally persuaded to undo the wrong which he has committed, Creon arrives too late after performing the burial which Antigone had begun. She has committed suicide as does Haemon and, later, his wife Eurydice.

Oedipus Rex (Sophocles, date uncertain — 420s[?])

As a result of an outbreak of plague in Thebes, its ruler, Oedipus, is beseeched to find a cure for the city's ills. Creon returns from Delphi with the demand that the polluter who killed the former king, Laius, should be expelled from Thebes. Oedipus, after formally pronouncing a curse on the malefactor, pursues a relentless investigation into the circumstances of Laius' death which eventually proves that he himself is the killer of his own father and that he is now living in wedlock with his natural mother. Jocasta, his wife/mother, commits suicide within the palace. Oedipus, polluted through no conscious knowledge on his part, puts out his eyes and bids farewell to his daughters and kingdom.

Electra (Sophocles, date uncertain)

Electra is implacably opposed to the rule of her mother, Clytemnestra, and consort, Aegisthus, who have gained the throne by the murder of Agamemnon. Her weaker sister, Chrysothemis, counsels submission to the present powers but Antigone is determined to wait for Orestes' return so that justice may be done. Electra is grief-stricken when a false report of Orestes' death is brought. When she learns of the reasons for the false tale and is reunited with the returned Orestes, she encourages him to carry out the killings. Clytemnestra is first put to death and at the end of the play Aegisthus is lured into a trap from which he will not emerge alive.

Oedipus at Colonus (Sophocles, posthumously produced, 401 BC)

After long wanderings with his daughter Antigone, Oedipus recognises that he has come to the end of his travels when he reaches the grove of the Eumenides, at Colonus, near Athens. He has to persuade the Chorus and Theseus, ruler of Athens, that he is a fit person to enjoy the protection of the grove. This he does by stressing his innocence of intention although he has incurred pollution. Polynices attempts to argue for the return of Oedipus' body to Thebes, so that he may secure the throne by virtue of its mystical powers, but Oedipus rejects him. The play ends with the miraculous passing of Oedipus into the earth, and the granting of his power after death to Athens.

Medea (Euripides, 431 BC)

In order to secure a place for himself and his sons in Corinth, Jason proposes to put away Medea in favour of a marriage with Glauce, daughter of the king of Corinth. Medea's fury at the rejection nearly results in her immediate expulsion from Corinth by the king, but he is persuaded to relent. Both he and Glauce die as a result of deadly gifts sent by Medea to her rival, and her revenge on Jason is completed when she kills their two sons. At the end, she glories in her abasement of Jason and departs in her sun chariot.

Hippolytus (Euripides, 428 BC)

To fulfil her plan to punish Hippolytus for his devotion to Artemis, Aphrodite inspires passion for him in his stepmother, Phaedra. To relieve her love-sickness, Phaedra's nurse reveals to Hippolytus his stepmother's desire for him. He violently repels these advances. Phaedra, mortified to be revealed in such a dishonourable light against her wishes, commits suicide after leaving a letter designed to incriminate Hippolytus. Theseus believes the contents of the letter and curses his son, who is mortally wounded as a result. Before his death, Hippolytus forgives Theseus for his hasty conclusions.

The Trojan Women (Euripides, 415 BC)

Produced, probably not coincidentally, the year after Melos was punished with the execution of its menfolk and the enslavement of its women and children, this play chronicles the fates of Hecuba, Cassandra, Polyxena, Astyanax and Andromache after the collapse of Troy. There is a debate in which Helen pleads for her life before Menelaus, while Hecuba champions her execution. At the end of the play, the city is put to the torch while its women are led off to the Greek ships and to slavery.

Electra (Euripides, date uncertain)

Electra has been married to a peasant by Aegisthus and Clytemnestra, but he has respected her maidenhood. Orestes returns to Argos with Pylades and has his identity revealed to his sister by means of an old tutor's recognition. Electra urges him on to take vengeance. He slays Aegisthus during a sacrifice, and then the pair lure Clytemnestra to the countryside on the pretence that her advice is needed in the rituals for the baby recently born to Electra and her peasant husband. After an argument between mother and daughter, Clytemnestra is taken within and slaughtered. Finally, Castor and Pollux appear as *dei ex machina* to pronounce the futures of the characters involved in the matricide.

Iphigenia in Aulis (Euripides [probably unfinished by him], *c.* 405 BC)

Agamemnon begins the play in his camp at Aulis, where the fleet have been becalmed, by expressing his anxieties about the decision to call Iphigenia to Aulis to be sacrificed. His old servant acts as his confidant, willing to carry a letter to the expected arrivals bidding them to return to Argos. When they arrive too soon for this to be effective, attempts to give up the sacrifice demanded for no very clear reason by Calchas, the prophet, are abandoned. Clytemnestra, who has accompanied her daughter against Agamemnon's wishes, learns of the plans to sacrifice Iphigenia and attempts to intercede for her. Iphigenia begins by pleading for her survival but suddenly declares herself ready to die for her homeland. The very end of the play is usually taken to be spurious. It may be that Artemis appeared as a *deus ex machina* making a speech about the substitution of a hind for Iphigenia, as in the other Iphigenia play by Euripides, *Iphigenia among the Tauri.*

The Acharnians (Aristophanes, 425 BC)

The crux of the play's narrative is the farmer Dicaeopolis' decision to negotiate a private peace with Sparta. Once he has defended himself against the charges of treason brought by the charcoal-burners of Acharnae, the play centres on the delights of peace as enjoyed by himself and his family.

Lysistrata (Aristophanes, 411 BC)

Lysistrata persuades the women of Athens to participate in a sex strike in a bid to force the men to make peace. 'Despite the extravagance of this reversal of nature,' writes Harsh, whose idea of nature seems fairly extravagant in itself, 'the play makes a powerful appeal for renovating the national texture and for establishing Panhellenic peace and unity.'[3]

Notes

1. Particularly helpful for this endeavour has been Philip Whaley Harsh, *A Handbook of Classical Drama* (Standford University Press, 1944).
2. Ibid., p. 47
3. Ibid., p. 292.

APPENDIX C: CREDITS OF FILMS OF GREEK DRAMA

Prometheus in Chains (Greece, 1927)

Directors	Costas and Demetrios Gaziadis
Based on the tragedy by	Aeschylus
Translated into modern Greek	Jean Gryparis
Mise en scène	Eva Sikelianos
Choreography	Eva Sikelianos
Costumes	Eva Sikelianos
Music	Constantin Psachos
Choir director	Philoctète Iconomidis (1927); N. Tsiliphis (1971)
Masks	Hélène Sardeau
Decor	Costas Foscolos

Cast

Prometheus	Georges Bourlos
Kratos	Avlonitis
Hephaestus	Destounis
Bia	Marika Kalogericou
Oceanus	Mavrogenis
Io	Katerina Kakouri
Hermes	Destounis
Coryphaeus	Coula Pratsica (1927); read by Clio Nicolaou (1971)
Oceanids	Mavretta Bourlou-Joachimidoi, Anna Psilianou-Phasoulioti, Vetta Raftopoulou-Kali, Viky Raftopoulou, Kaity Griva-Dascalaopoulou, Titiea Evmorphouli-Kiosse (1927); Sophia Tsiliphi, Anthoula Aga, Ermina Karadimitri-Lefeaditou, Hélène Contista, Christiane Pillard (1971)
Production/Commentary	Octave Merlier

Electra (Greece, 1962)

Director	Ted Zarpas
Original stage production	Takis Mouzenidis
Based on the tragedy by	Sophocles
Camera	G. Eptamenitis
Editor	E. Siaskas

Cast

Electra	Anna Synodinou
Orestes	Thanos Cotsopoulos
Clytemnestra	Kakia Panayotou
Tutor	Theodoros Morides
Aegisthus	Vassalis Canakis
Chrysothemis	Elly Vozikiadou

Oedipus Rex (Canada, 1956)

Producer	Leonid Kipnis
Director	Tyrone Guthrie
Screenplay	William B. Yeats
Based on the tragedy by	Sophocles
Photography (Eastman Colour)	Roger Barlow
Editor	Irving Lerner
Art Directors	Tanya Moiseiwitsch, Arthur Price
Music	Cedric Thorpe Davie

Cast

Oedipus	Douglas Campbell
Jocasta	Eleanor Stuart
Messenger	Douglas Rain
Priest	Eric House
Creon	Robert Goodier
Tiresias	Donald Davis
Man from Corinth	Tony van Bridge
Old Shepherd	Eric House

Chorus Leader   William Hutt
Nurse   Gertrude Tyas
Ismene   Nomi Cameron
Antigone   Barbara Franklin
An Irving M. Lesser Presentation

The Persians *(Les perses)* (France, 1961)

Director/Screenplay   Jean Prat
Based on the tragedy by   Aeschylus
Photography   Jacques Lemare
Art Director   Jean-Jacques Gambut
Original Music   Jean Prodromides
Orchestra Director   André Girard
Costumes   Christiane Coste

Cast

Coryphaeus   François Chaumette
Queen Atossa   Maria Meriko
The Messenger   Maurice Carrel
Darius   René Arrieu
Xerxes   Claude Martin
With Jean-Pierre Bernard, Jean Brassat, Charles Denner, Jean
Daniel Ehrmann, André Oumansky, Mario Pilar, André Thorent

Electre (France, 1972)

Play originally produced by Le Théâtre des Amandiers and filmed
during performances at Cité Universitaire Internationale.

Director   Jean-Louis Ughetto
Based on the play by   Sophocles
Translated into French by   Antoine Vitez
Stage Production by   Antoine Vitez
Parentheses by   Yannis Ritsos
Photography   Daniel Lacambre, François
                                 Migeat, Etienne de Grammont

Editor	Jean-Yves Rousseau
Sets/Costumes	Yannis Kokkos
Sound	Bernard Ortion, Gilles Ortion

Cast

Preceptor	Antoine Vitez
Orestes	Jean-Baptiste Malartre
Pylades	Colin Harris
Electra	Evelyne Istria
Chrysothemis	Jany Gastaldi
Clytemnestra	Arlette Bonnard
Aegisthus	Christian Dente

And the voice of Chrysa Prokopaki

Oedipus the King (Great Britain, 1967)

Producer	Michael Luke
Associate Producer	Timothy Burrill
Director	Philip Saville
Assistant Director	George Stamboulopoulos
Production Manager	George Sarris
Script	Michael Luke, Philip Saville
Based on the play by	Sophocles
Translated by	Paul Roche
Photography (Technicolor)	Walter Lassally
Editor	Paul Davies
Art Director	Yannis Migadis
Music	Yannis Christou
Costumes	Denny Vachlioti
Sound	Nikos Despotides, Rusty Coppleman

Cast

Oedipus	Christopher Plummer
Jocasta	Lilli Palmer
Creon	Richard Johnson
Tiresias	Orson Welles

Messenger	Cyril Cusack
Shepherd	Roger Livesey
Chorus Leader	Donald Sutherland
Palace Official	Alexis Mantheakis
Priest	Demos Starenios
King Laius	Friedrich Ledebur
Antigone	Oenone Luke
Ismene	Cressida Luke
Members of Chorus	Costas Themos, Paul Roche, Minos Argyrakis, Takis Emmanouel, George Dialegmenos
Jocasta's Handmaidens	Mary Xenoudaki, Jenny Damianopoulou, Diana J. Reed

Crossroads/Universal

Antigone (Greece, 1961)

Directed and scripted by	George Tzavellas
Executive Producer	Sperie Perakos
Produced by	Demetrios Paris
Music	Arghyris Kojnadis
Art Director/Costume Designer	G. Anemoyannis

Cast

Antigone (Greece, 1961)	Irene Papas
Creon, King of Thebes	Manos Katrakis
Ismene, sister of Antigone	Maro Kontou
Haemon, son of Creon	Nikos Kazis
Eurydice, Queen	Ilia Livikou
Tiresias, a blind prophet	T. Karousos
A sentry	John Arghyris
A messenger	Byron Pallis
Leader of the Chorus	T. Moridis

Electra (Greece, 1961)

Producer/Director	Michael Cacoyannis
Production Manager	Yannis Petropoulakis
Assistant Director	B. Mariolis
Screenplay	Michael Cacoyannis
Based on the tragedy by	Euripides
Photography	Walter Lassally
Editor	L. Antonakis
Art Director	Spyros Vassiliou
Music	Mikis Theodorakis
Costumes	Spyros Vassiliou
Sound	Mikes Damalas

Cast

Electra	Irene Papas
Clytemnestra	Aleka Catselli
Orestes	Yannis Fertis
Chorus Leader	Theano Ioannidou
Electra's Husband	Notis Peryalis
Pylades	Takis Emmanouel
Aegisthus	Phoebus Rhaziz
The Preceptor	Manos Katrakis
Agamemnon	Theodore Demetriou
Finos	

The Trojan Women (USA, 1971)

Executive Producer	Josef Shaftel
Producers	Michael Cacoyannis, Anis Nohra
Director	Michael Cacoyannis
Screenplay	Michael Cacoyannis
Based on the tragedy by	Euripides
English version by	Edith Hamilton
Photography	Alfio Contini
Art Director	Nicholas Georgiadis
Sound	Mikes Damalas

Sound Editor	Alfred Cox
Music	Mikis Theodorakis

Cast

Hecuba	Katharine Hepburn
Andromache	Vanessa Redgrave
Cassandra	Genevieve Bujold
Helen	Irene Papas
Menelaus	Patrick Magee
Talthybius	Brian Blessed
Astyanax	Alberto Sanz

A Josef Shaftel Production

Iphigenia (Greece, 1976)

Executive Producer	Yannoulla Wakefield
Director	Michael Cacoyannis
Screenplay	Michael Cacoyannis
Based on the tragedy by	Euripides
Photography (Colour)	Georges Arvanitis
Editors	Michael Cacoyannis, Takis Yannopoulos
Art Director	Dionysis Photopoulos
Music	Mikis Theodorakis

Cast

Clytemnestra	Irene Papas
Iphigenia	Tatania Papamoskou
Agamemnon	Costa Kazakos
Menelaus	Costa Carras
Ulysses	Christos Tsangas
Achilles	Panos Michalopoulos
Servant	Angelos Yannoulis
Calchas	Dimitri Aronis
Orestes	Georges Vourvahakis
Nurse	Irene Koumarianou
Messenger	Georges Economou

Greek Film Centre/United Artists

Phaedra (USA/Greece, 1961)

Producer/Director	Jules Dassin
Screenplay	Jules Dassin, Margarita Liberaki
Original scenario	Margarita Liberaki
Photography	Jacques Natteau
Editor	Roger Dwyre
Art Director	Max Douy
Set Decoration	Maurice Barnathan
Music	Mikis Theodorakis
Sound	Jacques Carrère, M. Karaksusian

Cast

Phaedra	Melina Mercouri
Alexis	Anthony Perkins
Thanos	Raf Vallone
Ercy	Elizabeth Ercy
Anna	Olympia Papadouka
Christo	Jules Dassin
Ariadne	George Saris
Andreas	Andreas Philippides
The Old Man	Giorgos Karoussos
Dimitri	Alexis Pezas
Dimo	K. Baladimas
Heleni	Depy Martini
Melinafilm	

The Cannibals (I Cannibali) (Italy, 1970)

Executive Producer	Giuseppe Franconi
Producer	Enzo Doria
Director	Liliana Cavani
Screenplay	Liliana Cavani, Italo Moscati
Based on the play *Antigone* by	Sophocles
Photography (Technicolor/ Techniscope)	Giulio Albonico
Editor	Nino Baragli

Art Director	Giovanni Baragli
Music	Ennio Morricone
Songs	'Vorrei Trovare un Mondo' by Gino Paoli, sung by Adryan Russ; 'The Cannibals' sung by Don Powell
Sound	Raul Montesanti
Production Supervisor	Giuseppe Butti
Director of Production	Federico Tofi

Cast

Antigone	Britt Ekland
Tiresias	Pierre Clémenti
Ismene	Delia Boccardo
Ismene's Fiancé	Marino Mase
Haimon	Tomas Milian
Haimon's Father	Francesco Leonetti

With Alfredo Bianchini, Alessandro Cane, Graziano Giusti, Carla Cassola, Massimo Castri, Francesco Arminio, Giampiero Frondini, Sergio Serafini, Antonio Piovanelli, Giancarlo Caio, and the Emilia Romagna Theatre Comapny
Doria Films/San Marco Films

Prometheus Second Person Singular (*Promitheas se Deftero Prosopo*) (Greece, 1975)

Produced, Directed and Written by	Costas Ferris
Based on 'Prometheus Bound' by	Aeschylus
'Theogony' by	Hesiod
and 'Bardo Thodol' Text	Costas Vrettakos
Photography (Eastman Colour)	Stavros Khassapis
Music	Stamatis Spanoudakis

Choreography/Costumes	Myrto Paraschi

Cast

Prometheus	Yiannis Canoupakis
Io	Myrto Paraschi
Mercurius	Vangelis Maniatis
Vulcanus	George Vouros
Oceanus	Costas Vrettos
Jupiter	Costas Ferris
Chorus	Members of the 'Theatre Re'

Stefi Film/Greek Film Centre SA

Elektreia (Elektra Szerelmem) (Hungary, 1975)

Producer	József Bajusz
Director	Miklós Jancsó
Script	László Gyurkó, Gyula Hernádi
Based on the play by	László Gyurkó
Adaptation	Miklós Vasarhelyi
Photography (Eastman Colour)	János Kende
Editor	Zoltán Farkas
Art Directors	Eva Martin, Tamás Banovich
Music	Tamás Cseh; excerpts from the work of Bela Bartók
Lyrics	Géza Bereményi, Gyula Hernádi
Music Director	Béla Vavrinyecz
Costumes	Zsuzsa Vicze
Choreography	Károly Szigeti
Sound	György Pintér

Cast

Elektra	Mari Töröcsik
Aegisthus	Jozsef Madaras
Orestes	Gyórgy Czerhalmi
Courtiers of Aegisthus	Mária Bajcsay, Lajos Balázsovits
Chrisothemis	Gabi Jobba

With Tamás Cseh, Tamás Jordán, Zsolt Körtvélyessy, Velecky

František, Aposztolisz Burulitisz, Dimitrisz Burulitisz, Anasztaszisz Florosz, Sándor Lovas, Janós Reimann, Takisz Tomosz, Balázs Galkó, László Pelsöczy, Iván Szendrö, József Bige, Balázs Tardy, György Delianisz, Janos Lovas, Csaba Oszkay, Tamás Szentjóby, Gyöngyi Vig
Hunnia Studio Mafilm

Oedipus Rex (Edipo Re) (Italy, 1967)

Producer	Alfredo Bini
Director	Pier Paolo Pasolini
Assistant Director	Jean-Claude Biette
Script	Pier Paolo Pasolini
Based on the play by	Sophocles
Photography (Technicolour)	Giuseppe Ruzzolini
Editor	Nino Baragli
Art Directors	Luigi Scaccianoce, Andrea Fantacci
Music	mainly African music
Musical Director	Fausto Ancillai
Costumes	Danilo Donati
Sound	Carlo Tarchi

Cast

Oedipus	Franco Citti
Jocasta	Silvana Mangano
Creon	Carmelo Bene
Tiresias	Julian Beck
Merope	Alida Valli
Laius' Servant	Francesco Leonetti
Messenger	Ninetto Davoli

Arco Film. With the collaboration of Somafis (Casablanca)

Medea (Italy/France/W. Germany, 1970)

Producers	Franco Rossellini, Marina Cicogna

Production Supervisors	Pietro Nardi, Sergio Galiano
Director/Script	Pier Paolo Pasolini
Based on the play by	Euripides
Photography (Eastman Colour)	Ennio Guarnieri
Editor	Giovanni Baragli
Art Directors	Dante Ferretti, Nicola Tamburro
Musical Supervision	Pier Paolo Pasolini, Elsa Morante
Costumes	Piero Tosi
Sound	Carlo Tarchi

Cast

Medea	Maria Callas
Jason	Giuseppe Gentile
Centaur Chiron	Laurent Terzieff
Creon	Massimo Girotti
Glauce	Margareth Clementi
Nurse	Anna Maria Chio

With Paul Jabor, Luigi Urbini, Gerard Weiss, Giorgio Trombetti, Franco Jacobbi, Gian Paolo Durgar
San Marco (Rome)/Les Films Number One (Paris)/Janus Film (Frankfurt)

Notes for an African Oresteia
(Appunti per un' Orestiade Africana) **(Italy, 1970)**

Director/Script	Pier Paolo Pasolini
Producer	Gian Vittorio Baldi
Photography	Giorgio Pelloni
Editor	Cleofe Conversi
Music	Gato Barbieri
Narrator	Pier Paolo Pasolini

with Pier Paolo Pasolini, Gato Barbieri, Marcello Melio, Donald F. Moye, Yvonne Murray, Archie Savage
IDI Cinematografica/RAI

A Dream of Passion (Switzerland/Greece, 1978)

Producer/Director	Jules Dassin
Production Manager	Stefanos Vlachos
Script	Jules Dassin
Based on the modern Greek version of Euripides' *Medea* by	Minos Volonakis
Photography (Eastman Colour)	George Arvanitis
Editor	Georges Klotz
Art Director	Dionyssis Fotopoulos
Music	Yannis Markopoulos
Costumes	Dionyssis Fotopoulos
Sound Editor	Françoise Orsoni
Sound Recording	Thanassis Arvanitis
Sound Re-recording	Jean Nény
Sound Effects	Daniel Couteau

Cast

Maya	Melina Mercouri
Brenda Collins	Ellen Burstyn
Kostas	Andreas Voutsinas
Maria	Despo Diamantidou
Dimitris/Jason	Dimitris Papamichael
Edward	Yannis Voglis
Ronny	Phaedon Georgitsis
Margaret	Betty Valassi
Creon	Manos Katrakis
Greek Chorus	Anthi Kariofili, Olympia Tolika, Rea Fortuna, Mary Chinari, Katerina Bourlou, Alexandra Pandelaki, Natasha Tsakarisianou, Sofia Sfiroera, Stella Yeromitsou, Eleni Georgiadou, Mariana Koutalou, Vicky Grammatica, Fotimi Filosofou, Mina Negreponti
Stathis	Andreas Philipidis
Bible student	Kostas Arzoclou

Diana	Irene Emirza
Manos	Panos Papaioannou
Lighting man	Nicos Galiatos
Attendant	Olympia Papadouka
Emma	Anna Thomaidou
BBC script	Litsa Vaidou
Soundman	Savvas Axiotis
Editor	Freddi Germanos
Shopkeeper	Stefanos Vlachos
Dr Pavlidis	Alexis Solomos

With Aleka Katselli, Rita Lambrinou
Brenfilm (Geneva)/Melinafilm (Athens)

Lysistrata (Lisistrati) (Greece, 1972)

Producer	Costas Kazakos
Director	Yorgos Zervoulakos
Screenplay	Yannis Negrepontis
Based on the play by	Aristophanes
Photography (Eastman Colour)	Nikos Milas
Editor	Nikos Kavoukidis
Art Director/Costumes	Joanna Papantoniou
Music/Music Director	Stavros Xarchakos
Sound	N. Achladis

Cast

Lysistrata	Jenni Karezi
Cleonike	Maria Marmarinou
Kinesias	Costas Kazakos
Myrrhine	Anna Fonsou
Lampito	Fouli Prodromidou
Magistrate	Dionysis Papayannopoulos
Spartan	Vangelis Kazan
Leader of Women's Chorus	Anna Mantzourani
Leader of Men's Chorus	Spiros Constantopoulos
Nea Kinimatografia	

The Acharnians (I Acharnis) (Greece, 1976)

Producer	Mimis Kouyioumtzis
Director	Mimis Kouyioumtzis
Director of Play	Karolos Koun
Screenplay	The play by Aristophanes
Photography	Dinos Katsouridis, Sakis Maniatis
Editor	Mimis Kouyioumtzis
Art Director	Karolos Koun
Sets/Costumes	Dionysis Fotopoulos
Music	Christos Leontis
Sound	D. Athanassopoulos

Cast

Dikaiopolis	Yorgos Lazanis
Lamachos	Kostas Tsapekos
Leader of Chorus	Mimis Kouyioumtzis
Kifissofon	Yorgos Armenis
Nikarchos	Antonis Theodorakopoulos
Amfitheos	Kostas Halkias
Pseudartabas	Haris Sozos
Euripides	Yiannis Deyaitis

SELECTED BIBLIOGRAPHY

Bachmann, Gideon, 'Jancsó Plain', *Sight and Sound*, vol. 43, no. 4, Autumn 1974.

Bazin, André, *What is Cinema?*, vol. 1, tr. Hugh Gray (University of California Press, 1967).

Causse, Michèle and Lapouge, Maryvonne, *Ecrits, Voix d'Italie* (Des Femmes, 1977).

Conacher, D. J., *Euripidean Drama: Myth, Theme and Structure* (University of Toronto Press, 1967).

Duflot, Jean, *Entretiens avec Pier Paolo Pasolini* (Editions Pierre Belfond, 1970).

Durgnat, Raymond, *Sexual Alienation in the Cinema* (Studio Vista, 1972).

Estève, Michel (ed.), *Pier Paolo Pasolini: le mythe et le sacré* (Minard, 1976).

Faas, Ekbert, *Tragedy and After: Euripides, Shakespeare, Goethe* (McGill-Queen's University Press, 1984).

Gássner, John, *The Theatre in our Times: A Survey of the Men, Materials and Movements in the Modern Theatre* (Crown Publishers, 1954).

Gervais, Marc, *Pier Paolo Pasolini*, Cinéma d'aujourdhui (Editions Seghers, 1973).

Harsh, Philip Whaley, *A Handbook of Classical Drama* (Stanford University Press, 1944).

Hurt, James (ed.), *Focus on Film and Theatre* (Prentice-Hall, 1974).

Jacob, Gilles, *Le Cinéma moderne* (Serdoc, 1964).

Jorgens, Jack J., *Shakespeare on Film* (Indiana University Press, 1977).

Kluckhorn, Clyde, *Anthropology and the Classics* (Brown University Press, 1961).

Knox, Bernard, *Word and Action* (Johns Hopkins University Press, 1979).

Kracauer, Siegfried, *Theory of Film: The Redemption of Physical Reality* (Oxford University Press, 1960, 1979).

Lloyd, Michael, 'The Helen Scene in Euripides' *Troades*', *Classical Quarterly*, 34, 1984.

Manvell, Roger, *Theater and Film: A Comparative Study of the Two Forms of Dramatic Art, and of the Problems of Adaptation of Stage Plays into Films* (Fairleigh Dickinson University Press, 1979).

Mast, Gerald and Cohen, Marshall (eds), *Film Theory ad Criticism*, 2nd edn. (Oxford University Press, 1979).

Mercouri, Melina, *I Was Born Greek* (Doubleday, 1971).

Muller, Herbert J., *The Spirit of Tragedy* (Alfred A. Knopf, 1956).

Murray, Oswyn, 'The dream of justice . . .', *The Times Literary Supplement*, 11 December 1981.

Nicoll, Allardyce, *Film and Theatre* (Harrap, 1936).

Noguez, Dominique, 'L'Oedipe de Pasolini', *ça*, October 1973.

Pasolini Cinéaste (Cahiers du Cinéma, 1981).

Pasolini, Pier Paolo, *Oedipus Rex*, tr. John Mathews (Lorrimer Publishing, 1971).

Pasolini: Séminaire dirigé par Maria Antonietta Macciocchi (Bernard Grasset, 1980).

Petrie, Graham, 'Style as subject: Jancsó's "Electra" ', *Film Comment*, vol. 11, no. 5, September–October 1975.

Prédal, René, 'L'Electre de Jancsó notre contemporaine', *Jeune Cinéma*, no. 90, November 1975.

Schuster, Mel, *The Contemporary Greek Cinema* (Scarecrow, 1979).

Siciliano, Enzo, *Pasolini: a biography*, tr. John Shepley (Random House, 1982).

Snyder, Stephen, *Pier Paolo Pasolini* (Twayne Publishers, 1980).

Stack, Oswald, *Pasolini on Pasolini* (Thames & Hudson/British Film Institute, 1969).

Steiner, George, *The Death of Tragedy* (Faber & Faber, 1961).

Taplin, Oliver, 'The Delphic Idea and After', *The Times Literary Supplement*, no. 4085, 17 July 1981.

——*Greek Tragedy in Action* (Methuen, 1978).

Taylor, John Russell, *Directors and Directions* (Eyre Methuen, 1975).

Tournès, Andrée, 'Liliana Cavani', *Jeune Cinéma*, no. 63, May–June 1972.

Vardac, A. Nicholas, *Stage to Screen: theatrical method from Garrick to Griffith* (Harvard University Press, 1949).

Vellacott, Philip, *Ironic Drama* (Cambridge Univesity Press, 1975).

Von Szeliski, John, *Tragedy and Fear: why modern tragic drama fails* (University of North Carolina Press, 1971).

Waller, Gregory A., *The Stage/Screen Debate: a study in popular aesthetics* (Garland, 1983).

Walton, Michael J., *Greek Theatre Practice* (Greenwood Press, 1980).

Webster, T. B. L., *The Tragedies of Euripides* (Methuen, 1967).

White, Robert J., 'Myth and *mise-en-scène:* Pasolini's *Edipo Re', Literature/Film Quarterly*, vol. 5, no. 1, Winter 1977.

Willemen, Paul (ed.), *Pier Paolo Pasolini* (British Film Institute, 1977).

Wilson, David, 'Edipo Re', *Monthly Film Bulletin*, July 1969.

——'Greek comedy: ancient and modern', National Film Theatre programme notes, March 1984.

——'Greek tragedy on film', National Film Theatre programme notes, June 1981.

Wollen, Peter, *Readings and Writings: Semiotic Counter-Strategies* (Verso Editions and NLB, 1982).

INDEX

People

Aeschylus 2, 13, 25, 31, 33, 35, 40-7
  passim, 55, 56, 64, 65n., 78, 79,
  86, 94, 97, 114, 116, 117, 121, 126,
  133, 154, 155, 165, 166, 174, 175,
  181, 182, 188
Amengual, Barthélemy 133, 134, 141,
  142, 144, 145, 162n., 163n.
Aristarco, Guido 140, 141, 163n.
Aristophanes 24, 32, 41, 41n., 56, 58,
  65n., 67, 94, 98, 169, 170, 172, 179,
  193, 194
Aristotle 8, 22-4 *passim*, 27, 31, 32, 35,
  40, 41n., 44, 51, 56, 69, 70, 77, 78,
  79, 86, 100, 132, 139, 154, 165, 167
Auty, Martyn 159, 160, 164n.

Barbieri, Gato 154, 191
Bazin, André 4, 6-15 *passim*, 21n., 22,
  66
Bergman, Ingmar 75, 158
Blessed, Brian 93, 186
Bourlos, George 44, 46, 180
Brecht, Bertolt 17, 35, 61, 86, 115
Bujold, Genevieve 81, 82, 93, 186

Cacoyannis, Michael 1, 2, 10, 48, 67,
  73-100 *passim*, 105, 122, 123, 161,
  165, 166, 167, 168, 185, 186
Callas, Maria 147, 191
Catselli, Aleka 75, 76, 185
Cavani, Liliana 1, 97, 98, 105-14
  passim, 120, 123, 124, 167, 187
Citti, Franco 128, 142, 190
Clémenti, Pierre 106, 107, 188

Dassin, Jules, 1, 40, 73, 97-104 *passim*,
  112, 123, 124, 126, 156, 158, 160,
  161, 165, 166, 187, 192
Davoli, Ninetto 129, 131, 141
Durgnat, Raymond 134, 135, 143,
  144, 145, 152n., 163n., 164n.

Eisenstein, Sergei 11, 21n., 76
Elley, Derek 105, 106, 108, 125n.,
  164n.
Euripides 2, 24, 26, 31, 32, 35, 38, 39,
  40, 47, 74-105 *passim*, 117, 119, 123,
  126, 146, 147, 150, 154-66 *passim*,
  177, 178, 179, 185, 186, 187, 191

Faas, Ekbert 33, 38, 39, 40, 42n.,
  132-8 *passim*, 142-5 *passim*, 152,
  162n., 167
Ferris, Costas 97, 112-16 *passim*, 123,
  188
Freud, Sigmund 36-42 *passim*, 132-8
  passim, 142, 143, 145, 152, 162n.,
  167

Gervais, Marc 137, 147, 154, 162n.,
  163n., 164n.
Godard, Jean-Luc 10, 12, 115
Guthrie, Tyrone 2, 51-6 *passim*, 61,
  63, 64, 66, 70, 71, 181
Gyurkó, László 117, 119, 120, 189

Haskell, Molly 81, 95n., 110, 125n.
Hegel, Friedrich 33, 39, 42n., 86, 95n.,
  142
Hepburn, Katharine 82, 93, 186
Hernádi, Gyula 118, 121, 189
Homer 98, 131, 132

Jancsó, Miklós 1, 97, 117-25 *passim*,
  165, 167, 189
Jorgens, Jack J. 18, 19, 21n., 24, 41n.,
  126

Kael, Pauline 81, 85, 95n.
Knox, Bernard 86, 95n., 96n., 137
Kracauer, Siegfried 7-12 *passim*, 20n.

Liberaki, Margarita 99, 100, 187

Malcolm, Derek 147, 159, 163n., 164n.
Mangano, Silvana 127, 129, 140, 145,
  190
Manvell, Roger 16-18 *passim*, 20n.,
  21n., 94n.
Marx, Karl 35-41 *passim*, 132, 135,
  136, 137, 142, 145
Menander 40, 169-73 *passim*
Mercouri, Melina 1, 98-100 *passim*,
  124n., 157, 159, 187, 192

Mitropoulos, Mrs Aglae 43, 48, 65n.
Muller, Herbert J. 26-8 *passim*, 33, 34, 38, 39, 41n., 42n., 134, 162n.
Munsterberg, Hugo 6, 7, 13, 20n.

Nicoll, Allardyce 7, 10, 11, 20n.
Nowell-Smith, Geoffrey 99, 124n., 143, 163n.

Olivier, Sir Laurence 5, 9, 66

Palmer, Eva 43, 44
Palmer, Lilli 67, 68
Panofsky, Irwin 6-10 *passim*, 20n.
Papas, Irene, 75, 76, 82, 87, 93, 96n., 184, 185, 186
Pasolini, Pier Paolo 1, 2, 41, 93, 126-67 *passim*, 190, 191
Perkins, Anthony 1, 100-2 *passim*, 187
Plato 22, 24, 27, 44, 69, 134
Powell, Dilys 54, 65n., 73, 94n.
Prat, Jean 55-7 *passim*, 64, 182
Pudovkin, V.I. 6, 13, 20n.

Racine, Jean 38, 100, 101, 104
Rayns, Tony 117-18, 125n.
Redgrave, Vanessa 82, 93, 186

Saville, Philip 2, 66-71 *passim*, 75, 183
Schickel, Richard 158, 159, 164n.
Schuster, Mel 3n., 112, 116, 125n.
Seneca 68, 100, 101, 147
Shakespeare, William 9, 10, 18, 24, 30, 35, 39, 66, 100, 146, 167, 173
Siciliano, Enzo 136, 156, 162n., 163n., 164n.
Sikelianos, Angelos 43, 44, 51, 64, 180
Simon, John 10, 21n., 81, 95n.
Snyder, Stephen 136, 137, 149, 153, 162n., 163n., 164n.
Sontag, Susan 10, 11, 14, 21n.
Sophocles 1, 2, 10, 24, 26, 30-2 *passim*, 35, 40, 43, 48, 49, 51, 54, 55, 60-72 *passim*, 77, 80, 94, 97, 98, 105-11 *passim*, 117, 119, 120, 126-46 *passim*, 154, 161, 165, 167, 175, 176, 181, 182, 184, 187, 190
Stack, Oswald 135, 144, 162n., 163n.
Steiner, George 36-8 *passim*, 42n., 101, 124n.

Taplin, Oliver 24, 25, 27-30 *passim*, 33, 41n., 42n., 43, 48-50 *passim*, 55, 56, 64, 65n., 94n., 101, 107, 112, 124n., 125n., 143, 153, 162n., 163n., 164n.

Theodorakis, Mikis 76, 185, 186
Tzavellas, George 72, 73, 76, 97, 184

Ughetto, Jean-Louis 60, 61, 64, 182

Vallone, Raf 1, 100, 101, 187
Vardac, A. Nicholas 4, 13, 20n.
Vitez, Antoine 60, 61, 63, 182, 183
Von Szeliski, John 34, 35, 37, 42n.

White, Robert J. 136, 137, 162n.
Wilson, David 22-4 *passim*, 41n., 87, 96n., 163n., 169, 173n.

Zarpas, Ted 48, 181

Works

Plays

Acharnians, The 172, 179
Agamemnon 13, 175
Antigone 43, 105-11 *passim*, 175, 184
Bacchae, The 2, 40, 47
Dyskolos 170, 172
Electra (Euripides) 2, 26, 40, 77-80 *passim*, 117, 165, 166, 178
Electra (Sophocles) 2, 48, 49, 60, 64, 80, 117, 119, 176
Eumenides, The 121, 155, 175
Frogs, The 32, 56, 58, 94
Hippolytus 24, 39, 100, 101, 177
Iphigenia in Aulis 39-40, 74, 85-9 *passim*, 178
Libation Bearers, The 2, 79, 117, 175
Medea 93, 98, 126, 146, 156, 158, 177
Oedipus at Colonus 26, 139, 140, 145, 176
Oedipus Rex 1, 27, 31, 51, 55, 57, 69, 126, 132, 134, 135, 137, 154, 165, 176
Oresteia, The 2, 25, 78, 126, 154, 155, 166, 175
Orestes 2, 75
Persians, The 41n., 55, 56, 57, 64, 174
Prometheus Bound 43, 44, 47, 51, 56, 57, 65n., 112, 174, 188
Trojan Women, The 74, 75, 80, 83, 98, 103, 178

Films

Acharnians, The 172, 194
Antigone 72-4 *passim*, 97
Cannibals, The 105-11 *passim*, 120, 123, 187
Chien andalou, Un 14, 115
Dream of Passion, A 126, 156-60 *passim*, 166, 192
Electra (Cacoyannis) 48, 71, 74-82 *passim*, 84, 91, 94n., 95n., 122, 166, 185
Electra (Meletopoulos) 48
Electra (Zarpas) 48-51 *passim*, 61, 63, 65n., 181
Electre 60-4 *passim*, 165, 182
Elektreia 111, 117-23 *passim*, 125n., 167, 189
Gospel according to St Matthew, The 140, 150, 151
Henry V 9, 66, 70
Iphigenia 74, 75, 82, 83, 85-92 *passim*, 99, 122, 161, 186
Lysistrata 170-2 *passim*, 179, 193
Medea 93, 126, 136, 146-56 *passim*, 159, 161, 190
Never on Sunday 98-100 *passim*
Notes for an African Oresteia 2, 126, 154-6 *passim*, 191

Oedipus Rex (Guthrie) 2, 51-5 *passim*, 61, 64, 65n., 165, 181
Oedipus Rex (Pasolini) 126-49 *passim*, 154, 156, 161, 164n., 167, 190
Oedipus the King 2, 66-72 *passim*, 94n., 183
Persians, The 55-60 *passim*, 61, 64, 182
Persona 158, 159, 164n.
Phaedra 1, 40, 73, 98-105 *passim*, 123, 165, 166, 186
Prometheus in Chains 43-8 *passim*, 64, 65n., 180
Prometheus, Second Person Singular 111-17 *passim*, 123, 188
Theorem 140, 147, 149
Trojan Women, The 74, 75, 80-5 *passim*, 91, 92, 93, 97, 185
Virgin, The 172

Books

Poetics, The 8, 22, 24, 27, 31, 35, 36, 165
Republic, The 22, 24, 27